Restructuring Eastern Europe

THE INTERNATIONAL LIBRARY OF STUDIES IN COMMUNISM

General Editor: Ronald J. Hill,
Trinity College, Dublin

The International Library of Studies in Communism is an important new series covering all aspects of communism, but focusing principally on communism as a system of rule. At a time when the Stalinist form of socialism is undergoing reappraisal and modification in the leading communist-ruled countries, and newly emergent nations are being led along the communist path, the need to understand this phenomenon has never been greater.

The series is edited under the sponsorship of Lorton House, an independent non-profit association which exists to promote the academic study of communism.

Restructuring Eastern Europe

Towards a New European Order

Edited by
Ronald J. Hill
Trinity College, Dublin
and
Jan Zielonka
University of Leiden

Edward Elgar

Published by
Edward Elgar Publishing Limited
Gower House
Croft Road
Aldershot
Hants GU11 3HR
England

Edward Elgar Publishing Company
Old Post Road
Brookfield
Vermont 05036

British Library in Cataloguing

British Library Cataloguing in Publication Data
Restructuring Eastern Europe: towards a new European order.
  (International library of studies in Communism)
  1. Eastern Europe. Politics
  I. Hill, Ronald J. II. Zielonka, Jan 1955 III. Series
  320.947

ISBN 1-85278-377-X

Printed in Great Britain by
Billing & Sons Ltd, Worcester

Contents

Preface

In the months while these essays were being prepared, what began as a study of political evolution rapidly turned into a study of revolution, as successive communist regimes collapsed and were replaced by non-communist — and in some cases avowedly anti-communist — governments, all of which promised to establish democracy on the basis of free elections. The process is still in train as the book goes to press.

For West Europeans, sharing a continent with peoples who have been ruled by communists for nearly half a century (approaching three-quarters of a century if the Soviet Union is included), these exciting events pose a number of challenges. The political, ideological, economic, military and cultural division of the continent has been the dominant feature of world politics since shortly after the Second World War. It has infused the everyday thinking of governments, scholars and citizens around the world. No one living in Europe since the 1940s has been unaffected by it. Yet now much of the rationale for such a division appears to be evaporating — or, at least, events are developing in such a way that the rationale needs to be adjusted if not abandoned. While the uniting of Germany proceeds apace, it is too early yet to speak of the reuniting of Europe. Nevertheless, clearly 'Europe' and the rest of the world will need to develop new ways of thinking before the twenty-first century is reached.

These developments were a natural cause of rejoicing, as regimes that had been called variously communism, socialism, state socialism, developed socialism, mature socialism, existing socialism and a variety of other names succombed to the pressure of their own failure to secure the economic well-being and to win the support, or even willing acceptance, of the populations over whom they ruled. The initial euphoria and triumphalism, both East and West, was quite understandable. However, such sentiments cannot serve as the basis for long-term policy or for creating a new relationship between the two parts of the formerly severed continent. The developments raise fundamental issues that have to be addressed by governments and peoples on both sides of the disappearing division. There is also much material for scholarly assessment, as we try to come to grips with the nature of the processes we are witnessing.

This set of essays is a contribution to such an initial reordering of thoughts, and it deliberately focuses on the responses of Europeans to events that affect them more directly than they affect citizens in other parts of the world. At the Netherlands Institute for Advanced Study in 1988/89, a number of the contributors to this volume participated in a variety of forums at which these and cognate isues were discussed. The editors have also invited other scholars to submit contributions on particular themes not addressed by the Fellows of NIAS, in order to round out the volume with topics on which they possessed special expertise. The result is a collection of essays by a dozen scholars drawn from eleven institutions in seven European countries, ranging from large powers — France, Germany and the United Kingdom — to the Netherlands and three European neutrals: Finland, Ireland and Sweden, ensuring an unusually broad perspective.

The editors are extremely grateful to all those who have generously devoted their time to this project, in some cases at fairly short notice. They express their profound gratitude to the administration and staff of NIAS for supporting the proposal, and particularly to the director, Professor Dirk van de Kaa, for his unstinting encouragement and his gracious contribution of a Foreword to this book. Without such moral and material support, it would have been quite impossible to bring this project to fruition.

Finally, we express our appreciation to our wives for their forbearance and patience at times when the pace and scale of change suggested that the project might consume the remainder of our lives.

R.J.H.

J.Z.

List of Contributors

Peter R. Baehr, University of Leiden, The Netherlands.

Godfried van Benthem van den Bergh, Erasmus University, Rotterdam, and Institute of Social Studies, The Hague, The Netherlands.

Kristian Gerner, Swedish Research Council for the Social Sciences and Humanities, University of Lund, Sweden.

Ronald J. Hill, Trinity College, Dublin, Ireland.

Egbert Jahn, Peace Research Institute, Frankfurt-am-Main, Germany.

Dirk J. van de Kaa, Director, Netherlands Institute for Advanced Study in the Humanities and Social Sciences, Wassenaar.

Kerstin Nyström, University of Lund, Sweden.

Krzysztof Pomian, Centre for Social Research, Paris, France.

Theodor Schweisfurth, Max Planck Institut, Heidelberg, Germany.

Alan H. Smith, School of Slavonic and East European Studies, University of London, United Kingdom.

Pekka Sutela, University of Helsinki, Finland.

Rachel Walker, University of Essex, Colchester, United Kingdom.

Jan Zielonka, University of Leiden, The Netherlands.

1. Foreword

Dirk J. van de Kaa

Unexpected, dramatic, revolutionary and unprecedented: such are the adjectives frequently used to describe the very rapid changes that have taken place in Eastern Europe since the last months of 1989. However, that Eastern Europe was in ferment had already become clear somewhat earlier, and on the initiative of two scholars from the University of Leiden, Dr Jan Zielonka and Professor Peter Baehr, The Netherlands Institute for Advanced Study in the Humanities and Social Sciences (NIAS) began planning a research theme group entitled *Approaching Eastern Europe* in the course of 1987. The international research group convened at NIAS for the full academic year 1988/89. It focused on two distinct sets of issues: first, changes in the social, economic and political fields and their meaning for Western Europe; and second, human rights and their significance for European security. Notwithstanding this element of duality present in the theme group, its programme became a resounding success. A monthly lecture series and an extremely well designed conference led to lively exchanges of views, provocative presentations and very thoughtful comments. The possibility that the Berlin Wall would come down, for example, was discussed many months before it became a reality, and I vividly remember how well the confusion and uncertainty it would cause in the rest of Europe was assessed. Similarly, the significance of nationalist movements was discussed with a good deal of foresight, even though no one dared to predict how soon developments in the Baltic states, in Armenia and in Romania would dominate world news.

The present book, *Restructuring Eastern Europe*, brings together a valuable series of contributions to our understanding of current changes in Eastern Europe and their impact on East-West relations. The two members of the research theme group who edited them, Professor Ronald Hill and Dr Jan

Zielonka, have done a marvellous job — as, indeed, have their authors. Their task was particularly demanding in that they had to work very fast in order not to be overtaken by new events.

2. Introduction: The Setting for Change

Jan Zielonka and Ronald J. Hill

As the world enters the last decade of the twentieth century, the observer of the modern history and politics of Europe has much to occupy his attention. Change is taking place at a rapid pace in a region that has long regarded itself as the centre of world events. Democratization and market-oriented reforms are progressing in countries that for decades have been under communist rule. Moscow is withdrawing from its European empire in response to demands for national and regional independence. Two German states are on the road to fully-fledged unification. The restructuring of the Warsaw Pact and NATO is also taking place as the traditional notions of threat and security are being re-defined and various forms of pan-European cooperation begin to flourish.

The ongoing change is so dramatic that we often lack the proper concepts or even the vocabulary to describe its pace, scope and implications. Even seemingly neutral terms used in this book (and more widely in thinking and talking about modern history and politics), such as 'Eastern' and 'Western Europe', reflect geopolitical realities that belong more to the past than to the future, or so it appears.[1] The bipolar division of Europe into two antagonistic ideological, economic and military blocs is fast disappearing, and the newly emerging multi-polar order is still indistinct and remains very unpredictable. What will be the future of the post-communist societies? What forms of European integration will decline and which will develop? Will the new security regime be more stable, or less, than the one that is being replaced? Will the gap between the poor and the rich countries be bridged as a result of current and future changes? What will be the new shape of Europe's Transatlantic connection? So far, there are no ready answers to these crucial questions.

However, the collapse of 'communism' in Eastern Europe, and the fall of the Berlin Wall, crude symbol of the cruel division of the continent by the 'iron curtain' — welcome as these and other manifestations of epoch-making change are — do not represent anything that might be termed the end of history.[2] Rather, they are part of a process that has been playing itself out throughout the century. The year 1989, in particular, in which the most dramatic sequence of changes took place in the countries of Eastern Europe, witnessed the acceleration of a process of evolution towards what might be called 'post-totalitarianism' in those countries, the seeds of which had been sown many years earlier, in those societies themselves (including the Soviet Union), and also elsewhere in the world. The evolution of Western Europe into a set of historically new economic and political relationships always served as a counter-attraction to the peoples subjected to a system of which they had no hand in the making (the USSR excluded). Moreover, the successes of the Western world, relayed not only through the activities of such agencies as Radio Free Europe, Radio Liberty and other Western sources, but in the reports of family members in emigration and from other 'private' sources, prevented the reality of communist rule from winning the allegiance of all but a minute segment of the societies concerned.

The preconditions for significant change were already in existence, and were to some extent being introduced: after all, with the sole exceptions of Romania under Ceausescu and Albania under Enver Hoxha and later Ramiz Alia, the full-blown Stalinist repression of the early 1950s had given way to generally less aggressive, perhaps more insidious, forms of political control. In such circumstances, ideas that challenged the *status quo*, whether devised and circulated illegally by 'dissidents', or created and developed in the academies and universities and given circulation in the scholarly journals, had become part and parcel of social and political reality in the Soviet Union and other countries of the 'bloc'. Given the rising educational levels of the people, the increasingly sophisticated division of labour, the enhanced leisure time, and the technological revolution which made it ever more difficult for governments to control the circulation of ideas, it was really only a matter of time before the inadequacies of the system to cope with the pressures on government made themselves felt. What could, of course, never be predicted was the precise course of events — where, when and how the necessary changes would be brought about — and, more especially, its speed. It is the pace of change — in which the single year 1989 has been compared with the revolutionary year of 1848 — that has led observers to simplify the processes involved, and to overlook the complex of factors that influenced the changes, and will continue to influence further developments, in ways that cannot all be foreseen. What is clear already is that the course of the changes that are being deliberately introduced is not identical. Not only did each 'revolution' have its own peculiarities, with certain features shared by several countries, but the likely course of development will vary. What is being witnessed, as the different nations break away from the remnants of the uniform straitjacket imposed by Stalin (a process of diversification that was already under way), is a reassertion of national characteristics at an enhanced pace, as each nation rejects uniformity and seeks its own forms of democracy, including its own relations with its neighbours and the outside world.

What this means that greater Europe is being established (or re-established), whose political and economic contours are barely discernible at this stage. Western Europe, where a process of integration had been gaining momentum, is being forced to assess the changes with considerable urgency. The countries that are emerging from communist rule require investment and economic aid that would otherwise have been channelled into the poorer areas of the European Community. In addition, the changes raise anew questions of the identity of 'Europe' from which the eastern portion was excluded, and in which the Nordic countries (apart from Denmark) and even Switzerland, in Europe's very heart, declined to participate. 'Europe', in other words, is regaining and being forced to reassess its identity, culturally, economically and politically. This has, of course, implications for international political relationships that go well beyond the borders of Europe (wherever they may lie). In this introductory chapter, we examine the background to the changes, their nature, the internal and international consequences, and the prospects for development towards and into the twenty-first century.

THE NATURE OF CHANGE IN EASTERN EUROPE

Whatever the precise sequence of events that brought about the collapse of the established communist rule in individual countries, a number of common features of the revolutionary situation can be identified. They can be separated for analytical purposes; however, it is important to bear in mind that the various features are interlinked in an organic process.

The first point, which goes to the very heart of the original justification for the regime, was the recognition that the ideology was less and less helpful in resolving the everyday problems of government and policy making in a complex society. As a philosophy that offered an attractive vision of a future society characterized by peace, justice and social harmony, in which 'exploitation of man by man' had been abolished, the state had withered away, and citizens ran their own affairs through 'communist self-administration', Marxism's appeal was undermined by the practice of communism as a system of rule. As a guide to action in a complex world, in which the pace of technical change was creating ways of life that were not dreamt of by the founding fathers, the ideology was singularly inappropriate. It may have helped to identify friends and enemies, but it had nothing to say about competition in a world where the microchip was transforming whole economies and people's everyday lives in much of the world. It had long been treated as a series of dogmas, and calls for its 'creative development' — no more so than in the Soviet Union — appeared as little more than forlorn cries for new justifications for the unjustifiable. Communists themselves recognized this, particularly in countries like Hungary. Acknowledgement of the value of a competition in ideas was implicit in Gorbachev's phrase, 'socialist pluralism', and the abandonment of Marxism-Leninism as the 'official' ideology has been an almost universal feature of the East European revolution.

A consequence of that has been the abandonment of the communist party's traditional leading role, with deliberate repeal of the constitutional guarantee of its position in a number of countries; the party's role has been further modified as a consequence of the restructuring of the state representative institutions as organs for the genuine exchange of opinions. The move towards a recognizable parliamentary democracy has been a central element of the East European revolution, accompanied by a number of additional necessary features: the establishment of the rule of law or a *Rechtsstaat*, independence of judges and the courts, thoroughgoing legal reform, abolition of the secret or political police, or curtailment of its role (an issue that was of particular concern in Romania and the German Democratic Republic), electoral competition, freedom of the press (sponsored in the Soviet Union under the slogan of *Glasnost*), and, in almost all countries, the establishment or revival of alternative political parties in competition with (rather than alongside, as was formerly the case in Poland, the GDR and Czechoslovakia) the communists; the communists, indeed, felt a need to change the name of their party in what is perhaps the most eloquent symbol of the discrediting of the whole system.

All of this is part of a process whereby civil society is being re-established after the stultifying effect of decades of imposed orthodox thinking and behaviour. Apart from newly emerging or re-emerging political parties, other broad social movements, trade unions, political discussion clubs and a whole variety of spontaneous organizations are being created without the need for formal sanction by the party or state authorities. Even without the creation of new parties, the political monopoly of the communist party has been or is being broken. In Poland — Solidarity, in Soviet Lithuania — Sajudis: movements, rather than parties, have succeeded in sweeping the polls in elections. And within months, oppositionists have taken over power: Solidarity led a new government in Poland from August 1989; the playwright Václav Havel, imprisoned for three months for his dissident activity (not for the first time) earlier in the year, was elected president of the republic in December, and Alexander Dubcek, reformist leader of 1968 who had lived for over twenty years in disgrace and obscurity, became speaker of the parliament. Elsewhere, communists struggled to establish credibility as they prepared for elections that would determine the evolutionary fate of the systems that had led into a blind alley.

A key movement in the reform has been that for national independence, whether seeking freedom from control by the Soviet Union on the part of nominally independent states, independence of the Soviet Union (as in the case of the three Soviet Baltic republics), or unification with another state (as in the case of Soviet Moldavia, demanding reunion with post-Ceausescu Romania, or Azerbaijan, seeking association with northern Iran). In some cases, demands for greater cultural, economic and political autonomy developed into calls for secession, or for administrative and territorial adjustments. The dispute between Armenia and Azerbaijan over control of the enclave of Nagorny Karabakh flared into violence and blockade during 1988 and 1989; in Yugoslavia, inter-ethnic rivalries and tensions led to violent demonstrations over the autonomy of Kosovo (inhabited principally by Albanians, but administratively subordinated to Serbia), and to a virtual rupture of relations between the constituent republics of Slovenia and Serbia.

The rising tide of nationalism, often with triumphalist overtones, is one of the more disquieting aspects of the East European revolution. The issues of German and Romanian reunification, the independence of Poland, federalism in Czechoslovakia and Yugoslavia, the rights o minorities in Romania and Bulgaria: these and other issues that became topical after years in which the issues had been officially taboo demonstrate both the failure of the Marxian stress on proletarian internationalism in changing people's basic values, and the intractability of a phenomenon that has more than once in history led to disaster in Europe. Ancient rivalries, hatreds and suspicions have resurfaced, placing Eastern Europe somewhat out of tune with deliberate attempts in Western Europe since the Second World War to overcome the traditional enmities among states and nations. Blood has been spilt — and will probably continue to be spilt — over divisions that are seen as no less acute in the last decade of the twentieth century then they were in the first. The repression of these animosities has not dissipated them. And the philosophical question arises as to whether it is morally preferable that ethnic groups should express their anger against fellow citizens, or that they should be forced to keep their passions in check. A fundamental question that has to be faced as these countries establish new institutions and mechanisms for the resolution of society's conflict is what is their attitude towards ethnic minorities and towards state borders. Quite clearly, the issue of Europe's identity and the identities of its constituent nations and states is little closer to resolution than a century ago.

A final socio-political issue that has been of considerable significance in these developments is the role of religion and the churches. The strong support given by the Roman Catholic church to Solidarity in Poland, initially under Cardinal Wyszynski and later under his successor, Cardinal Glemp (with the crucial support of the Polish Pope John Paul II), is but the most prominent example. A widespread revival of religious observation throughout the countries of Eastern Europe had been in train for a decade or more, with Churches giving sanctuary to anti-regime manifestations in a number of countries, including the GDR and Czechoslovakia. In Soviet Lithuania, the Roman Catholic church threw its weight behind the movement for national independence of the Soviet Union. In the GDR, it was a series of mass demonstrations following meetings in the Cathedral of St Nicholas (Nikolaikirche) in Leipzig that kept up the pressure on the communist authorities. In Romania, it was an attempt by the regime to arrest pastor László Tökés that sparked demonstrations in the city of Timisoare, leading to nationwide demonstrations in which the army joined the rebel population. The struggle for religious freedom was, indeed, a central element in the push for human rights and democratic reform.

In the economy, the heavy-handed mechanism of centralized state planning was severely modified, and a significant private sector is being introduced, in a number of cases with the involvement of foreign capital and expertise. Cooperative and individual labour was permitted in the Soviet Union, and in other countries the express intention of establishing a market economy has been announced, with rapid movement in that direction in Poland, in particular. There are, of course, formidable practical difficulties in taking such a major step, in countries where managerial and business expertise is almost completely lacking, since it was not required under the central planning system; moreover, suspicions of profiteering on the part of those who charge high prices for goods and services in chronic short supply are widespread among the populations. But so incapable had the traditional system proved itself at supplying a highly differentiated market with goods of a range and quality demanded by an educated, articulate and relatively wealthy consumer that drastic measures were vital simply in order to regain basic confidence. Indeed, the failing economy was the initial impetus for Gorbachev's reform policy, as it was in Poland and Hungary. And even where the economic performance was, by East European standards, tolerably good, the reformist leaders quickly abandoned their predecessors' adamant refusal to acknowledge the need for market-oriented reform. Several countries of the area were saddled with massive external hard-currency debt, and practically everywhere there was a flourishing black market in Western currencies, which had to be tackled if economic order were to return. Adjustment of the official exchange rates, as a prelude to the longer-term convertibility of East European currencies, is one mechanism that has attempted to inject realism into economic affairs, but deep reform of the system of economic management and of property relations would be required in order to lift those countries out of their difficulties. This, in particular, has implications for their relations with the rest of the world, especially Western Europe.

IMPLICATIONS OF THE EASTERN EUROPEAN REVOLUTION

The changes are still under way, with moves towards apparent liberalization in the last Stalinist stronghold, Albania, in the late spring of 1990. Their ultimate scale is therefore still uncertain. However, it is quite clear that many of the assumptions that have governed attitudes and policies in East and West over the past half century are in need of radical revision, if not complete abandonment. Three areas are of particular concern for relations between Western and Eastern Europe: the problem of international security;

the question of building a new economic order; and the issue of human rights.

International security

Much of West Europe's thinking about its security since the Second World War has had as its premise the assumption of a threat from the countries of the communist world. However, the developing revolution in Eastern Europe, even before the overthrow of communist regimes in 1989, was already causing a diminution in both the perception and the reality of the threat. The concept of the threat from the East was a complex one, embraced not only military factors such as the overwhelming numbers of manpower under arms in the countries of Eastern Europe compared with the West, but also the onslaught of hostile propaganda, and certain ideological statements that were taken to imply potential aggression on the part of communist regimes. In this equation, the Soviet Union played the key role, with subordinate and even minor parts allocated to that country's allies in the Warsaw Treaty Organization. Gorbachev's 'peace offensive' on attaining office has involved many concessions to the West and embracing a series of diplomatic summit conferences leading to arms reduction treaties, the withdrawal of troops from Afghanistan, and the withdrawal of some Soviet troops and equipment from Eastern European countries.

From the perspective of the East European countries, the ideological confrontation had been affected by the increasing commercial and cultural contact that had been built up over many years, and the capitalist West had become a source of vital capital and expertise for a number of countries: indeed, indebtedness to Western banks was one of the causes of the economic crisis that precipitated the reforms in Poland and Hungary; in Romania, the Ceausescu regime's repression in the cause of repaying foreign debt at an unreasonable speed led to desperation on the part of the people, who had very little to lose economically — and nothing at all politically — by revolting against the regime.

All this had already undermined the rationale for the permanently hostile posture between East and West Europe; and the abandonment of Marxism-Leninism as the official ideology in favour of 'democracy' (whatever that may mean in practice) has removed continued justification for the cold war, with its intellectual simplicity and its bipolar thinking (frequently interpreted as political stability). The Greater Europe of the 1990s and beyond is bound to be far less simply structured, and is therefore potentially less stable to a significant degree. Moreover, the clear loosening of ties between the Soviet Union and the former satellites is leading to a reassessment of the functioning and role of the economic organization Comecon (Council for Mutual Economic Assistance) and the Warsaw Treaty Organization. In the past, both of these international organizations were dominated by the Soviet Union; in the new situation, the other members are questioning their utility from a national standpoint. The effect is to undermine the cohesion of what was formerly the Eastern bloc, and this imposes a need on the part of Western Europe to reassess its own defence requirements and its economic relationships with Europe's 'other half'.

In terms of security, the collapse of the communist regime in East Germany immediately placed on the European political agenda the question of the unification (or reunification) of Germany through some new arrangement between the Federal Republic and the Democratic Republic. The prospects for an immediate move towards that are not universally welcome, if only because many of Germany's neighbours fear the potential threat of a resurgent German nationalism and possible calls for the re-establishment of greater Germany. Elsewhere, the revival of ethnic tensions in the wake of the greater freedom to give political expression to public concerns holds the risk of instability in several areas of Europe, and could well feed back on to the nationalist movements in Western Europe. The animosities between the Bulgarians and the Turks, the Serbs and the Albanians, the Slovenes and the Serbs, and perhaps — again — the Czechs and the Slovaks inside individual countries might well be joined by renascent suspicions and hostilities between nation states: Germany and Poland, Hungarians and Romanians. Already the long-repressed desire of the three Baltic states of Estonia, Latvia and Lithuania to regain their independent statehood appears to herald the eventual dismemberment of the Soviet Union, with similar developments elsewhere on the periphery of the old Russian Empire.

These actual and prospective developments, as nations assert their individual identity, will lead to as yet unknown political and military alignments, with consequences that can hardly be guessed at. One thing they clearly demonstrate is the abysmal failure of the communist experience to replace ancient sentiments with the noble ideals, embodied in Marxism-Leninism, of proletarian internationalism, fraternal assistance and tolerance — some of which ideals are required to sustain living democracy. A divided Europe that has enjoyed peace through the repression of such national feelings is being replaced by a Europe in which a number of contiguous nations are exulting in their new-found separate identity, at a time when in the western part of the continent nations have been deliberately encouraging the opposite development: a measure of pooling of sovereignty in the interests of the peace and prosperity of the broader community.

The international economy

Similar considerations may apply in the field of European economic collaboration. Ostensibly, the democratization of Eastern Europe opens the way to greater economic co-operation, as private firms are established and begin to trade freely in place of the state foreign trade monopoly. Bureaucratic barriers to trade are being dismantled and the principles of the market are being introduced; the economic agencies and governments look westward in search of capital and expertise to revive and modernize their economies; and price reforms accompanied by other moves towards economic rationality are expected to lead eventually to freely convertible currencies in Eastern Europe. At the same time, the change in the strategic and defence equation undermines the security rationale for strict export controls through CoCom and other agreements.

However, the extent to which the economies of Eastern and Western Europe are complementary is still open and remains to be tested. At present, and in the immediate future, economic relations will be dominated by the need to get the collapsed economies of some of the Eastern countries moving again, principally by rescheduling debts and injecting fresh capital, either as loans, as joint ventures, or as direct investment, and providing managerial expertise and training. Again, the decline of the strategic factor should permit export of computer and similar advanced technology that would permit the modernization of those backward economies. Complementary development could lead eventually to the creation of a market of some 300 million with a colossal productive capacity — significantly greater if the Soviet Union is included. Such a Europe could be brought into competition with other major economic powers, with whom there is already a measure of rivalry for increasingly scarce energy and other resources: the United States, Japan, and the rapidly modernizing economies of the Third World, notably Taiwan, South Korea and Malaysia. The prospect of a revitalized Europe, collaborating economically and politically, if not already on the way to a greater union, may change the prognosis for the twenty-first century as the century of the Pacific basin.

In this connection, the role of the European Community becomes quite crucial. The proposed aid from EC countries to Eastern Europe will help to overcome the immediate difficulties of countries emerging from half a century of 'socialist' economic planning, with stress on relatively inefficient and dirty heavy industry. However, it will not resolve the long-term structural problems of inequality in levels of income and wealth across what has until now been the East-West divide. Overcoming that will require a pan-European extension of the European Community — including possibly the involvement of such wealthy states as Sweden. At the same time, this will inevitably lead to a re-direction of some resources envisaged to support regional development in the present Community. The special economic relationship between the two German states already changes the working assumptions of the European Community, and could lead to great advantages for that state, exacerbating the problems of regional variation.

Quite clearly, the long-term economic problems and opportunities raised by the development away from the Stalinist form of economic management will require great patience and foresight, and indeed new thinking about the strategies of development pursued in Europe over the past forty years.

The importance of human rights factors

The revolution in Eastern Europe, involving as it does a break with what, in its heyday, was one of the most repressive types of regime to exist in modern times, involves a whole variety of dimensions, in which the striving for human, civil and political rights became transformed into a striving for democracy and national independence. It is also at the heart of the entire process of restructuring the Soviet type of system in the direction of a *Rechtsstaat*, or state based on the rule of law.

It is already clear that this process of establishing notions of human rights in post-communist societies that had never previously enjoyed such a tradition is going to be fraught with difficulties. The thorny problem of national minorities has already been mentioned, but religious and linguistic diversity — whether or not complicated by the ethnic question, as in Yugoslavia or the Soviet Union — is also a problem that will demand great tact on the part of governments, East and West. Yet the question of human rights is central to the whole issue of democratization, and it is therefore one that cannot be ignored or treated lightly.

The issue of human rights has sometimes been used by the West as an ideological weapon in the struggle against 'communism', rather than as an instrument for inducing internal democratic changes. Current developments

in Eastern Europe militate against treating human rights as a mere
propaganda instruments: let it not be forgotten that the new Europe includes
nations whose spontaneous evolution was suspended for much of the present
century. Progress in the field of human rights is likely to proceed unevenly,
as the various countries experience their historic opportunity of transition
from communist rule to democracy. The West, and Western Europe in
particular, can render assistance on both the political and the economic fronts,
and this assistance should be tied in with its human rights policy. In addition,
the West can try to expand the role of the Helsinki process in providing
mechanisms for the exchange of information and the monitoring of
governments' performance in the field of human rights.

ASSESSING THE CHANGES

In attempting to assess the historic significance of the events in Eastern
Europe, and thereby assess future prospects as a means of defining our own
approach in the coming years, there are difficult questions that have to be
addressed. There may be no 'correct' answer: the interpretation may be
different in the various countries in the region, and indeed the policies that
result from the particular interpretation are likely to have some impact on the
course of development.

A central question relates to the nature of the system that is being
discarded. Much instant comment at the end of the 1980s spoke of the
collapse of 'socialism' or of 'communism' and the victory of 'freedom' and
even of 'capitalism'. While it is gratifying to Western Europe to think in
such terms, since quite plainly its society proved far more attractive to the
peoples of Eastern Europe, such instant assessments do not address the
searching questions of the nature of the 'socialism' or 'communism' that is
being abandoned. This is a complex question that has been addressed by
many scholars over the years, and one to which a definitive answer is not
possible. It is, however, important to appreciate the issues, central among
which is the relationship of Stalinism to the whole enterprise of attempting to
build a 'communist' society.

It is, of course, true that no country has ever claimed to have created a
communist society such as that presented in the utopian vision of Marx and
Lenin. Hence, reference to 'communist countries' could mean nothing more
than countries ruled by communists, that is, by individuals dedicated to the
creation of 'communism'. The most that was ever claimed what that the

Soviet Union had entered the phase of the rapid building of communism, with the prediction that by the early 1980s the technical base for communism would 'in the main' have been built. That assessment was made by Khrushchev in 1961 at a time of very rapid growth in the Soviet economy, and it was quickly abandoned by his successors. Brezhnev substituted the term 'developed socialist society' to characterize the stage attained in the Soviet Union, and the other countries of Eastern Europe claimed to be building such a society. Moreover, in a further refinement of this ideological assertion, Brezhnev's successor, Andropov, indicated that 'developed socialism' was a historically lengthy period which had only just been entered. Quite clearly, then, the notion of 'communism' remained purely theoretical.

What is being judged, therefore, in the whole world — including those countries that are ruled in this fashion — is communism *as a system of rule*, or 'real socialism' ('existing socialism'), as it came to be called in the 1970s. As a system of rule, it is derived very heavily from the experience of the Soviet Union in the 1930s, when, under Stalin's leadership, the country was being forced to modernize at breakneck speed: to make good in a decade the lag of fifty or a hundred years behind the advanced industrial countries, and to do so in a largely hostile world. The ideology and the backwardness of Russia permitted Stalin to justify his methods: state ownership of the economy, the planning system, the terror, the lack of freedom. Moreover, the uniqueness of the experience — disregarding Mongolia and Tannu Tuva (later to be incorporated into the Soviet Union in any case) — allowed Stalin to define the Soviet system as 'socialism', with both its positive features and its extremely deleterious effects on the individual, and on political life in general. The imposition of this system on other societies — or the adoption of it by leaders who won power of their own accord — including countries of quite different traditions from the Soviet Union in the 1930s, is what has led to the present situation. The Stalinist version of 'socialism' is being deliberately remodelled and in some cases, apparently, totally abandoned.

A question to which there is no clear answer as yet is whether it is Stalinism that is being abandoned, or the very idea of 'socialism', which for many people does indeed mean Stalinism.

Gorbachev's approach to these issues is to deny the exclusive validity of Stalinist socialism, asserting that there are other conceptions of socialism that pay greater attention to the human factor. Socialism, in other words, does not simply mean a state-owned and planned economy with a relatively high priority given to heavy industry and to welfare provision. Socialism is also democratic, and must provide for popular involvement in the running of society, as a prelude to 'communism', when people will run their own affairs. The Soviet approach, therefore, is to attempt to reform the system, but with an open-ended agenda. Hungary initially attempted a similar approach, and obviously communists would still wish to retain certain features of the system through which they have ruled.

It is perfectly clear, however, that for significant numbers of citizens in those countries the communists' own definition of their system as 'socialism' has so tainted the very concept that it is rejected overwhelmingly. Whatever appeal 'socialism' and 'communism' may have had has been dissipated by the reality of repression, exacerbated by the failure of the planned economy to meet the needs of an increasingly complex, sophisticated, educated and demanding population. When ancient smokestack industries have polluted the rivers, lakes and atmosphere, and produced impressive defence capacity, but denied the population of the range of goods and services their neighbours on the same continent have come to take for granted; when even basic products such as soap are not available, and food has to be rationed; and when leaderships display scant awareness of the real suffering of their peoples under a system that they constantly proclaim to be the most humane of all social systems: in such conditions, the assurance that you are 'building communism' is of little comfort.

So much is clear, and the motives of the peoples of Eastern Europe in overthrowing the system are not hard to fathom. What is not yet clear is whether the experience of half a century or more of living in such a system has had any other impact. The planned economy may have led to an insoluble crisis, yet it was notwithout its social benefits. For many years, prices remained relatively stable, and certain key products and services were heavily subsidized by the state. Employment levels were high, and economic development created opportunities for new jobs and social mobility from which millions have benefited. Welfare provision meant education and health care free of direct charge. This says nothing about the quality of the provision; but it is not yet clear that at least some of the 'cradle to grave' provision has not become part of a whole generation's expectation of their system. We should not therefore assume that unbridled capitalism is to be the immediate goal of societies emerging from Stalinism. There could well be bitter political struggles, as the countries of Eastern Europe engage in debates similar to those that preoccupied Western Europe in the three decades following the Second World War.

By the same token, we should not necessarily assume that full-blown liberal democracy is an immediate target, or that it can be attained without difficulty. For forty years, and in the Soviet case for considerably longer, the peoples of Eastern Europe have been deprived of the experience of open, democratic politics. A whole generation — two generations — who have grown up since the Second World War have lived under an authoritarian system, which denied them opportunities for genuine participation in the political process. Moreover, the ethos of 'communist' politics was summed up in Lenin's phrase *kto kogo?* — 'Who whom?': who shall win and who shall lose: politics is about victory and defeat. The democratic principle that politics is about the search for the optimal compromise, and that the very process necessarily involves self-restraint, respect for one's opponents and similar values, has not been part of the political culture of the system from which they are emerging. Nor, in the majority of cases (Czechoslovakia being the prime exception), did the political experience before the advent of communist rule prepare those nations to function in a democratic manner. The slogan common in Gorbachev's Soviet Union, 'We are learning democracy', is perfectly apt, and is highly relevant in the context of the conflict between the Armenians and Azeris and other ethnic disputes, and the attitudes towards ethnic Turks in Bulgaria and Hungarians in Romania, along with other forms of social diversity noted above.

A further difficulty associated with this history is that the group with the most direct experience of running society and dealing with foreign governments is, of course, the discredited communist party. That partly explains the attempts by such parties, after changing their names, to take the lead in creating the new system; and it certainly explains much of the popular disenchantment once the euphoria of popular revolution had passed. The attempt by the reforming leader in East Germany, Hans Modrow, to replace the communist secret police by a non-communist equivalent indicates the tendency of former rulers to think in certain patterns; and it is not certain that non-communists — or even anti-communists — who come to power in the first genuine elections for half a century will avoid using methods with which they and their whole society are familiar.

What this means, at the very least, is that we cannot assume the smooth and steady evolution of a liberal democratic society such as West Europe and the United States enjoy. The establishment of democratic forms is in itself not sufficient to guarantee democratic functioning, and again there is no place for smugness or complacency on the part of West Europeans.

THE CHALLENGES OF THE FUTURE

What has been written above suggests that the next half-century of European development is likely to be significantly more complex than the previous half-century. The economic problems are perhaps the most amenable to solution, particularly if all parties identify the opportunities offered by pan-European collaboration. The politics of European evolution pose greater challenges, and perhaps even threats.

Europe as a whole faces a struggle between autocracy and democracy, which is not simply the struggle between decaying Stalinism and West European liberalism: it is a continuation of a far older struggle in Europe's political evolution. To some extent, the rigidities of the Cold War froze that evolution, and perhaps exacerbated it by reinforcing traditional authority patterns in a different guise. It is conceivable that the renascent social conflicts of Eastern Europe, now attempting to find expression in democratic processes after repression for half a century, will rekindle embers of conflict in Western Europe.

In that context, the revival of nationalism poses perhaps the greatest threat to stability and perhaps to peace. We should not forget that the existence of many distinct cultures in a relatively small geographical area is one of the characteristics of 'Europe', and that a number of conflicts have been merely repressed, not resolved. West Europe liberated from nazism and fascism learned one particular lesson from the experience of unbridled nationalism and took steps to prevent a recurrence. The mechanisms that enforced peace and collaboration in Eastern Europe, the Warsaw Treaty Organization and Comecon, are collapsing, and there is so far nothing to replace them. The role of Western Europe in extending a friendly and understanding hand to her neighbours could be quite crucial in the coming decades — while not overlooking West Europe's own struggle to accommodate minority aspirations. A peaceful Europe — indeed, a peaceful world — has to be built on the basis of an internationalist outlook, no matter how much we each pledge allegiance to our own society.

As the eastern part of the continent embarks on the task of restructuring itself after half a century under a system that has proved inappropriate and unacceptable, the prospects for Europe as a whole are both exciting and ridden with risks and challenges. There are no guarantees in human life, and in politics the unpredictable may always astound us: the pace of change in Eastern Europe took everyone by surprise, even though it appears to have a certain inevitability about it. In some cases, problems are being taken up that had been in suspense for several decades, and these will undoubtedly require delicate handling.

But the fact is that Europe and the world have not stood still. There can be no returning to the world of 1939. The process of West European integration has already changed the identity of 'Europe', and that process seems set to continue. The countries of Eastern Europe, too, are very different from what they were when the communists came to power: in terms of social structure, educational levels, economic base, substructural links and in a variety of other ways, those societies have evolved in parallel with those of the West. Whatever the present difficulties, the countries of Eastern Europe are by world standards relatively wealthy and modern, and they are more capable of partnership with their more advanced western neighbours than any Third World countries would be.

Moreover, there exist new mechanisms to assist Europe in facing its challenges and overcoming its problems. New international bodies such as the United Nations, the International Court of Justice and the European Court of Human Rights are in place to help particular societies overcome internal difficulties and settle inter-state disputes. The Helsinki (or CSCE) process has already had some impact in setting standards of behaviour which states are expected to observe, and it should receive a fillip from the developments in the east. The existence of such pan-European bodies as the Council of Europe likewise can ease the process of education in Europe, as the two halves set about getting to know one another. And technological advances, particularly in the field of communications — not only telecommunications, but even basic physical communication by ordinary citizens of east and west — has opened up borders and created a new generation of Europeans willing and eager to travel to their neighbours. These processes can enhance the integrative effect of economic and political cooperation.

There is therefore much scope for interaction, convergence and a common evolution between the two halves of Europe, to the benefit of the individual nations of Europe, Europe as a whole, and the world. The evolution of a new Europe, in which the identity of the whole is created on the basis of fostering the identities of its constituent parts, could properly constitute the political agenda of the next half-century.

NOTES

1. As Timothy Garton Ash has suggested, 'We should no longer talk of Eastern Europe, at least with a capital "E" for Eastern. Instead, we shall have a central Europe again, east-central Europe, southeastern Europe, eastern Europe with a small "e", and, above all, individual peoples, nations, and states': see his 'Eastern Europe: The Year of Truth', *The New York Review of Books*, 15 February 1990, p. 17. In the present book, for the sake of simplicity, the term 'Eastern Europe' is used throughout.
2. See Francis Fukuyama, 'The End of History', *The National Interest*, 16 (Summer 1989), pp. 3-18. This article attracted widespread critical interest in the summer of 1989.

3. The Institutionalization of Reform

Ronald J. Hill

In the complex of changes taking place in the countries of Eastern Europe, including the Soviet Union, that have been subjected to rule by the Stalinist version of 'socialism', one of the most critical is the establishment of new institutional arrangements to guide the societies towards new prosperity and participatory political processes. The collapse of the system followed different patterns, with a number of common elements; the chances are that future developments will lead to substantial diversification in the forms and practices of East European public life.

Two principal factors have been instrumental in promoting the institutionalization of change: the arrival of a reformist leader in the Soviet Union;[1] and the adoption of contested elections, which gave citizens a political way of demonstrating their opposition to the ruling communist elites. Further back in the chain of logic is the economic crisis that revealed the inability of the Stalinist planning system to manage a complex modern economy and society. Associated with that, the weapon of the strike, deployed by workers for increasingly political purposes, has served as a powerful form of pressure for change.

In the Soviet Union, in Poland and in Hungary, previous attempts at economic reform by essentially administrative methods, unaccompanied by political concessions, had enjoyed only temporary success, while storing up difficulties that eventually required a wide battery of thorough-going reforms. The failure of those earlier attempts has inspired aspects of the current changes.

EARLIER REFORM ATTEMPTS

In the Soviet Union, Khrushchev moved from authoritarianism by abolishing the political use of terror and capricious repression — his major contribution to Soviet political development.[2] He attempted to redistribute power away from the central ministries and their massive apparatus, to the party (in which he was largely successful) and to the representative soviets (in which his success was limited).[3] Attempts at economic reform under Aleksei Kosygin in the mid-1960s failed, mainly because there was no attempt to extend the reforms to the political system; in the 1970s, what is now officially designated 'stagnation' (*zastoi*) set in. Reformist ideas were still being generated and circulated but they had little political impact: at best they prepared for reform under Mikhail Gorbachev, by developing ideas that have now been taken up and implemented, and by educating the post-Brezhnev leadership generation to think of reform while holding responsible posts below the political summit.[4]

In Eastern Europe, reform was attempted at different times via various mechanisms in several countries. Yugoslavia, expelled from the Communist Information Bureau (Cominform) in 1948, devised its own form of 'socialism', markedly different from the Soviet model. It stressed worker participation in the work-place through 'self-management by the direct producers' (*samo-upravljanje*), and offered far greater individual freedoms than were permitted elsewhere in the region; the political structures attempted to accommodate national distinctions in ways not attempted elsewhere.[5] Nevertheless, lacking strong central direction since Tito's death in 1980, this approach has not proved durable, and the stability of the system is in doubt.

After Stalin's death and Khrushchev's denunciation of him at the Twentieth CPSU Congress, popular uprisings took place in the German Democratic Republic in June 1953, and in Poland and Hungary in the autumn of 1956. The events in Hungary had the most dramatic immediate impact and conceivably the greatest long-term influence on reform. The reinstalled 'dissident' communist Prime Minister, Imre Nagy, advanced proposals that would have led to sharply different domestic and external political relationships, including a multi-party system and Hungary's withdrawal from the Warsaw Treaty Organization.[6] Over the next thirty years, under János Kádár, important economic reforms were introduced (in 1968) and society was significantly liberalized under the continuing political monopoly of the communist party (the Hungarian Socialist Workers' Party).

The most sustained reform programme until the 1980s came in Czechoslovakia in early 1968. Under Alexander Dubcek, the communist party proposed an Action Programme that would have amounted to democratization had its implementation been allowed.[7] It included abolition of censorship, extending citizens' rights (including the right to travel abroad), federalizing the state to give Slovaks a greater voice in national politics, and opening the economy to world trade, leading eventually to a convertible currency.

In Poland, although the political system as such was not affected, workers' demonstrations and mass action in December 1970 forced the resignation of Wladyslaw Gomulka and in June 1976 made Edward Gierek cancel proposed food price rises. In 1980-81, the creation of the independent trade union Solidarity, and the concomitant rise in the Catholic Church's political role and influence, appeared to signify a sharing of power with the ruling Polish United Workers' Party (PUWP). The apparent genuineness of the negotiations between the authorities and Solidarity, together with the Church's conciliatory role, suggested that the communists were willing to compromise with political and social reality, with possible evolution into a new social partnership under public ownership. Hence the appropriateness of the concept of the 'self-limiting revolution',[8] which would have represented a fundamental break with the communist party's traditional political monopoly.

These repeated efforts showed that the Stalinist model had not been accepted in Eastern Europe, and the people were not prepared to tolerate the restrictions in their political rights and their economic wellbeing that the system imposed on them. Indeed, it demonstrated that legitimacy — acceptance by the populations of the validity of a particular system of rule — cannot be attained by repression.[9] Furthermore, the constant refusal of the mass of citizens to accept the regime, even as wealth steadily accumulated in the 1960s and 1970s, raised fundamental doubts about the communists' assumptions concerning the supremacy of material factors in winning support. The importance of religion in Russia and Poland, and the universal desire for freedom from controls, inspired the working masses' refusal to be bought off with material wealth.

The failure of the reformist efforts, and the forceful — sometimes brutal — way they were terminated, demonstrated that the Soviet Union, exercising dominance over six of the eight countries in the region, would not tolerate infringement by its allies of certain basic 'rules': the communist party's leading role, democratic centralism to ensure discipline, and censorship to stifle competing viewpoints, as the 'pillars' of the system.[10] Moreover, the so-called 'Brezhnev doctrine', which sanctioned Warsaw Pact intervention in Czechoslovakia in August 1968, supposedly justifed the USSR's right to 'rectify' the course of 'socialist' countries that deviated from the orthodox model.[11] It required the passing of the Brezhnev generation, and the arrival of a new, more sophisticated leadership in circumstances of economic and political crisis, to acknowledge the need for fundamental reform in the system as such. In part, this entailed a recognition that Stalinism, however effective in mobilizing resources for the basic industrial development of a peasant society, could not cope with managing the product of that initial success: a complex society with a highly-developed division of labour, comprising relatively wealthy, well-educated, well-informed citizens, making multifarious demands which it is the purpose of a political system to acknowledge and respond to. The need for reform lies in the contrast between the system's origins and capabilities and the tasks that now face it — including the winning of acceptance and support.

THE ORIGINS OF THE SYSTEM

The Bolsheviks seized power in a country that, by the conventional standards of Marxist theory, was not ripe for socialist revolution. Most features of the revolutionary society, depicted by Marx and Engels in *The Communist Manifesto*, were absent in Russia in 1917 and for many years thereafter. A peasant society ruled by a distant autocratic monarchy, in which illiteracy and ignorance were the predominant characteristics of the bulk of the population, it had a tiny working class which was in no position to exercise the 'dictatorship of the proletariat' called for by Marxists. Hence, the party deemed itself the 'vanguard of the proletariat', and exercised that dictatorship 'on behalf of' the working class. It also undertook to modernize the society — a task that should have been achieved by a bourgeoisie which was largely absent in Russia. Those circumstances dictated different methods from what might have been contemplated in different conditions, and forms of rule devised to overcome backwardness came to be regarded as natural and even necessary for a society attempting to build socialism and communism.[12] These included certain organizational principles such as democratic centralism, the communist party's leading role (in fact, political monopoly), and the ban on fractionalism within ruling parties, and also a culture in which the rulers claimed to possess higher wisdom because of their superior understanding of 'scientific' Marxism-Leninism. Moreover, manipulation of the ideology permitted Stalin to justify vicious methods to impose harsh discipline on all members of society, communists and non-communists alike. This, too, became a kind of dogma: class enemies must be exposed and rooted out mercilessly; nothing must be allowed to stop the march of the victorious proletariat towards communism.

In its heyday, that system achieved rapid growth rates, and changed the social structure of the Soviet Union and other countries around the world; it did so essentially by repressing political development in favour of economic growth. In its evolved, post-Stalin form, policy was made by the communist party Politburo, headed by the General Secretary, and endorsed by the Central Committee. It was given legal status by the parliamentary institution (the Supreme Soviet, the Volkskammer, the Sejm), comprising carefully screened deputies whose 'election' was little more than a formality, and who almost never voted against party-approved policy. Policy was then implemented, under communist supervision, by the ministries, whose heads formed the Council of Ministers or 'government'. The hierarchy of command spread downwards, and interlocking membership of party and state bodies helped to ensure compliance at all levels.

It also, however, led to gross interference by party organs and officers in the work of the state — a phenomenon called in Russian *podmena* (substitution) — to the extent that the state had no genuine authority, and certainly no political independence. The ministries, to be sure, possessed power through their control of sectors of the economy. But they functioned under the 'leadership' of the party, whose members staffed the administrative apparatus and occupied all positions of responsibility and authority.

None of the major institutions was in any real sense accountable: at most, some individual deputies took their representative functions seriously, and intervened with the bureaucracy on behalf of their electors. So long as policies appeared broadly acceptable to the populations, some legitimacy, however grudging, was accorded to the system. Once the economy began to fail, the regimes could do nothing to win even a minimum of acceptance, and the authority of the party and state collapsed. This was intensified by the revelations of corruption on the part of the self-styled leaders in the building of 'developed socialism'.

In some respects, the Soviet Union originated the reforms, but increasingly it has followed changes introduced elsewhere. By the spring of 1990, communist parties accustomed to unfettered power buttressed by constitutional guarantees had abandoned or lost their political monopoly in Poland, Hungary, the GDR, Bulgaria, Romania, Yugoslavia and the Soviet

Union itself. The astonished world witnessed a wave of radical reformist and revolutionary change, as old institutions yielded to political pressure, leading to the establishment of new frameworks.[13] The circumstances of communist rule, as established in Eastern Europe in the past two generations, help to explain the swiftness of the collapse of communist power; they also present a wide range of problems for the democratic development of the countries in the region. The task is, of course, to dismantle the monopolistic structures and power relations and replace them with new forms, while simultaneously stabilizing weakened economies and keeping society in general functioning. The task of breaking with traditional communism and establishing new, democratic rule followed different courses in the various countries.

PARTY-LED REFORM

In three countries the ruling party initiated the reform following a leadership change. First, Gorbachev in the Soviet Union signalled reform. Initially part of an attempt to inject dynamism into a stagnant economy, political reform later acquired its own justification.[14] Greater openness and frankness in public discourse (*glasnost*), intended to engage the population's attention and undermine the position of opponents of reform,[15] was followed by a more radical approach. Political reform, hinted at in February 1986 in connection with the electoral system,[16] came to be seen as indispensable for the system's very survival. Both the methods of government and the administrators who had guided the decline were so discredited that only a radical transformation could hope to prevent collapse, even as the loosening up seemed to threaten the integrity of the manifestly fragile multinational union.

The party leader led the reform, fighting 'conservatives' opposed to change (including probably the bulk of the apparatus, appointed through the system of *nomenklatura*) and radicals keen to push towards a market economy and political pluralism. In contested elections in 1987, 1989 and 1990, communist party candidates performed badly, losing to national movements and to radical reformers. Whether such countermeasures as the creation in March 1990 of a presidential system of government — giving Mikhail Gorbachev powers so sweeping as to cause considerable consternation in liberal and radical circles[17] — will save the reforms and the union remains an open question.

More successful, in terms of securing radical political change, was the reformist wing of the Hungarian Socialist Workers' Party. Even under János Kádár, Hungary had led economic and political reform. In the late 1980s, however, the economy deteriorated, and after thirty years in office Kádár proved incapable of responding in a forthright and imaginative way: he was dropped unceremoniously from the party leadership in May 1988. In the struggle for reform, the running was made by Imre Pozsgay, a radical Politburo member firmly committed to democratizing socialism. Specifically, the communist party must stand on its record and compete for power with other parties in elections scheduled for 1990. New parties began to form, including a Hungarian Socialist Party, inheritor of the Socialist Workers' Party mantle. A reform organization, the Hungarian Democratic Forum, and more than fifty parties took part in the country's first contested elections in April 1990: the former communists were roundly defeated.

In Bulgaria, too, with apparently no great pressure from below for change,[18] Politburo member Petar Mladenov played a role comparable with that of Pozsgay in Hungary, precipitating a Politburo crisis that preceded the ousting of Todor Zhivkov, and becoming party leader in his place. The party agreed on 11 December to abolish its constitutionally guaranteed political monopoly, and promised elections for the summer of 1990; in these, in a contest of more than thirty parties, and with a high turnout, the former communists polled strongly — and even secured victory.

REFORM INDUCED FROM BELOW

Poland was the first communist-ruled country in which pressure from below forced the hand of the communist regime, after a decade in which it had failed to resolve the economic, political and social crisis. There, more than elsewhere, the social preconditions for a participatory system already existed: most importantly, the experience of earlier attempts to bring about change, particularly in the 'Solidarity' era of 1980-81. That era ended in repression, yet the sense that things could be different, and in identifiable ways, was part of the accumulated national experience, and Solidarity survived underground, a vehicle for political reform ready to emerge.

In November 1987, after years of unmitigated economic failure, the government held a referendum on a package of economic reforms, warning that two or three years' further hardship was inevitable. The very idea of a referendum on a broad policy issue was quite novel, yet it did not win over the population. Urged by Solidarity to boycott the proceedings, the electorate rendered a sharp rebuke to the Jaruzelski government by not supporting the package in the required numbers.[19] The government proceeded in any case with its measures, with only slight modifications, warning of a prolongation of the people's economic plight.[20]

The underlying problem remained unsolved: motivating a people who rejected the system as an alien form imposed by Stalin for strategic reasons and accepted at Yalta by the Western allies. By 1988 the political situation was markedly worse than a decade earlier. The 1980s had done nothing to win over public opinion, and stalemate was reached. It was, in the perceptive words of one commentator on the eve of historic talks between the Polish government and Solidarity in the spring of 1989, a particular application of a wider problem:

> The crisis is not Poland's — it is a crisis of the system. It engulfs the Soviet Union. In Poland, the crisis is particularly pernicious because, unlike the Soviet Union, no one believes the system deserves to be saved.[21]

Strikes during 1988 demonstrated Solidarity's continuing potency, and the communists had to recognize this. Talks in which Solidarity and the government were 'condemned to agree' on a pluralist approach to resolving the crisis[22] began on 6 February 1989: Solidarity was re-legalized in return for supporting a package of economic and political reforms, which opened the possibility of radical political evolution. A new institution, the Senate, was created alongside the Sejm (parliament), and in elections in June Solidarity swept the board, taking all its allocated constituencies in the Sejm and all but one Senate seat. In the subsequent negotiations, the role of the quasi-independent non-communist parties became crucial. Having functioned for decades in the communist-dominated 'hegemonic party system'[23] within the National Front, the Democratic Party and the United Peasants' Party asserted their independence — in effect, withdrawing from the 'coalition' — leaving the PUWP politically impotent. On 19 August, the country gained in Mieczyslaw Rakowski its first non-communist prime minister since the Second World War, and his largely non-communist government set about dismantling the 'socialist' system that had served the population so ill.

The reform gathered pace in the summer of 1989, as Hungary — still ruled by the communists — moved to liberalize society. New parties formed, and from May the barbed wire that formed the 'iron curtain' border with Austria was dismantled. Taking advantage of this opening, and the abrogation by Hungary of a twenty-year agreement with the GDR, thousands of East

Germans on vacation fled to Austria; others invaded the German Federal Republic's embassy compounds in Prague and Warsaw, where they were given FRG passports and transported to West Germany. In such an atmosphere, the GDR celebrated its fortieth anniversary on 7 October. The presence of Mikhail Gorbachev, seen universally outside the Soviet Union as a force for reform and democracy, cut no ice with the long-standing leader, Erich Honecker; but the popular mood meant that change could not be resisted indefinitely. In addition to the haemorrhage of young, well-trained refugees, weekly demonstrations in Leipzig and other cities put further pressure on the regime. Within two weeks of the anniversary, Honecker was removed from office and replaced by the interior minister Egon Krenz, who in less than two months changed the Socialist Unity Party's policy and even breached the Berlin Wall.

By late autumn, the pressure of events became apparently unstoppable. In Czechoslovakia, repeated mass demonstrations in Prague, Bratislava and elsewhere — in which large crowds cheerfully jangled keys in confidence at their eventual victory — forced the hand of the communist regime of Milos Jakes. The reformist leader of 1968, Alexander Dubcek, reemerged to encourage the reformers, a leading figure among whom was the playwright Václav Havel,[24] a thorn in the side of the authorities, imprisoned as a dissident earlier in the year, who now led the Civic Forum democratic movement. After the communist regime collapsed in late November, Hável became President, and Dubcek chairman of the parliament.

The most forceful example of pressure from below came, however, in Romania, where in Christmas week bitter and brave street fighting in support of the army against the well-armed Securitate (political police) brought to a bloody end the 24-year rule of Nicolae Ceausescu. A provisional government was set up in which communists played a leading role, but which pledged to work towards free elections (held on 20 May 1990) and to create a new system of government.

THE WAVE OF REFORM

That event, watched by millions around the world — revolution by television[25] — was the culmination of an astonishing year in Eastern Europe. Communists had lost power in Poland, Czechoslovakia and Romania; in Hungary, the GDR and Bulgaria, they were committed to elections allowing other political parties a genuine opportunity to win power. Events continued rolling. On December 19, the communist party in Lithuania resolved to sever its links with Moscow: in effect, the party split, with the majority moving for independence — under political pressure from the separatist movement Sajudis — and a rump staying with 'the CPSU platform', a pattern repeated in Estonia in March and Latvia in April 1990. These were but the more spectacular signs of disarray within the Soviet Communist Party, which advanced its Twenty-Eighth Congress, due to be held in the spring of 1991, first to the autumn of 1990 and then to July. Such was the state of morale, and so great the differences over the merits and prospects for *perestroika* (restructuring), that a permanent split in the Soviet party was openly discussed from late 1989. Apart from the splinter parties in the Baltic republics, a 'Democratic Platform' was established on 21 January 1990 and a 'Marxist Platform' also published a manifesto:[26] the pattern of Eastern Europe fed back to the USSR.

Barring a reactionary coup, pluralist politics are firmly now in view. On 7 February, following an unprecedented demonstration in Moscow of upwards of a quarter of a million protesters, the party Central Committee voted to abandon Article 6 of the Constitution, and the Congress of People's Deputies complied on 13 March, inserting a reference to 'other political parties'. Some already existed in embryo, in regional nationalist movements and in the variety of political clubs that sprang into existence as a result of the reforms. On their basis, competitive politics will develop.

COMMON FEATURES

This brief chronology reveals several common features. While each nation has abandoned traditional communist rule in its own way, certain symbolic elements and behavioural patterns are shared. The first is the crucial step of allowing citizens to express an opinion, in place of the phoney elections and plebiscites of the past. The mould was broken by Poland, with its referendum of 29 November 1987. The electorate, in rejecting the proposals, showed itself no longer prepared to accept communist rule unquestioningly. In the Soviet Union, too, given a choice of candidates in an electoral experiment in June 1987, many electors voted to remove local party and state officers from the 'organs of state power'.[27] In the spring of 1989, they repeated the message to leading communist candidates for election to the Congress of People's Deputies, and again in the spring of 1990 at republican level. Polish voters did the same in the summer of 1989. And, as the various countries went through an electoral contest, a similar result was witnessed:

rejection of the former communists in favour of 'democrats'. In Hungary, indeed, the architect of reform, Imre Pozsgay, failed to secure election on March 25; in the GDR, where leading politicians from West Germany (including the federal Chancellor, Helmut Kohl) played an active, even crucial, part in the campaign, the Christian Democrats (senior coalition partners in Bonn) were victorious, largely on promises of early unification of the two German states on economic terms favourable to GDR citizens. Whatever the precise results in individual cases, the message is clear: half a century of unopposed rule by communists is enough.

A second common feature, clearly tied in with competitive elections, is the abandonment of the communist party's monopoly, in most cases enshrined in the state constitution. Moreover, once that particular bandwagon began to roll, it seemed unstoppable, as the Soviet experience indicates: the speed of Mikhail Gorbachev's conversion to the idea of a multi-party system — from rejection in December 1989 to acquiescence in February 1990[28] — shows the force of example. Party reformists appeared content to allow the CPSU to take its chances alongside emergent new parties.

Across the region, the creation of viable alternative parties has proceeded. In some cases, such as Poland and the GDR, that entailed the invigoration of parties that had nominally existed under communist rule. Elsewhere, it took the form of the creation of a multiplicity of new parties, many of which (as in Hungary) are unlikely to survive long in competitive politics. And in some cases, the transformation of other organizations into parties or quasi-parties enabled them to win substantial successes at the polls: Solidarity in Poland, the reformist coalition Civic Forum in Czechoslovakia, Democratic Forum in Hungary, Sajudis (Lithuania) and Rukh (Ukraine) in the Soviet Union.

Equally important — indeed, perhaps ultimately more important than these auxiliary measures — was the reconstitution of the parliament as a genuinely authoritative law-making institution. The communist state legislature was essentially the party's dutiful handmaiden, containing hand-picked deputies, selected for their sociological characteristics rather than their political qualities or capacities as representatives; they met too infrequently to control current policy-making; their 'rubber-stamp' role made the typical communist parliament virtually impotent. The transfer of genuine authority to these bodies, if necessary by restructuring them, was a *sine qua non* for advance towards a working democracy. In the Soviet case, the old Supreme Soviet was replaced by a Congress of People's Deputies which elected a smaller

Supreme Soviet comprising almost professional representatives; in Poland, as noted above, Solidarity claimed overwhelming victory in elections to the Sejm and the Senate, allowing it to force a change in the nature of parliament.

INSTITUTIONALIZING REFORM

The transfer of power from a self-coopting oligarchy to a genuinely representative parliament is the basic task in the process of institutionalizing reform — even if in the future the communists manage to win a parliamentary majority. This is not a straightforward process. The establishment of a stable, working democracy entails far more than simply setting up a parliament through competitive elections. The society's political culture to some extent governs both the functioning of the electoral process and the performance of the representatives in their institution. The mastery of procedures and willingness to submit to them — indeed, the initial establishment of procedures and standing orders — is a vital element in the success of representative bodies. While the halting, hesitant attempts in the USSR Congress of People's Deputies to establish its own working rules had an amusing side, the minute attention paid to this area of 'learning democracy' by the newly-elected deputies had an extremely serious purpose. The almost total absence of a tradition of thinking in such terms, either before the communists came to power in a number of countries, or during several decades of communist rule, meant that those thrust into such positions had to feel their way with little in their experience to guide them. 'Getting the rules right' — a necessary condition for democratic government (as the eighteenth-century makers of constitutions plainly understood) — is not a sufficient condition, given the propensity for much 'politics' to take place secretly, outside formal institutions.

More broadly, these countries face the task of establishing completely new procedures for taking authoritative decisions. Setting up a parliament and acquiring experience on the part of its members is but part of the problem. As in the newly emergent Third World countries, the transition from opposition to government — a common experience for post-communist societies — presents the new incumbents with a quite different set of tasks and requires attitudes very different from those of hostility to the regime. They are faced with taking extremely hard decisions to rectify a disastrous economic situation not of their making — a task that Solidarity, for example, was reluctant to undertake. The enormous fund of good will, born of the euphoria of successful revolution, carries the new institutions only so far. As the policies required by the situation begin to take effect (with expected price rises, unemployment and other unpopular consequences), the electors' mood is likely to swing sharply, and with it, possibly, suspicion of the new institutions: yet, without stabilizing the economy, the medium-term prospects for establishing the legitimacy of the new parliamentary bodies are exceedingly bleak. Either way, the institutionalization of reform is fraught with difficulties: policies for long-term success will not win short-term popularity, which could undermine the stability of the new parliaments. There are many highly practical questions to be resolved, including such matters as the number of chambers, the committee structure (if any), the electoral system, the rights and privileges of parliamentarians, the principle of immunity, the frequency and duration of sessions, procedures for drafting, introducing and adopting legislation, centre-local relations, the financial powers of parliament and procedures for scrutinizing and adopting the budget.[29] These are new problems.

To some extent, the success will depend on such supplementary institutions as political parties, whose fortunes will be affected in turn by the electoral system. There are dangers for the stability of new institutions in a proliferation of small parties: shifting coalitions do not facilitate bold decision-making. In such conditions, proportional representation may not be ideal, even though it has many advantages in democratic theory. A threshold of, say, five per cent (as in West Germany) is a simple but effective mechanism for facilitating the growth of a small number of strong parties, while smaller organizations might be expected to promote the development of other forms of representation, such as interest groups and lobbying bodies associated with the new parliaments. In the present circumstances of widespread national distress, it may be argued that 'getting the economy right' takes the highest priority. Eventually, however, the establishment of secure, pluralist political institutions and processes must be the desired goal, with a complex of forms for interest articulation and political expression. At the present time, these institutions are all feeling their way, and would doubtless benefit from the experience of established democracies. Even basic experiences such as setting up and running organizations that are not under the auspices — whether directly or indirectly — of the ruling party are quite new in these societies, and it is not yet certain that the legal systems provide adequate protection for members of parties and other organizations against unscrupulous officers. Hence, the establishment of a firm legal system — called in the Soviet Union a 'socialist Rechtsstaat' — is absolutely vital.[30] Extending democracy to the local level, after decades of centralized control, presents similar challenges.

NON-INSTITUTIONAL ASPECTS

Some of these problems are compounded by the Leninist political culture, which identifies politics as concerning victory and defeat, victors and vanquished. Such a view of politics — a maxim for communists — was succinctly encapsulated in the phrase, '*kto kogo*' ('who whom'): who shall defeat whom? The notion of compromise was alien, representing a 'solution' in which both (or all) sides lose. In democracy, compromise represents victory, in which both or all sides gain something of their goal. Replacing the Leninist values by the democratic alternative requires far more than simply allowing representative institutions to be formed on the basis of electoral choice, or even establishing new institutions. Given the ethnic and other tensions in the region, it cannot be assumed that the tyranny of a communist minority will not give way to a tyranny of the majority. The demonstrations in Bulgaria in January 1990 against civic rights for citizens of Turkish background; the dominance of Serbs in the Albanian-inhabited province of Kosovo; the violence perpetrated by Romanians in March 1990 on the Hungarians of Transylvania; the attempts to legislate the denial of certain rights to non-ethnic inhabitants of the Soviet Baltic republics: these suggest a triumphalist nationalism that may prove inimical to the establishment of justice and democracy, as numerically dominant groups use their preponderance to exploit majorities in democratic institutions. The question of new kinds of federalism or regional autonomy as the solution to some problems of this kind — say, in the USSR, Yugoslavia, Romania and Czechoslovakia — must be high on the political agenda.

In addition, communist bureaucrats have formed a select coterie who possessed power and influence and created an *esprit de corps* that led some observers to see them as a ruling class.[31] Claiming quasi-professional status,[32] their supposed superior understanding of the 'scientific' ideology justified their control, excluding the masses in whose name they purportedly functioned. The political atmosphere in the Soviet Union and elsewhere was characterized by Leonid Brezhnev's *laissez faire* approach to administration: cadres were permitted independence in exchange for securing political peace or the implementation of the economic plan. In fact, in the Soviet Union, the GDR, Romania, Bulgaria and elsewhere (where former communist leaders faced trial on charges of corruption and treason), the *apparatchiki*, headed by the 'leader', established intricate networks of privilege and high living quite out of keeping with the system's ostensible goals. In a real sense, they were the system: they designed it, controlled it, and spoke in its name; they rewarded one another materially and with honorific benefits (medals, titles and so forth) for their services to the cause. Reform, therefore, entails above all rescuing society and the system from the bureaucracy, and returning politics to the people.[33]

The bureaucrats will not surrender their privileges or power willingly. The Soviet bureaucracy has repeatedly been identified as a principal obstacle to reform, and with reason: its resistance led to the stalling of earlier reforms, and it has responded similarly to Gorbachev's far more vigorous campaign. Despite intra-party discipline and democratic centralism, the bureaucrats — almost entirely communists — have been running a vigorous rearguard campaign of resistance, partly under the patronage of leading party officers. The reformers' dilemma is that they rely on the same bureaucrats to keep the country running and to implement the reforms: they cannot all be sacked and replaced by enthusiasts.[34]

Even following a decisive break with communist rule, the bureaucrats of the communist era possess expertise and experience unrivalled among the largely untested politicians who have to dismantle the old system and replace it with a democratic administration. The difficulty of attaining this change, and the opportunity for foot-dragging by entrenched officials, is obvious. Hence, part of the effort of restructuring must entail breaking up established institutional links and teams of functionaries so as to prevent cohesion in defence of the discredited and overthrown system.

This highlights the complex relationship between the communist party and reform. By the late 1980s — indeed, long before then — ruling communist parties contained both passionate reformers and equally ardent conservatives (who usually presented themselves as defenders of 'genuine' socialism).[35] The clash was seen sharply in the exchange between Nina Andreeva in *Sovetskaya Rossiya* and *Pravda*'s editorial response in the spring of 1988.[36] Similar clashes have been resolved in some countries by splitting the party, with the reform wing changing its name: in the case of the Hungarian Socialist Workers' Party, the reformers (the majority) adopted the name of Hungarian Socialist Party; in Poland, the Polish United Workers' Party split into Social Democracy of the Polish Republic and Social Democratic Union. The prospects in the spring of 1990 appear to be for a similar split within the Soviet party, beyond the splintering in the Baltic region, noted above. In the contested elections, however, the embracing of reform and the change of name cut little ice with the electorate: the Party of Democratic Socialism in the GDR and the Hungarian Socialist Party surrendered power following their poor showing (16 and 10 per cent respectively) in the national elections.

In such a situation, where the power of the dominant institution has collapsed, new relationships have to be created to fill the power vacuum. This demands a new distribution of power among the elected legislature, the government (administration) and the president or head of state, whose symbolic position as embodiment of the nation may not be matched by powers commensurate to the tasks the nation faces. There is a very real dilemma for the creators of the new system. The overthrown communist system invested the leader with great power and in some cases encouraged dictatorship, disguised by a cult.[37] The individual possessed extensive powers of patronage and was supported by a loyal political police (the KGB, the Securitate, the Stasi and their equivalents). The 'circular flow of power', whereby the leader used *nomenklatura* to secure the appointment of supporters to positions that brought membership of bodies (such as the central committee) that formally elected the leader,[38] established a tradition of relying on the leader for authoritative judgments. The role model for some potential leaders is therefore that of the strong leader, and public servants (and possibly sections of the public, too) are trained to respond to such leadership. Moreover, the economic plight may be such that tough leadership is needed. Yet the values of democracy are not entirely compatible with such a role, and shifting coalition governments may deprive an executive president of the capacity to act effectively. For such reasons, the details of any new constitutional arrangements take on an exceptional significance.

PROBLEMS OF DEMOCRATIC REFORM

There exist, then, potentially serious obstacles to institutionalizing democracy, including direct opposition and resistance by communists and bureaucrats on whom the leadership depends for administration, and the lack of appropriate experience and culture on the part of the whole society. Possibly of greater concern are the unpropitious circumstances in which the new governments are coming into office. While instrumental in discrediting and inducing the collapse of communist rule, economic ruin is not the most fertile ground in which democracy might take root. Western financial and technical assistance may require harsh economic decisions. Bankruptcies, unemployment and sharp price rises on basic goods are demanded by the situation. Yet the new regimes face populations accustomed to full employment, relatively generous welfare provision (including 'free' health care and education), subsidies on basic foods, housing, utilities and other necessities, and a range of other features of 'socialism'. Those under the age of 50 have known nothing else, and the inflation of recent years is an aberrant experience. Now that citizens have the democratic right to turn out governments that produce unpopular or unsuccessful policies, the outlook for continuity and stability looks quite bleak. Similarly, freshly emancipated workers making profligate use of their new right to strike do nothing to improve the economy. Ethnic tensions further complicate the picture.

Equally significant is the right to create political parties — like the right to strike, a highly symbolic prize, demonstrating the overthrow of a political monopoly. Yet the proliferation of narrowly based and local parties, including some with a clear ethnic dimension, does not augur well for stable government. Coalitions are likely to be common for several years, hindering resolute government.

Finally, the distinct nationalistic element in the current wave of reform, involving the overthrow of a foreign-imposed system of rule, brutally reinforced more than once by military might, may take the form of triumphalism and inward-looking self-congratulation. The prospect of popular discontent at the presence of foreign capital, employers, economic advisers and others cannot be ruled out — although, paradoxically, the fact that hard economic decisions are imposed by an external agency such as the International Monetary Fund may help insecure governments. The precise political effect will vary from country to country and over time: the capacity to 'blame' the IMF may crumble under popular discontent at domination by foreign concerns if the economic measures fail.

These are some potential difficulties associated with transforming communist rule into effective democracy. Success is more likely in some countries than in others, and the outcome will depend on how far new arrangements cope with the major cleavages in society: are there significant ethnic or religious minorities which hinder the establishment of a homogeneous, nationwide set of representative institutions?

CONCLUSIONS

The institutionalization of change in the new, post-communist world of Eastern Europe is a developing phenomenon, in which the characteristics of individual nations come to take precedence over the shared experience of several decades of communist rule. The peoples of Eastern Europe have gained a fresh opportunity to deploy the experience, and to enjoy again the exhilaration, of political self-expression, yet we cannot assume that the road towards reform and democracy will be smooth. This 'breaking away' from communism may lead to manifestations of national pride, self-assertion and even triumphalist nationalism, which encourages the expression of long-suppressed animosities — such as the conflict between Romania and Hungary over Transylvania, or between Poland and the USSR over the Western Ukraine. The ties of the Warsaw Pact and the Council for Mutual Economic Assistance (Comecon) are already weakening, and independent roles are being sought in the world — including new relations with a Western Europe that was moving rapidly towards economic and political integration. Hence, alongside the institutionalization of democratic procedures there is also a need for new frameworks for international relations, which will involve Western Europe as well as relations among newly assertive East European nations.

The problems are potentially formidable, and in addition to practical matters, questions of interpretation arise. For if self-styled 'socialist' countries governed by self-styled 'communists' have abandoned the hallmarks of 'communism' as a form of rule, how is the system to be characterized? At what stage do we say that the system has changed? And, particularly, at what stage short of fully-fledged, stable liberal democracy are we to acknowledge that 'communism' is something different from what it was? Already, the communist parties' political dominance has been challenged, and in some cases rejected. But it is by no means clear how, say, a Bulgaria in which the former communists have won a parliamentary majority is to be classified and treated.

As philosophical problems, such questions are quite intractable. Yet in practical politics they matter, as the example of, say, South Africa also demonstrates. Pragmatism can suffice for a certain time, but at some point a country such as the Soviet Union will be recognizable as fundamentally different from the Stalinism of the late 1940s, whatever its political rhetoric, just as Britain at some point in the last 150 years adopted the features of a modern liberal democracy, without having a revolution that permitted it to start from scratch. Such philosophical musings are, however, of less immediate concern for the peoples of Europe, east and west. The experience of 'communism' is part of their common history, and its immediate legacy is almost wholly negative: the political task is to overcome that legacy, by creating new institutions that will protect the societies from a recurrence.

NOTES

1. See Archie Brown, 'Gorbachev: A Reformer in the Kremlin', *The Nation*, Vol. 244, No. 23 (1987), pp. 792-5.
2. F. Burlatskii, 'Khrushchev (Shtrikhi k politicheskomu portretu)', in Yu. N. Afanas'ev (ed.), *Inogo ne dano* (Moscow: Progress, 1988), pp. 424-40 (p. 424).
3. See Ronald J. Hill, 'Ideology and the State', in Martin McCauley, *Khrushchev and Khrushchevism* (London: Macmillan, 1987), pp. 46-60.
4. See Ronald J. Hill, *Soviet Politics, Political Science and Reform* (Oxford: Martin Robertson, 1980).
5. See Duncan Wilson, *Tito's Yugoslavia* (Cambridge: Cambridge University Press, 1979); Fred Singleton, *Twentieth-Century Yugoslavia* (London: Macmillan, 1976), ch. 9; April Carter, *Democratic Reform in Yugoslavia: The Changing Role of the Party* (London: Pinter, 1982).
6. For further details of this event and the 'Polish October', see Zbigniew K. Brzezinski, *The Soviet Bloc: Unity and Conflict*, rev. edn (New York: Praeger, 1961), chs 10-11; François Fejtö, *A History of the People's Democracies* (Harmondsworth: Penguin, 1974), ch. 5; Roger Pethybridge (ed.), *The Development of the Communist Bloc* (Boston, MA: D. C. Heath, 1965), pp. 160-74 and 156-60, contains excerpts from relevant contemporary documents.
7. The fullest account is H. Gordon Skilling, *Czechoslovakia's Interrupted Revolution* (Princeton, NJ: Princeton University Press, 1976).
8. See Jadwiga Staniszkis, *Poland's Self-Limiting Revolution* (Princeton, NJ: Princeton University Press, 1984).
9. This was confirmed by survey data in Czechoslovakia in 1968, when adherence to pre-communist values and symbols was greater after 20 years of communist rule than at the time of the communist takeover: see Archie Brown, 'Czechoslovakia: Revival and Retreat', in Archie Brown and Jack Gray (eds), *Political Culture and Political Change in Communist States*, 2nd edn (London: Macmillan, 1979), p. 176; for details of survey results, see Jaroslaw Piekalkiewicz (ed.), *Public Opinion Polling in Czechoslovakia, 1968-69* (New York: Praeger, 1972).
10. See Archie Brown, 'Eastern Europe: 1968, 1978, 1998', in *Daedalus*, Winter 1979, p. 152.
11. The 'Brezhnev doctrine', used to justify the invasion, stated that any 'deviation' from genuine socialism by a member of the movement was not the internal affair of that country alone but directly concerned the whole socialist world, which had a duty to intervene to protect the gains of socialism. For assessments of the doctrine, see Peter Summerscale, 'The Continuing Validity

of the Brezhnev Doctrine', in Karen Dawisha and Philip Hanson (eds), *Soviet–East European Dilemmas: Coercion, Competition and Consent* (London: Heinemann, 1981), pp. 26-40; Karen Dawisha, *Eastern Europe, Gorbachev and Reform: The Great Challenge* (Cambridge: Cambridge University Press, 1988), ch. 7. Gorbachev has abandoned the 'doctrine': see Kevin Devlin, 'Brezhnev Doctrine Dead: No More Invasions', *Radio Liberty Report on the USSR*, Vol. 1, No. 39 (29 September 1989), pp. 14-15.

12. This anachronistic approach has been characterized as using feudal methods to create what should have been accomplished by capitalism, in the name of socialism, leading to a 'syncretic' system: see Felipe García Casals (pseud.), *The Syncretic Society* (White Plains, NY: M.E. Sharpe, 1980).

13. A useful account of the various East European revolutions of 1989 is *Tearing Down the Curtain: The People's Revolution in Eastern Europe* (London: Hodder & Stoughton, 1990); see also Timothy Garton Ash, *We the People: The Revolution of '89* (Cambridge: Granta Books, in association with Penguin Books, 1989).

14. The literature on Gorbachev's reforms is substantial. For example, David A. Dyker (ed.), *The Soviet Union under Gorbachev: The Prospects for Reform* (London: Croom Helm, 1987); Peter Juviler and Hiroshi Kimura (eds), *Gorbachev's Reforms: US and Japanese Assessments* (New York: Aldine de Gruyter, 1988); R.F. Miller, J.H. Miller and T.H. Rigby (eds), *Gorbachev at the Helm: A New Era in Soviet Politics?* (London: Croom Helm, 1987); Walter Joyce, Hillel Ticktin and Stephen White (eds), *Gorbachev and Gorbachevism* (London: Cass, 1988); Ronald J. Hill and Jan Åke Dellenbrant (eds), *Gorbachev and Perestroika: Towards a New Socialism?* (Aldershot: Edward Elgar, 1989). On the evolution of Gorbachev's strategy, see John M. Battle, '*Uskorenie, Glasnost'* and *Perestroika*: The Pattern of Reform under Gorbachev', *Soviet Studies*, Vol. XL, No. 3 (1988), pp. 367-84; and, more recently, Hans-Hermann Höhmann, 'Interaction between Economic, Political and Social Reforms', *Soviet Economic Reforms: Implementation Under Way* (Brussels: NATO, 1989), pp. 41-55.

15. On the political importance of *glasnost*, see Nick Lampert, 'The Dilemmas of Glasnost'', in Joyce, Ticktin and White (eds), *Gorbachev and Gorbachevism*, pp. 48-63; Ronald J. Hill, '*Glasnost'* and Soviet Politics', *Coexistence*, Vol. 26 (1989), pp. 317-31.

16. See his speech to the Twenty-Seventh CPSU Congress, in *XXVII S''ezd Kommunisticheskoi partii Sovetskogo Soyuza: Stenograficheskii otchët* (Moscow: Politizdat, 1986), Vol. 1, p. 79. On the early implementation of electoral reform, see Stephen White, 'Reforming the Electoral System', in Joyce, Ticktin and White (eds), *Gorbachev and Gorbachevism*, pp. 1-17.

17. On the powers vested in this post (to which Mikhail Gorbachev was elected on 15 March 1990), see Elizabeth Teague, 'The Powers of the Soviet Presidency', *Radio Liberty Report on the USSR*, Vol. 2, No. 12 (23 March 1990), pp. 4-7; also Dawn Mann, 'Gorbachev Sworn In as President', ibid., pp. 1-4.

18. A demonstration of a mere 10,000 in Sofia prompted the resignation of the veteran party leader, Todor Zhivkov, on 10 November, although an ecology

movement put pressure on the government for some months before the change in political leadership.

19. With a turnout of 67 per cent, and 66 per cent in favour of economic reforms and 69 per cent supporting democratic reforms, the referendum failed to secure the endorsement of the requisite 51 per cent of registered electors.
20. See the report in *Tearing Down the Curtain*, p. 21.
21. William Pfaff, 'For the Poles, an Enormous Act of Faith', *International Herald Tribune*, 4-5 February 1989, p. 6.
22. Solidarity leader Lech Walesa, quoted in Pfaff, ibid.
23. See Jerzy Wiatr, 'Political Parties, Interest Representation and Economic Development in Poland', *American Political Science Review*, Vol. 64, No. 4 (1970), pp. 1239-45; also Marian Grzybowski, 'The Polish Party System in Transition', in Sten Berglund *et al.*, *East European Multi-Party Systems* (Commentationes Scientiarum Socialium, 38) (Helsinki: The Finnish Society of Science and Letters, 1988), pp. 30-55.
24. Havel has been called 'Czechoslovakia's dissident-in-chief' and the events of November–December 1989 the country's 'velvet revolution': see *Tearing Down the Curtain*, pp. 100-23, esp. p. 107; the experience has also been called a 'laughing revolution': see Ash, *We the People*, p. 129.
25. See, for example, Jonathan Alter, 'Prime-Time Revolution', *Newsweek*, 8 January 1990, p. 18.
26. See Julia Wishnevsky and Elizabeth Teague, '"Democratic Platform" Created in CPSU', *Radio Liberty Report on the USSR*, Vol. 2, No. 5 (2 February 1990), pp. 7-9; the programme of the Democratic Platform was published in *Pravda*, 3 March 1990, p. 3; that of the Marxist Platform in ibid., 16 April 1990; and the official platform of the CPSU appeared in ibid., 13 February 1990.
27. See Jeffrey W. Hahn, 'Moscow's Electoral Experiment', *Journal of Communist Studies*, Vol. 4, No. 2 (1988), pp. 208-13; Jeffrey W. Hahn, 'An Experiment in Competition: The 1987 Elections to the Local Soviets', *Slavic Review*, Vol. 47, No. 3 (1988), pp. 434-47; Stephen White, *op. cit.*
28. At the Congress of People's Deputies session on 12 December 1989, 'Gorbachev kept a firm hand on proceedings.... In this way he ensured that debate on Article 6 was rejected': Vera Tolz, 'The USSR This Week: Tuesday, December 12', *Radio Liberty Report on the USSR*, Vol. 1, No. 51 (22 December 1989), p. 33; Elizabeth Teague, 'Gorbachev Discusses Possibility of Multiparty System', ibid., Vol. 2, No. 5 (2 February 1990), pp. 3-4; by the time of the Central Committee Plenum of 5 February 1990, Gorbachev was prepared to argue that the party should 'give up its constitutionally guaranteed monopoly on power and instead fight and win its leading role in Soviet society': Vera Tolz, 'The USSR This Week: Monday, February 5', *Radio Liberty Report on the USSR*, Vol. 2, No. 7 (16 February 1990), p. 30; Elizabeth Teague, 'Gorbachev Proposes Dropping Communist Party Monopoly', *Radio Liberty Report on the USSR*, Vol. 2, No. 6 (9 February 1990), pp. 6-8.
29. This list is deliberately taken from the chapter headings of a work published in the Soviet Union under the auspices of the Inter-Parliamentary Union: Mishel Ameller, *Parlamenty* (Moscow: Progress, 1967); originally published as Michel Ameller, *Parliaments: A Comparative Study on the Structure and*

Functions of Representative Institutions in Fifty-Five Countries (London: Cassell, 1966).
30. See Theodor Schweisfurth's contribution to this volume.
31. See, for example, Michael Voslensky, *Nomenklatura: Anatomy of the Soviet Ruling Class* (London: Bodley Head, 1984). A classic analysis from the 1950s is Milovan Djilas, *The New Class* (London: Unwin Books, 1966).
32. See Alex Simirenko, *Professionalization of Soviet Society* (New Brunswick, NJ: Transaction Books, 1982), especially ch. 1.
33. Compare Czechoslovakian President Václav Havel's 1990 New Year Address: 'Tvá vláda, lide, se k tobe navrátila!' (People, your government has returned to you!': quoted as an epigram in Garton Ash, *We the People*, p. 7).
34. This is an ironic reversal of the position the Bolsheviks found themselves in after 1917, when, on Lenin's insistence, they employed so-called 'bourgeois' specialists, whose expertise and experience were vital to the survival of the regime.
35. For discussions of previous generations of reformers within the Soviet Communist Party, see Stephen F. Cohen, 'The Friends and Foes of Change: Reformism and Conservatism in the Soviet Union', reprinted in Stephen F. Cohen, Alexander Rabinowitch and Robert Sharlet (eds), *The Soviet Union since Stalin* (Bloomington, IN: Indiana University Press, 1980), pp. 11-31; also Hill, *Soviet Politics, Political Science and Reform*.
36. See Nina Andreeva, 'Ne mogu postupat'sya printsipami', *Sovetskaya Rossiya*, 13 March 1988, p. 3; 'Printsipy perestroiki: revolyutsionnost' myshleniya i deistvii', *Pravda*, 5 April 1988, p. 2. This exchange is discussed briefly by Stephen White in Joyce, Ticktin and White (eds.), *Gorbachev and Gorbachevism*, pp. 136-9. Nina Andreeva, a chemistry teacher in Leningrad, continues to surface from time to time with her hostile criticism of Gorbachev and his policies.
37. This led to quite grotesque features in the case of the late Nicolae Ceausescu, whose inauguration as state president of supposedly 'socialist' Romania was accompanied by formal portraits of himself wearing a sash in the blue, yellow and red Romanian national colours and bearing a sceptre!
38. The notion of the 'circular flow of power' was put forward by Robert V. Daniels: see his 'Soviet Politics Since Khrushchev', in John W. Strong (ed.), *The Soviet Union under Brezhnev and Kosygin* (New York: Van Nostrand-Reinhold, 1971), p. 20. More broadly on the nomenklatura, see Voslensky, *op. cit.*; also various essays in T.H. Rigby, *Political Elites in the USSR: Central Leaders and Local Cadres from Lenin to Gorbachev* (Aldershot: Edward Elgar, 1990).

4. The Assertion of Democratic Movements

Jan Zielonka

The manner in which democratic movements have recently come to power in various countries of Eastern Europe has been truly impressive. What was still unthinkable in the mid-1980s had become a reality by the end of 1989: democratic groups had broken the political monopoly of communist parties and begun to form their own governments, first in Poland, and later in other countries. It is difficult to give a simple definition of these democratic forces. They include hundreds of groups with different programmes and organizational structures.[1] They are all, however, united in their struggle against the communist system and their desire to introduce (or re-introduce) basic forms of parliamentary democracy. It should be borne in mind, however, that not all anti-communist organizations can be called democratic.

This chapter will, first, indicate the origins of the unprecedented growth of democratic organizations. Second, it will indicate the common features of political thinking within various groups. Third, it will point to elements of diversity within the democratic movement. And finally, it will try to indicate major challenges that the movement is likely to face in the 1990s.

THE ORIGIN OF SUCCESS

At least three major factors have contributed to the unprecedented strengthening of democratic organizations. First of all, the assertions of the old dissident groups should be mentioned, with their persistent striving for the observance of human rights and the reconstitution of civil society. Without the continued work of both 'revisionist'.and 'neo-positivist' currents of dissent from the 1960s and 1970s the popular movement of democracy could hardly have developed as a well-organized and self-aware actor in the politics of Eastern Europe.[2] Initially, small and seemingly marginal groups of dissenters managed to break the paralysing barrier of fear among East European societies and manifested moral standards which were crucial to mobilizing the support of the wider masses. The same groups developed an initial programme of social change in the direction of democracy and national independence.[3] They were also the first to put these programmes into action by establishing a network of independent initiatives and campaigning for basic civil rights. Subsequently, members of these dissident communities provided the leadership in spontaneous popular protest actions.[4]

Another factor contributing to the success of democratic organizations is the multi-dimensional crisis of communist rule in Eastern Europe. The crisis sharpened social conflicts and uncovered the inefficiency, inhumanity and injustice of the system led by the administrators appointed through the party-dominated system known as *nomenklatura*. For instance, the ideological crisis deprived the system of true believers in the Marxist-Leninist doctrine and created a vacuum arising from a lack of motivation for, and belief in, the legitimization of one-party rule. This naturally opened the doors to popular pluralistic and libertarian ideas.[5] The economic crisis made it impossible for the regimes to apply a policy of consumerism as a substitute for all the demands for political changes. Moreover, the economic crisis discredited the centrally planned economy and stimulated the trend towards privatization and market forces advocated by the opposition. The crisis within state institutions made possible the legitimation of oppositional programmes to create alternative independent clubs and associations in all spheres of public life. And the identity crisis of the industrial working class and blue-collar workers created an audience for the revival of patriotism, nationalism and solidarism that was promoted by the democratic opposition.

Finally, the successes enjoyed by democratic forces are also a result of the internal developments within the communist elites. First, the growing confusion and disintegration within communist circles weakened their ability to combat the democratic campaign. Second, the emergence of the reformist circles within the communist elites opened the doors for political compromises that allowed a smooth and relatively painless transition towards democracy. In this context, the impact of Gorbachev's *perestroika* has been especially crucial. Reformists within various communist parties accepted or even absorbed a part of the democratic programme of change. They also entered into dialogue with the democratic opposition that paved the way for free elections and the subsequent victories of democratic campaigners.

The use of governmental violence could not prevent democratic changes, but as the Polish (1981) and Romanian (1989) experiences have shown, violence imposed enormous human, economic and political costs on those societies, with only negative consequences for the progress of democracy.[6]

ELEMENTS OF CONTINUITY IN THE THINKING OF DISSENTERS

The political programmes of nearly all democratic groups in Eastern Europe contain certain common characteristics. Many of these features are well known to students of dissent in the late 1970s and the early 1980s.

Support for an evolutionary rather than a revolutionary pattern of change is one such common feature. Democratic groups have persistently argued that far-reaching political, social and economic reforms are needed, but that they should be introduced gradually, and preferably in a spirit of cooperation rather than confrontation between the rulers and the ruled. Jacek Kuron has expressed this idea in the following words:

> The world has always seen dozens of revolutions. It is an old story: people invest all their hopes in a revolution which cannot fulfil them. And they are always followed by crisis and hatred.... Today a revolution would not rebuild the country but destroy it further. Our duty is to try a course of action which would enable the whole of society to organize itself and the existing order to change gradually.[7]

The evolutionism of the democratic opposition is linked to its commitment to non-violence. Violence as a means of social change is condemned as being unethical and self-destructive. As Václav Havel put it: 'I myself and all the independent groups do whatever is possible to make developments peaceful, to prevent bloodshed, casualties, violence, and unrest'.[8]

Another long-standing common feature of nearly all democratic programmes is the idea of social self-organization. Citizens should organize themselves, it is argued, into various grassroots alternative organizations that will help them to re-establish social links and overcome atomization within the communist-ruled society. Self-organization allows the people to take the initiative in public affairs; it allows them to exert effective pressure from below against the autocratic government. A statement by the East German group, Initiative for Peace and Human Rights, has expressed this succinctly: 'Fundamental change ... is not to be expected from the "all-powerful" perfect state. To achieve this, decentralization and the self-organization of society, as well as self-management in all areas of life is required'.[9]

The idea of social self-organization is linked with a characteristic anti-statism. Democratic groups frequently insist that the state should serve man and not dominate him. State organizations should serve society, they argue, and should not be identified with a single party; the state should work for the common good of the whole nation. As one of the Polish Solidarity programmes stated: 'We are united in our protest against the state which treats citizens like its property'.[10] And a programme of the Hungarian Federation of Free Democrats added: 'We demand a radical reduction of excessive state authority ... local autonomy, and guarantees for the rights of individuals and communities against the power of the state'.[11]

Emphasis on the rights of the individuals is also present in nearly all the official statements and programmes of democratic organizations. Challenging the Marxist doctrine, the opposition expresses concern about the autonomy and dignity of the individual. As, for instance, Oleg Rumyantsev from the Moscow club Democratic Perestroika put it: 'The basis of our movement is the sovereignty and self-esteem of the individual ... our movement is about humanism'.[12]

Opposition groups criticize the government for trying to deprive the individuals of their personal dignity, and for denying them their basic human and civil rights. The commitment to defend these basic rights represents a major platform of all oppositional actions. Václav Havel described this very vividly:

> The post-totalitarian system is mounting a total assault on humans and humans stand against it alone, abandoned and isolated. It is therefore entirely natural that all the 'dissident movements'... exist to defend human beings and the genuine aims of life against the aims of the system.[13]

A characteristic 'pan-Europeanism' is also constantly present in nearly all pro-democracy statements. 'We belong to Europe' is the repeated cry of Eastern European activists. In their view Europe possesses a special kind of identity, which is based on certain cultural and legal traditions, on common principles of democracy and the common religious roots of Christianity and Judaism. Certainly, such a notion of Europe can hardly be limited to countries west of the river Elbe. According to Eastern European writers, a notion of Europe must therefore include all nations that cultivate the tradition of a European identity regardless of forty years of Soviet domination. The

Association of Young Democrats in Hungary echoed other independent programmes when it stated: 'In spite of our political situation, our history and culture bind us to Europe. We consider ourselves as belonging here: no armies nor tanks can force us to give up this belief'.[14]

NEW COMMITMENTS AND ASPIRATIONS

Despite elements of continuity in democratic programmes throughout the last twenty years, the late 1980s introduced several new elements in pro-democracy thinking.[15] First of all a characteristic rehabilitation of politics took place among the leading democratic organizations.

For years dissidents insisted on carrying on their struggle on ethical rather than political grounds. Politics was the domain of the communists, and the opposition preferred to stay in a domain of 'anti-politics', as György Konrad put it.[16] In consequence, the opposition campaigned for basic human rights rather than for free parliamentary elections. It advocated the creation of alternative social institutions rather than alternative political parties. It spoke about truth, hope, dignity and conscience with the intention of depoliticizing social life. The opposition should — as Jacek Kuron puts it — 'carry out a moral revolution rather than a political one'.[17]

In the late 1980s we could already begin to observe a dramatic transformation of the dissident attitude towards politics. This is well illustrated by the 1988 manifesto of the Czechoslovak Movement for Civil Liberties:

> Let us enter the field for which people have felt a general distrust because of its domination by those who were saturating it for decades with dictatorship and incompetence. This field must be rehabilitated. Politics must once again become an environment in which the authentic interests of society are reflected and realized.... It is high time for society, for all of us, to enter politics.[18]

Entering the sphere of politics resulted in the spontaneous creation of political parties and broad public movements which clearly had political aims. At the top of the opposition agenda emerged pure political issues such as elections, parliament, government. The traditional struggle for human rights has been transformed into the struggle for parliamentary democracy. Since 1989 democratic groups have begun to campaign in — and win — parliamentary elections. This has naturally opened new opportunities for transforming the old authoritarian system into a fully-fledged democracy.

In the late 1980s rehabilitation could also be observed in another important area of public life, namely economics. Economics has traditionally been the area ignored, or at least neglected, by the dissident organizations. The democratic opposition regularly criticized communist mismanagement of the economy, but it hardly ever tried to develop its own programme for running economic affairs. This has changed recently, first in Hungary, and later in other Eastern European countries.

Two major factors contributed to this involvement in economic affairs. One of these was linked to the progress of market-oriented reforms conducted by the communist regimes; another factor resulted from the sharp deterioration of the economic situation in virtually all Eastern European states.

Economic reforms brought about the extension of private initiative in agriculture, services and small-scale industry which in turn produced the emergence of new groups of entrepreneurs pressing for the protection of their economic rights, including the right to private ownership. These groups soon found themselves in conflict with the party and state bureaucracy, especially at the local level. Communist-led reforms produced few new entrepreneurial groups in heavy industry, but they increased the worker's sensitivity to economic issues directly affected by the ongoing economic changes. Moreover, the initiation of market-oriented reforms by the communists contributed to the destruction of the myth that state-owned enterprises would remain in Eastern Europe for ever. This of course enhanced the development of the liberal economic thinking.

The economic reforms conducted by the communists were, however, inconsequential and insufficiently deep, and they concentrated on protecting the leading role of the party. In effect they stimulated industrial chaos, increased inequality, and led to a general deterioration of the standard of living. In this situation democratic groups could no longer maintain a passive posture: they had to assume economic responsibility by elaborating comprehensive programmes for economic change and creating opportunities for putting them into effect.

Characteristically enough, several leading democratic groups overwhelmingly endorsed the neo-liberal model of the economy, supporting massive reprivatization, essential reductions in state intervention in the economy, and the free play of market forces. The ideas of Milton Friedman, Friedrich Hayek or Michael Novak have been increasingly influential in stimulating this new economic thinking, especially in countries such as Poland, Hungary and Czechoslovakia.

Economic factors became especially crucial as democratic groups began to assume governmental responsibilities. From then on, the entire future of the democratic experiment became closely linked with the economic successes or failures of the newly established non-communist regimes. The late 1980s also witnessed not so much rehabilitation as a dramatic upgrading of the national question within the opposition. This was especially true in the Soviet republics where the Popular Fronts of the Balts, Ukrainians, Belorussians and Moldavians have been able to set the pace of political life in the European part of the Soviet Union. The national question has also dominated political debates within the opposition movements in Yugoslavia, Hungary, Romania and Bulgaria. Even in relatively nationally homogeneous Poland a heated debate developed about minority rights of the Jews, Germans, Ukrainians and Belorussians.

Of course, questions of nationalism often divide rather than unite the opposition. Some democratic groups, especially in the federal states such as the Soviet Union or Yugoslavia, fear a violent disintegration of their countries caused by nationalist unrest. They are, in turn, accused of neglecting, if not totally ignoring, the national question. For instance, according to the Coordinating Committee of Non-Russian Nationalities (in the Soviet Union), 'Many of the activists in the Russian democratic opposition have not yet grasped the primary axiom of democracy: nations cannot be genuinely free if they oppress other nations, or if they serve as instruments of such oppression'.[19]

Democratic campaigners in countries which do not fear violent partition or disintegration are also concerned about nationalism. After all, certain forms of nationalism can act as a locomotive for autocratic rather than democratic systems by promoting national egoism and chauvinism, if not national hatred, by restricting the rights of national and ethnic minorities, and by subordinating the interests of the individual to the 'objective' interests of the nation. Václav Havel expressed the hopes and desires — not always fulfilled — of Eastern European democrats when he observed that

> Thanks to this [communist] regime we have developed a profound distrust of all generalizations, ideological platitudes, clichés, slogans, intellectual stereo-types, and insidious appeals to various levels of our emotions, from the baser to the loftier. As a result, we are now largely immune to all hypnotic enticements, even of the traditionally persuasive national or nationalistic variety.[20]

In the late 1980s the increased importance of religious questions among the opposition was also in evidence. What was traditionally a relevant phenomenon only in Poland has recently become a reality more broadly, especially in Czechoslovakia and the German Democratic Republic (and on a smaller scale also in Hungary, Bulgaria, Yugoslavia and the Soviet Union). Thus democratic groups began to ally themselves with the Evangelical, Catholic or Orthodox churches in campaigning for the moral revival of society, for greater religious freedom, and for equal public rights for both believers and non-believers. The religious rights of the Jews are today also on the agenda of many democratic organizations.

Finally, the unprecedented concern about ecological issues should be mentioned. Ecology was not an issue anywhere until at least the mid-1980s. Since then, however, there has been evidence of growing concern about environmental devastation that has given birth to the emergence of influential ecological groups, and to the incorporation of ecological statements into the programmes of nearly all the leading democratic movements in Eastern Europe.

PROBLEMS WITH TYPOLOGY

Despite a great number of common features, the opposition in Eastern Europe is very diverse. The division lines, however, are not clear-cut, and they hardly reflect Western stereotypes of left and right or of conservatives *versus* socialists *versus* liberals. Consider, for instance, the political profile of the Hungarian Democratic Forum. According to its leader, Csaba Gy. Kiss, the Democratic Forum is

> an all-national party that is not tied to any single class or social stratum. Neither is it an ideological party, but a sort of German-type 'Unionpartei' that operates within three main ideological currents: a liberal, Christian and the so-called 'third road' current between socialism and capitalism. Political pragmatism and avoidance of extremes represents the most important principle.[21]

The classification of oppositional groups and movements in countries other than Hungary is equally difficult. Polish Solidarity is conservative, socialist and liberal at the same time.[22] The same is true of the Bulgarian Union of Democratic Forces, Czechoslovak Civic Forum, the Romanian National Salvation Front, East German New Forum or the National Fronts in the Baltic Soviet Republics. The programmes of Moscow-based groups are usually very general. For instance, the Democratic Union presented the following aims to the public: the establishment of a multi-party system in the

USSR; the adoption of a new constitution to replace the existing document, which made the CPSU 'the leading and guiding force' of Soviet society; the creation of independent trade unions and a free press; and the withdrawal of Soviet troops from Eastern Europe, the Western Ukraine, and the Baltic states.[23] None of these aims could be classified as either conservative or progressive in Western terms.

Since the application of Western stereotypes is inappropriate, if not virtually impossible, scholars construct typologies based on the local national characteristics of democratic forces. Aleksander Smolar, for instance, distinguishes four major currents in the Polish democratic opposition before 1989:

1. the legitimists who want to continue the Solidarity movement;

2. the realistic opposition that attempts to expand the sphere of freedom by taking the situation created by the December 1981 coup and the elimination of Solidarity as its point of departure (without morally accepting it);

3. political radicals for whom winning national sovereignty and building a democratic system is more important than attempts to expand the level of freedom; and

4. the Church-oriented opposition which places its hopes in the Roman Catholic Church in Poland.[24]

Ivan Baba reveals another characteristic division line in Eastern European politics when he refers to two different types of Hungarian democratic organizations: first, the so-called older independent organizations, involved in a democratic campaign for the last 5-12 years (for example, the Alliance of Free Democrats or the Hungarian Democratic Forum); and, secondly, the 'new old' parties which were active before 1948 and re-born in the late 1980s (for example, the Social Democratic Party or the Smallholders' Party).[25] In Bulgaria, Poland, the GDR and Czechoslovakia new umbrella-type organizations have been created such as the New or Civic Forum already mentioned.[26] They play de facto the role of political parties without calling themselves by that name. Beyond coordinating the work of various democratic groups in their countries, the umbrella organizations nominate their own candidates in local and parliamentary elections.

If one is looking for ideological rather than historical or organizational division lines within democratic groups in Eastern Europe, then at least two separate, if not opposite, currents might be apparent. The first can be called 'populist' or 'nationalist', the second 'urban', 'occidental' or 'pluralist'.[27]

The latter current consists of advocates of a Western-style democracy as practised in Scandinavian countries. The reasoning of the 'occidentalists' proceeds from universal principles as distinct from that of the 'populists' who see as their point of departure the fate of their nation. 'Occidentalists', in fact, frequently criticize national egoism and the instrumental treatment of the national question.

'Occidentalists' acknowledge the importance of moral values in politics, but prefer to build the public order on purely democratic rather than religious principles. For instance, in contrast to some 'Populists' they believe that a parliamentary majority rather than principles derived from the Gospel should be decisive in shaping the legal order.[28] 'Occidentalists' support the need for market-oriented reforms in the economy, but stress the role of trade unions and industrial democracy. They also believe in the active role of democratic governments in securing the basic principles of distributive justice.

The 'occidentalist' current promotes many ideas that are close to the Western notion of the political left. Remarkably enough, however, 'occidentalists' try to distance themselves from the vocabulary and image associated with both reformist communism and democratic socialism. (Owing to their unfortunate post-war experience with collectivist slogans, the general public in Eastern Europe often treats not only communism and Marxism but even the most democratic forms of Western socialism as a threat to freedom.) Moreover, the 'occidentalist' current also includes a group of liberal or even conservative activists. For instance, the liberal wing of the Hungarian Free Democrats, or the Polish conservative group around the monthly *Res Publica*, can certainly be included in the 'occidentalist' rather than the 'populist' current.

The 'populist' current within the democratic groups of Eastern Europe resembles what the West used to call the 'conservative right', but it is also strongly rooted in a specific Eastern European culture and tradition. The 'populist' current emphasizes the idea of the 'nation', advocates a 'third road' towards democracy rather than copying the Western example, and manifests strong adherence to the moral values of Christianity. As distinct from the universalist approach, 'populists' are basically concerned with their national destiny, especially its moral integrity and cultural vitality. Their common prescription for dealing with communism is to 'nationalize' it rather than improve it, as some 'occidentalists' would argue. 'Populists' are especially concerned about the peasantry and problems of the countryside. They emphasize the crucial role of the family and request various legal and economic measures aimed at its protection. They also argue against Western-style consumerism, and condemn the 'moral relativism' of the 'urban' circles.

Representatives of these two major ideological currents can often be found in the same organization. In Poland, for instance, typical 'occidentalists' such as Jacek Kuron or Adam Michnik are working hand-in-hand with many 'populist' leaders of Solidarity. Czechoslovakia's Civic Forum also unites activists from different ideological backgrounds. In Hungary, on the other hand, 'occidentalists' such as Janos Kis or Ferenc Köszeg are in conflict with the populist movement formed by the Hungarian Democratic Forum.

CHALLENGES OF THE 1990s

Despite the remarkable successes of the late 1980s, democratic groups face several enormous problems in dealing with the volatile developments in Eastern Europe. Democrats have not only taken power: they must also shoulder the responsibility for getting their countries out of deep economic, moral and political crisis, and there are no simple remedies for this. Moreover, democrats are still faced with the challenge posed by communist (or former communist) organizations. Although the communist elites seem no longer to aspire to a political monopoly, they are nevertheless far from forfeiting all their influence and privileges. Finally, democratic movements are faced with an identity crisis. Their internal strategic and ideological differences become increasingly apparent as successive new problems begin to affect the processes of democratic transformation.

It would be no exaggeration to say that the democratic groups came to power basically unprepared for running a country. Their programmes were clear about why the old system ought to be replaced and what was necessary to achieve this. These programmes, however, have been much less specific on how to organize post-communist states and societies. Democratic groups have gained enormous public trust, largely thanks to their moral qualities, but in government they have increasingly been faced with economic rather than moral pressures. The 'resistance mentality' that allowed these groups to endure years of repressions has proved to be of little help in creating a new ethos of civic service and private entrepreneurship. Moreover, democratic groups often lack qualified cadres able to put new policies into practice. This problem is especially apparent in countries that lacked well-established democratic opposition before the upheavals of 1989.

The creation and implementation of concrete programmes for transforming Eastern Europe is a task without historical precedent: there is no experience of moving back from communism to democracy and a market economy. Even in the most 'Western' countries, in a cultural sense, such as Hungary, Poland, the GDRand Czechoslovakia, democrats will have problems in applying new policies of political pluralism, ideological tolerance, the rule of law and economic competitiveness. In other countries, such as Romania, Bulgaria and especially the Soviet Union, the political culture is even less receptive to the eventual assimilation of liberal democracy. For instance, the autocratic tradition virtually precludes abolishing statism and the *nomenklatura* system. Excessive populism and nationalism competes with pluralism and legalism. Messianic Slavophilism clashes with liberalism and the economic need for a mercantile outlook. This linkage between the political culture, on the one hand, and the progress of a democratic experiment, on the other hand, is well illustrated in the Baltic republics. The remarkable success of democratic movements in that region is closely linked to the existence of a strong, Western-style, liberal political culture.

The complex relationship between democratic groups and communist parties represents another important challenge for the 1990s. In countries such as the Soviet Union, the communist party is still very much in charge, especially in the crucial Russian republic. But even in countries where the communists have lost parliamentary elections or have given up important governmental posts, their role is still crucial to the future of democracy. Communists usually maintain control over the police and the army. Top civil servants, managers and judges are usually members (or former members) of the communist party. Old-style trade unions, important sections of the media and several non-governmental organizations are still influenced by the old guard. Of course, the communist parties no longer wield the influence they used to. Some of them have not only changed their names, they have also adopted social-democratic programmes. In fact, many democratic groups appreciate Gorbachev's leadership in pursuing *perestroika*. Whether communists should be excluded from political life or integrated into the new system is a major dilemma for democratic movements in Eastern Europe.

Although Romania is the one country that has proposed outlawing the communist party, there is apparent public support for further curbs on communists' powers in several other countries. It is the communists, even those supporting reforms, who are held responsible for the current crisis. Their new reformist credentials are not widely trusted. It is practically impossible to proceed with fully-fledged democratization without challenging their remaining privileges.

However, a tough policy towards communists would certainly evoke fierce resistance which could paralyse governments and bring the economies to a standstill. In a situation of prolonged conflict and anarchy military coups cannot be discounted, with all their negative consequences for the progress of democracy.

A conciliatory policy towards communists might therefore facilitate rather than hamper democratic transformations. Communists could be integrated into a new system by a series of corporate agreements between democratic and communist organizations (similar to the Round Table agreements completed in 1989 in several countries). Individual party members would then be able to pursue further careers within the reformed government or in private business. Institutions such as the army and police would retain their budgets and independence. Communist parties would be invited to share certain powers without being exposed to devastating electoral defeats.

The corporate policy of conciliation has already been tried by democratic groups in Poland, Czechoslovakia, the GDR and Hungary, but evoked public criticism and opposition from the more radical democratic organizations.[29] There is controversy over the scale and scope of successive compromises, and also about the secretive nature of corporate agreements. Arguments have also arisen over the principle that corporatism and conciliation ignore the ballot box and the opinions of those who are outside such corporate agreements. Furthermore, ideological closeness between reformed communists and groups of an 'occidentalist' democratic orientation, especially on issues such as abortion, privatization or religious education, has evoked the suspicion that a new left-wing alliance is in the making.

This leads us to another major dilemma of democratic organizations evoked by the identification crisis within their own ranks. In the early stages of democratic transformation, democrats showed a remarkable degree of unity and self-discipline. Faced with a seemingly powerful *ancien régime*, democratic groups silenced their differences and established close cooperation. Solidarity in Poland, the Civic Forum in Czechoslovakia or the Union of Democratic Forces in Bulgaria provided a broad platform for joint action by many groups with different, if not conflicting, programmes.

The democratic successes of 1989 reduced the need for united action only to a certain degree. Eastern Europe still faces a multi-dimensional crisis and political turmoil. Should democrats maintain the centralized structure which constrains their internal freedom, but prevents internal disintegration? Or should they rather split into several competing political parties — the option that could strengthen democracy within the movement as such, but might weaken its position *vis-à-vis* non-democratic forces, and even lead to anarchy?

Timothy Garton Ash has compared this conflict between the political imperative of rapid, decisive, united action and the moral imperative of internal democracy to Bertold Brecht's dilemma: 'We who fight for democracy cannot ourselves be democratic'.[30] This dilemma manifested itself particularly acutely on the eve of parliamentary elections, when democratic groups had to choose between campaigning under either a united or a multi-party front. It will subsequently be echoed by all controversial decisions of new parliaments (or governments), be they in the field of politics, the economy, education or culture.

Characteristically enough, democratic transformations in Eastern Europe did not automatically lead to a Western-style multi-party system. Despite the spontaneous emergence of many new and different parties, it is the national umbrella democratic organizations that dominate politics in most of the countries in the region. The formation of coalitions and finding the balance between over-centralization and disintegration of the democratic movement will therefore remain crucial in the years to come.

Breaking the communist monopoly has opened up new opportunities for democratic organizations. Nevertheless, the transition from autocracy to democracy is not likely to be either painless or smooth. The continuing instability and state of crisis complicates the process of change. Democrats are not immune to internal conflicts; they are affected by the general rise in nationalism, and there is no magic route to the solution of economic problems. Democratization will probably continue to proceed in fits and starts, and the future of democratic movements is far from certain.

NOTES

1. Several different types of democratic organizations can easily be distinguished, such as political parties, religious organizations, independent trade unions, human rights organizations, national groups and movements, political clubs and associations, and apolitical associations in the field of culture, information or education. Political groups linked to well-known magazines or journals such as *Beszélo* in Hungary, *Glasnost*' in the Soviet Union or *Znak* and *Res Publica* in Poland can also be placed in a separate category. Independent individuals who are difficult to identify with any specific organization (for

example, Roy Medvedev in the Soviet Union, Stefan Kisielewski in Poland or Mirea Dinescu in Romania) represent yet another sort of 'non-aligned' democratic campaign.

2. The terms 'revisionists' and 'neo-positivists' were first used by Adam Michnik in his well known essay 'The New Evolutionism', *Survey*, Summer/Autumn 1976, pp. 292 and vv.

3. It might be argued, however, that the dissident groups elaborated merely a programme for combatting totalitarianism, rather than a programme for creating democracy as such in their respective countries.

4. For a comprehensive analysis of the dissident movement in the 1960s and the 1970s see especially Rudolf L. Tökés (ed.), *Opposition in Eastern Europe* (London: Macmillan, 1979).

5. It should be observed that the rise of pluralism opened the door to anti-libertarian ideas as well.

6. Martial law repressions in Poland, for instance, worsened Poland's economic crisis which currently represents a major threat to democracy in that country. Violence in Romania drastically sharpened political divisions between the old and new political elites; this made it difficult for Romanians to reach a broad consensus on the path of democratic change and contributed to political chaos, if not anarchy. One can multiply similar examples.

7. Jacek Kuron, 'Instead of Revolution', *Eastern European Reporter*, Spring-Summer 1989, pp. 32-3.

8. Václav Havel in an interview for Radio Free Europe, in *Radio Free Europe Research*, 2 August 1989, p.15.

9. Published in *East European Reporter*, Summer 1988, p. 59. See also an interview with Václav Havel in *Eastern European Reporter*, Summer 1988, p. 5; also Adam Michnik, 'The New Evolutionism', p. 272.

10. The Programme, 'Self-Governing Commonwealth', adopted by the First National Congress of Solidarity in October 1981.

11. Published in *Radio Free Europe Research*, 9 May 1989, p. 21.

12. Oleg Rumyantsev, 'An Alternative' (paper presented at the International Conference 'Glasnost and Perestroika', Amsterdam, 29-30 September 1989; unpublished), p. 9.

13. Václav Havel, 'The Power of the Powerless', in Václav Havel et al., *The Power of the Powerless: Citizens Against the State in Central-Eastern Europe* (London: Hutchinson, 1985), p. 67.

14. Programme adopted by the First Congress of the Association of Young Democrats (FIDESZ), published in, for example, *Eastern European Reporter*, Spring-Summer 1989, p. 19.

15. This evolution of pro-democracy thinking, it should be stressed, took several years in, for example, Poland; several months in the GDR, and only several days in Bulgaria and Romania. Moreover, not all elements of pro-democracy thinking cited are equally present in all East European countries.

16. György Konrad, *Antipolitics* (New York: Harcourt Brace Jovanovich, 1984), esp. pp. 116-24.

17. Jacek Kuron, *Polityka i Odpowiedzialnosc* (London: Aneks, 1984), pp. 184, 84), esp. pp. 116-24.

18. 'Democracy for All: A Manifesto of the Movement for Civil Liberties', published in, for example, *Radio Free Europe Research*, 21 October 1988, p. 23.
19. A statement of the Coordinating Committee of Non-Russian Nationalities issued in Lvov, 12 June 1988, and quoted in Vojtech Mastny (ed.), *Soviet/East European Survey, 1987-1988* (Boulder, CO: Westview, 1989), p. 240.
20. Václav Havel, 'Words on Words', in *Listy: Journal of the Czechoslovak Socialist Opposition*, November 1989, p. 5.
21. An interview with Csaba Gy. Kiss published in *Gazeta Wyborcza*, 6 July 1989, p. 6. In another interview Kiss stated that the Democratic Forum wishes to express the views of a broad social spectrum, including 'bourgeois radicalism, Christian humanism, classical Hungarian liberalism, and democratic socialism': quoted in *Radio Free Europe Research*, 28 October 1988, p. 23.
22. I have written more about this problem in Jan Zielonka, *Political Ideas in Contemporary Poland* (Aldershot: Avebury, 1989), pp. 2 *et seq.*
23. Vera Tolz, 'Soviet "Informal Groups" Organize', in Mastny, *op.cit.*, p. 233.
24. Aleksander Smolar, 'The Polish Opposition', in Aleksander Smolar and Pierre Kende (eds), *The Role of Opposition Groups on the Eve of Democratization in Poland and Hungary (1987-1988)*; research project 'Crises in Soviet-Type Systems', Munich, 1989; Study No. 17-18, p. 10.
25. In an interview in *East European Reporter*, Spring-Summer 1989, p. 4.
26. The Civic Forum is, in fact, a Czech umbrella organization. Its sister organization in Slovakia is called the Public Against Violence (PAV). In Poland, the umbrella role is formally played by the OKP (Ogolnopolski Komitet Porozumiewawczy) and in Bulgaria by the Union of Democratic Forces. The National Salvation Front in Romania played the role of a provisional government rather than of an umbrella organization uniting various democratic forces.
27. The second current is also named 'Westerners', 'revisionists', 'reformists' or 'syndycalists'. None of the many terms used is widely accepted. Terms 'populists' and 'nationalists' are frequently used to describe the first political current discussed here.
28. See, for example, Stefan Niesiolowski, 'Spor o Zasady i Metody', *Gazeta Wyborcza*, 3 August 1989, p. 6.
29. See, for example, Jadwiga Staniszkis, 'Grozba Latynizacji', *Tygodnik Solidarnosc*, 10 November 1989, p. 3.
30. Timothy Garton Ash, 'The Revolution of the Magic Lantern', *The New York Review of Books*, 18 January 1990, p. 44.

5. The Marketization of Eastern Europe

Pekka Sutela

The East European states are facing substantial economic problems as they move from central planning to the market economy, in addition to the social, political and ideological issues discussed in other contributions to this volume. Over the medium term, at least, the efficiency gains from the transition to a mixed market may well prove to be less than expected. However, the retention of central planning is neither possible nor desirable. Rather, those countries have to face the fact that, both during the transition and afterwards, their formerly centrally planned economies will be heavily burdened by a particular inheritance of resource endowments, industrial structure and built-in inefficiencies, which will adversely affect their performance.

THE CENTRALLY PLANNED ECONOMY

The geographical area which outsiders usually call Eastern Europe — the CMEA seven: that is Bulgaria, Czechoslovakia, German Democratic Republic, Hungary, Poland, Romania and the USSR — is historically, culturally and geographically an artificial creation of the Second World War. Nevertheless, the economies of the region were transformed into such close resemblance with one another that to talk of an East European or even a Soviet type of economic system of central planning was for decades justified. It is useful to look at some of the constituent parts of an 'East European' economy.[1] This helps to highlight the crucial change that has already taken place in some of the economies of the region. At the same time it helps to differentiate between changes of greater and lesser importance. Finally, it also underlines the inevitable incompleteness and contradictions of any real-world transition from central planning to market.

All the East European economies have shared certain fundamental *institutional* characteristics: the declared priority of state ownership over other property forms; the organization of the state sector in a hierarchical bureaucracy of branch ministerial management; centralized planning of production by means of mandatory plan targets; the centralized supply of the means of production; and, in various forms, a state monopoly of foreign trade. The far-reaching fusion of crucial political and economic power in the same hands, defined as totalitarianism, is another way of looking at such characteristics.

Such institutional fundamentals were not the only similarities among those countries. Certain *strategic goals* were closely related to the institutions. These included rapid economic growth and, in the early phases of the system, rapid economic transformation, full employment, stability of consumer price levels and other forms of economic security and relative equality.

These and other strategic goals were pursued by various economic *policies*. During the post-war decades such policies included high investment ratios, high priority given to heavy industry in the allocation of investments, highly centralized price and wage setting, and a tendency towards national and regional economic autarky.

This description of the 'East European economy' is not exhaustive. In particular, an analysis of the linkages between the variables is missing. Still, the description should remind us of the probability that institutions, goals and policies are really parts of a single setting. To some degree at least, institutions have often come into being as answers to particular strategic goals which can then — within the given institutional setting — be pursued only through particular policies. If this is so, institutional reform can promise little without a corresponding change in policies and *vice versa*. This, in fact, is among the foremost lessons of current reform experience.

Two examples may clarify the range of issues involved. The post-1985 Soviet policies first attempted an institutional change without abandoning the goals of rapid growth and superpower status. This contributed to the deepening economic crisis. Not only were the consequent resource needs in contradiction with the slackness necessary for structural change, but such goals continued to reproduce the old administrative system through measures such as state orders. *Perestroika* and *uskorenie* (acceleration) were soon found to be contradictory goals. The attempts to increase the efficiency of investment by means of cutting its growth rates are another example met with in many East European countries. Given the institutional setting, the economy simply needs huge investments to keep on growing: cutting them does not bring about efficiency but an open economic crisis.[2] The strength of linkages between institutions, goals and policies should not be exaggerated. As shown by comparisons among countries and over time, differences in resource endowments, traditions, policies pursued and even the personal values of the leadership go a long way in explaining the observed variation in economic performance. The emphasis on systemic properties is not meant to minimize national differences or to deny the existence of important policy alternatives within a given institutional framework. In fact, recent change in Eastern Europe has to a remarkable degree abolished what used to be the quite uniform Eastern European or Soviet type of economy. Outlining the logic of the stages of economic reform helps to explain why this is so.

THE FIRST STAGE OF ECONOMIC REFORMS

The initial idea for reforming central planning was simple. Could not direct centralization and management by mandatory targets be replaced by indirect centralization, management by 'economic levers' or such parameters as prices, wages and interest rates? Mathematicians showed that this is theoretically feasible while economists argued that it not only leads to better static and dynamic efficiency through giving more leeway to enterprise initiative but also increases the degree to which the planners' preferences are implemented in the economy.[3] These reform theories were not about marketization: they were about simulating the role that markets have in a market economy by means of computers and modern mathematical methods. The goal of such simulation was to increase the control that the centre has over the economy.

It is easy to see that such theories of the modified centrally planned economy (MCPE) had several faults. First of all, the expected savings in bureaucratic costs with the transition to indirect centralization were simply not forthcoming: the centralized calculation of optimal prices to be used for enterprise guidance requires in general exactly the same amount of information as the calculation of mandatory plan targets. Second, the use of computers and related methods for simulating markets may be somewhat feasible in a static sense, but it cannot possibly perform better than the information given by enterprises allows. Third, as long as enterprises are still the subordinate units in the hierarchy of the state monopoly of ownership, they will have plenty of reason to give false information about their production possibilities. Any plan based on such information, whether calculated by abacuses or by computers, is faulty. Market simulation therefore cannot in general give the efficiency looked for. Fourth, such theories of MCPE do not even try to address the crucial issues of dynamic efficiency connected with competition. They have an extremely crude image of enterprise motivation. Issues of personal motivation, creativity and entrepreneurship are neglected. And finally, as long as ministries retain their position as hierarchically responsible for the performance of 'their' respective branches, they will not and really cannot allow any increased autonomy of enterprise decision-making. Indirect centralization will therefore keep reverting to direct commanding of the classical kind. This does not constitute a feasible economic system.

THE SECOND STAGE OF ECONOMIC REFORMS

In the USSR theories of MCPE have strongly influenced reform legislation, from the aborted Kosygin reforms of 1965 to the Law on the State Enterprise in 1987. Some other countries as well, the GDR in particular, have long subscribed in general terms to this mode of reform thinking. Its appeal was never overwhelming, however. In Poland and Hungary the number of economists believing in the simulation of goods markets by means of computers was never great. The reform experience of these countries has been strongly moulded by what could be called theories of reformed centrally planned economies (RCPE).

The classic exposition of RCPE was the 1961 book by Wlodzimierz Brus.[4] Brus argued that while the planning centre had also in the future to decide upon net investments for reasons of growth, structure, stability and employment, it could and should be 'freed' from the day-to-day management of the economy. The centre should concentrate on what only it could do; the enterprises would decide upon their day-to-day operations on the basis of profit-oriented market criteria. This was to be 'a planned economy with a built-in market mechanism'.

For two decades Hungary generally followed the basic outlines of Brus's model. RCPE is a radical reform of the centrally planned economy, which abolishes many classical features of central planning. RCPE is also a feasible economic model, as the two decades of Hungarian reform history show. Still, as Hungarian experience also shows, while RCPE contributes to making the society a nicer place to live in, the efficiency gains of RCPE are modest at best. Why? Polish, Hungarian and increasingly also Soviet economists have come up with several answers to this question.[5] First, even RCPE does not really address the question of competition. It is difficult to see how competitive behaviour can be implemented as long as enterprises remain parts of a unified state monopoly of ownership. Second, as long as the centre decides upon investments, the economic destiny of enterprises is to a large extent dependent upon decisions made outside them. The budget constraint of the enterprises thus remains essentially soft, and all kinds of inefficiencies remain. And finally (for the purposes of this chapter), as long as the centre remains true to the strategic goals of full employment and security, creating market competition is rendered impossible by a high number of enterprise-specific policy measures.

In practice, therefore, RCPE degenerates into a situation of 'neither planning nor markets',[6] where the informal control by the centre (or, in large countries, by the regional authorities) limits the real degree of enterprise sovereignty in the same way as central management does in the traditional centrally planned economy. The economy is ready for the third stage of economic reforms.

THE THIRD STAGE OF ECONOMIC REFORMS

The third stage of East European economic reforms is a transition towards a mixed market economy (MME) with a dominant non-state sector, market pricing and freedom of entry and exit for foreign capital. If accomplished, it will prove the validity of the well-known Soviet joke about socialism being the longest road from capitalism to capitalism. In that sense the time of reforms has gone and that of revolutions has arrived. That has already been witnessed in Poland and Hungary and partially in the USSR, and it will undoubtedly follow in other countries as well.

In order to look at the reform situation in each of the countries involved it is appropriate, while discussing the Soviet Union as a separate case, to group the other six countries into three pairs. On the basis of developments until Autumn 1989 Hungary and Poland are the *radical reformers*, Bulgaria and Czechoslovakia the *radicals in words* and the GDR and Romania the *conservatives*.[7] As will be shown below, this division retains much of its validity, even after the political revolutions of late 1989, but before the first free elections. If only for reasons of prudence, the post-communist caretaker cabinets tended to leave all crucial economic decisions to be taken by the future democratically elected governments.

THE DIVERSITY OF REFORM EXPERIENCE

The Soviet Union

The Soviet Union is not the most radical or consistent of the reformers, but still it should be the first to be discussed. Eastern Europe is a Soviet creation, and for decades the repercussions in the Eastern European countries of any Soviet policy change have been closely watched in the Kremlin. On the other hand, the Soviet presence has been used to constrain reforms in many of the countries involved. Much of this has changed. Not only has the Brezhnev doctrine been abandoned, but the present Soviet changes are in many respects deeper than anything openly contemplated during the Prague Spring of 1968. In retrospect, the Czechoslovak reform movement may be seen as the last one to remain within the limits of classical socialism. And even if the USSR leadership did not approve of some of the developments in the (formerly) Soviet-type societies, there is little that it can do about them economically, politically or militarily within the broad contours of its own reform policies. This has opened a historic window of change for those ready to take advantage of it in Eastern Europe.

The internal Soviet reform position is uniquely discordant. Whatever the reasons, the USSR seems to be simultaneously in all the three reform phases outlined above. The main planning changes so far have been of the Stage One type, while there is much pressure to create markets of the Stage Two kind. Finally, the new policies on cooperatives and leaseholding might in the best of cases be first steps towards creating a workable private sector: this is now openly advocated in the USSR. The regional dimension further blurs the picture. Private market production is party orthodoxy in Estonia, while even rudimentary *perestroika* has hardly reached Turkmenia. The question of how such discrepancies are to be handled is an open one, and they are contributing to the social tension that may well wreck the policy of reforms.

The speed with which the Soviet reform agenda has changed is the main lesson to be drawn from the past four years. This speed was later repeated in the hitherto tranquil East European countries — notably the GDR, Czechoslovakia and Romania. The GDR, in fact, traced the political changes that took decades in Poland and Hungary in a few hectic weeks in autumn

1989, while the *political* revolution was even swifter in Romania in December 1989. There are two other important lessons to be learned from the Soviet case. The USSR has seemed to be repeating mistakes earlier made by other economic reformers. No market-like allocation mechanisms were originally drafted as the substitution for the mandatory central planning that was supposed to be abandoned. This, more than anything else, has brought about a rapid deterioration of the economy. *Perestroika* has been dubbed *catastroika*.[8]

This is something that could have been avoided by learning from the Hungarian and Polish experiences. Still, some repetition of mistakes seems to be an unavoidable form of learning. Apparently the logic of reform stages is made convincing only by learning from errors. The social support for consistent marketization and privatization did not exist in 1985. It is unclear whether it exists even in 1990. So far transitions from one stage to another have been mostly brought about by an open crisis.[9]

Another lesson also remains to be fully absorbed by the Soviet leadership. While they seem to be beginning to understand at least some of the linkages between institutions and policies, the future of Soviet reforms is still threatened by a deficient understanding of the importance of correctly sequencing the reform measures. To give just one example: since the traditional economy has been plagued by shortages, any market-oriented reform is necessarily inflationary. While an activization of the price mechanism is much needed, the creation of a market can succeed only if the economy can maintain a degree of macro-economic equilibrium. The recent Soviet *débâcle* of a huge budget deficit and indiscriminate money supply — itself a combination of incompetence and the pressure of vested interests — strongly implies that the financial system has to be put in order before any liberalization of price and wages policy can be contemplated.[10] This seems to be an experience which can be generalized.

The radical reformers

Hungary and Poland both qualify, although in somewhat different ways, as radical reformers that are set to leave the framework of socialism as understood until now. The *Hungarian* experience was long one of a reformist muddling through. Although it has suffered its share of setbacks and even reversals, the basic policy of reform which already surfaced in the early 1950s has survived since the early 1960s. Yet changes within the state sector have been small, competitiveness has been deteriorating and productivity is still low. Balance of payments problems have been recurrent, investments have been declining and consumption levels have stagnated. Most analysts agree that the roots of the present economic crisis lie in the willingness of economic policy-makers to continue informal centralized management. Without trusting in market adjustment, they have tried to save the Hungarian political consensus by continued subsidies and import licensing. Inefficient industries and existing jobs have been protected. In the Hungarian case consensus has masked an increasingly weak government, and reformist talk has all too often been substituted for determined policies.

Still, the situation in Hungary offers some hope. The institutionalization of a multi-party system might in the best of cases bring about a strong coalition government, and a sweeping programme of reprivatization already exists. The development of the financial system is also well under way, and foreign investment is encouraged. Even the communist leadership has been forced to abandon its traditional doctrines. Unfortunately, a pessimistic scenario is also easy to envisage. It would spell a political system paralysed by infighting, further debt crises and declining standards of living, finally leading to civil unrest and a further deteriorating productive capacity. Within the new Europe, Hungary would be given a semi-colonial position.

This brings us to *Poland*, the first East European country with an institutionally pluralist political system but with less real marketization than Hungary. In the 1980s, the radicalism of official reform decrees left little further to demand: the problems have been in their implementation. For one thing, martial law strengthened centralizing tendencies. And in the absence of real legitimacy, the possibly genuine reformist aspirations of the communist leadership have been incapacitated by the need to appease vested interests. The lack of structural change amid a deep recession has been a conspicuous feature of the Polish economy, and the existence of a militant labour movement has further complicated matters from a technocratic economic point of view.

So far, the Polish case demonstrates how reforms are often attempted only when the economy is already in such a crisis condition that the costs of transition seem overwhelmingly heavy. It also shows how the government in such a situation may become the weak prisoner of vested interests, unable to implement its own programmes. It would be extremely naive to expect that a democratic government — especially one with a background in militant labour — would necessarily be less subject to the pressure of vested interests. Certainly, if the history of Solidarity is anything to go by, it will have great problems in implementing structural change and equilibrium prices for consumer goods in its new situation. Indeed, desirable as democracy is for several reasons, an ability to push through the transition to a market economy is not necessarily one of them. It is more important that the government is liberal, committed to a more modest state with less power over markets.[11]

The declared policies of the Solidarity government are without precedent. The willingness to engage in a shock transition to a market is a measure of the deplorable state into which the Polish economy had been taken.

Radicals in words

Outside observers have long had difficulties with defining the economic position of *Bulgaria*. For a decade already, the country has accepted various measures which — if implemented — would have abolished several of the main pillars of the traditional economic system. Legislation since 1987 has envisaged the use of world market prices (in practice mostly CMEA prices) as the basis of domestic prices, the abolition of enterprise-specific taxation and subsidies, and the creation of a two-tier banking system. In late 1988 and early 1989 new measures were announced. These are supposed to encourage the pluralism of ownership forms, create real independence for enterprise management, and abolish both the state monopoly of foreign trade and mandatory plan targets for enterprises. These decisions have been characterized as 'the most coherent and detailed economic reform document to come out of Eastern Europe yet'.[12]

Why, then, have observers had little confidence in the actual implementation of such measures? First of all because the legislation has generally been vague and contradictory. The state leadership has also repeatedly announced that it does not intend to relinquish its control over such fundamentals of the economy as income distribution, pricing and basic production. Furthermore, the Bulgarian economy is exceptionally closely tied to the CMEA market. From this point of view Bulgarian changes are not endogenous, but acknowledged to be reflections of current Soviet legislation. Finally, the Bulgarian authorities have had the most unfortunate habit of changing even the basic rules of the economy almost every year. Such an environment is too unstable to facilitate a fundamental change in the routines of the economy. The situation altered little during the first few months after the leadership change in November 1989.

The *Czechoslovak* authorities long walked on a political tightrope. From 1972 onwards, the public use of the word 'reform' was unthinkable. After December 1987, however, the communist authorities engaged in a relatively open criticism of the existing traditional system. They also talked of an economic reform (*prestavka*), of a transition to 'economic' instead of 'administrative' methods of management, and also of a price reform. The Czechoslovak reform programme seemed at best to attempt a transition to an MCPE. As a leading Czech reformer of the 1960s saw *prestavka* 'the credibility of the reform programs and economic policies is very low' (Kouba, 1989). This does not mean that the economy is not in need of reform. Growth rates have approached zero, standards of living have stagnated, the productive capacity has been antiquated, what remained of international competitiveness has been mostly lost, and environmental deterioration is among the worst in the world. At the same time the economy still has assets which facilitate a reformist programme. The economy is relatively balanced (though on a low level of activity), most consumption goods are easily available, and the external debt is small. Also, there is a strong tradition of reformist thinking, which is now heavily represented in the post-communist Prague government. Interestingly, the main economic spokesmen of the caretaker government were among the vocal free-marketeers of Eastern Europe. Whether Czechoslovakia actually joins Poland and Hungary on the road to capitalism remains to be seen after the 1990 elections.

The conservatives

In the *German Democratic Republic* the 1970s began with a conservative reversal: the economic reforms of the 1960s were dismantled, all ideological innovations were repudiated and a traditionally centralistic form of economic and political rule was reasserted. The reversal was obviously connected with changes in Soviet policies. But after 1985 the Honecker leadership abandoned any comparisons between the needs of their country and the USSR, openly condemned many of the developments in Hungary and Poland and dismissed any market-oriented change in the CMEA. It took a virtual rising of the population to force Honecker down and push the country on to the path of political reform.

The GDR reforms of the 1960s — later abandoned — were somewhere between the first and second phases of economic reforms as defined above. Even if the fact that the only alternative to the traditional system is far-reaching marketization should have been obvious even on the basis of this experience, large parts of the East German intellectual elite spent months after the November revolution harking back to a 'better' socialism. The economic policies of the post-Honecker cabinets were powerless in the face of the continuing outflow of population. The economy simply melted away. By early 1990, this left an unconditional capitulation and speedy unification with the Federal Republic as the only option left.

Nowhere is economic progress so clearly tied to leadership change as in *Romania*. That country's adherence to the traditional model of central planning, together with almost inhuman social and economic policies, has turned a country with plentiful resources into the poorest in Europe. No real change was possible without major political upheavals. Following the revolutionary change of December 1989, the new regime has the consolation that even minor reforms should bring about notable progress in the economy, such is its present state; and the Ceausescu regime's policies at least eliminated the burden of foreign indebtedness.

ECONOMIC AND POLITICAL POWER

We have seen that only in Hungary and Poland does a political understanding clearly exist about a transition to an economy predominantly based on the market. The GDR is a somewhat special case. Soviet economists are only starting to contemplate such a strategy, while for the other East European countries the prospect of a consistently market-oriented reform is a matter for the future democratic governments. Still, as we have seen, there are good theoretical grounds for arguing that only a market economy can be a credible alternative to traditional central planning. Half-way houses are feasible, but they are not efficient.

But how does one institute a market economy, given the existing political and ownership structure? The true answer is short: one does not. Although political pluralism and marketization do not necessarily go hand in hand, a substantive transition to a market economy does have political and ownership preconditions. Politically, a liberal government is needed; socially, a pluralist ownership structure with a dominant non-state (private) sector seems necessary. This more than anything else helps to explain the sources of opposition to market reforms in Eastern Europe.

Markets cannot function without a separation of political and economic power. Such separation is never total: some economic decisions will always be made on political grounds. Still, a permanent predominance of political motives — vested interests — is too expensive to be feasible. Profitability has to be given priority in most instances. On the enterprise level the umbilical

cord between enterprise managers and branch ministries has to be cut —
without replacing it by a strong link with regional authorities. This is a
crucial political change.

Even in the new system, managers have to be responsible to somebody.
One possibility is to subordinate them to the enterprise workers: this is the
self-management option. The other possibility is to institute a joint-stock
company structure with managers' responsibility to share-owners. This does
not necessarily mean the return of capitalism in the technical sense of private
share ownership: state share ownership is also possible, as are various
institutional owner solutions. Self-management is one of the few things that
might possibly survive of the 'Great Socialist Project' of the last hundred
years. As a potential solution, however, it is strongly handicapped by the
rather catastrophic Yugoslav experience, which seems to entail a very short
decision-making horizon, galloping wage inflation and a neglect of
investment. Is self-management thus doomed in the same way as central
planning and general state ownership? To a certain degree, the answer has to
remain open. Some of the Yugoslav problems can be readily explained by the
specific features of the country. With a virtual absence of national cohesion,
a highly monopolistic production structure, very little mobility of resources
and erratic economic policies, no economic model could function efficiently.
Self-management without markets or democracy is doomed to fail.[13]
Furthermore, some Yugoslav problems are dependent on the technical form
in which self-management has been instituted. Theoretically at least, they
could well be alleviated.

One can thus argue that the self-management option has not been really
tested. World-wide experience seems to show that to be successful it needs a
well-motivated labour force, but even then it has great problems with raising
equity capital and nurturing entrepreneurship. It is not for nothing that
organized labour has been more willing to concentrate upon issues of wage
levels than of enterprise management.[14] The social support necessary for a
'socialist' solution like self-management may well be missing in the Eastern
Europe of the near future. The reputation of self-management is going to be
further undermined by such slogans as the Soviet *arenda* (leasing of
enterprises), which is presented as a variation of self-management but all too
easily becomes corrupted into an ordinary incentive scheme.[15]

The enterprise level is not the only one relevant for the separation of
political and economic power. Regional party officials have long been crucial
economic arbiters, a position that has to be given up. The Central Bank has

been subordinated to government, yet without its independence no rational monetary policy — one of the quintessential preconditions of functioning markets — is possible.

OWNERSHIP

Economic theory is not very good at discussing the consequences of different ownership arrangements. The arguments against comprehensive state ownership are, however, strong. Three arguments seem crucial. It seems exceedingly difficult to have workable competition — including the real possibility of bankruptcies — between enterprises with the same owner. Second, the pressure of non-economic interests is stronger upon state enterprises than on private entrepreneurship, and various social and political arguments easily overwhelm the logic of profit maximization. In some cases this is perfectly acceptable, but as a general rule policy-making for non-economic reasons becomes all too expensive. And finally, any state administration is too sluggish to be given the monopoly of entering into new ventures.

State-owned enterprises, working in a somewhat competitive environment, are capable of reaching their economic goals in a satisfactory way, as has been seen in many countries. The question then is, how large should the non-state sectors of the economy be to make a competitive environment possible? There is no exact answer to this question beyond saying that the share of state ownership must be much smaller than it is today. It is therefore better to ask what can be done to give the private and cooperative sectors a real possibility of developing.

Outright prohibitions and limits of size, naturally, have to be abolished. But is that enough to make the private sector 'grow quite spontaneously ... like mushrooms in a forest after rainfall'?[16] Admittedly, the actual size of private enterprises usually remains much smaller than what the officially sanctioned limits allow. This, however, can be readily explained by the many and sometimes subtle ways of discrimination still remaining. No diligent capital accumulation can be expected as long as market imperfections permit the demanding of huge rents, while uncertainty and the fear of future repression discourages strategic investment.

Communists have long opposed any small-scale private production, for the fear of its growing — as Lenin and other Bolsheviks prophesied in the 1920s — into genuine capitalism. As Janos Kornai points out, they have been right:

small-scale private production does develop into capitalism, if the constitutional framework and confidence in the future needed for capital accumulation exist. The irony of the matter is that as long as such guarantees of capitalism are missing or they cannot be trusted, the capitalism existing within socialism will show some of its most unpleasant features. To change private profiteering and conspicuous consumption into diligent accumulation, not only are instruments like workable capital markets needed, but a profound political and ideological change is also necessary. So far the constitutional security needed for private capital accumulation has been absent from all the East European countries, Hungary included.

Socialist governments find it easier to accept private entrepreneurship in areas which have earlier been unexploited by state enterprises. Direct private competition with state enterprises is much more difficult to accept, and the outright privatization of state property is the least favoured form of private ownership. Privatization also faces problems of a different kind. State property can hardly be simply handed over to willing individuals because of equity considerations. It is also difficult to sell, as the absence of realistic asset valuation will make pricing difficult. Domestic capital to buy state property hardly exists, while the wide use of foreign buyers causes problems of sovereignty. Moreover, popular resistance to privatization cannot be excluded.[17] Many enterprises will be unable to command a positive price. They should really be simply scrapped, but this has employment and regional implications, which will probably be dominant for a weak reforming government.

In the foreseeable future, then, the state sector will continue to be relatively large, probably overwhelming in the manufacturing branches. Within this sector structural change will quite probably be slow in coming. Forms of informal bureaucratic control continue to dominate within the state sector not only in Hungary but in the capitalist countries as well. Are the post-reform mixed market economies with their large state sectors therefore condemned to relative inefficiency and lack of competitiveness? There are two answers to this question. First, as we saw above, the degree to which the state sector can be subjected to meaningful market signals and profit criteria depends on the relative size of the non-state sector. Making private activities dominant in the economy may well take decades. Even then, as the experience of market economies helps to explain, the managers and workers of the state sector, assisted by powerful regional interests, will do the utmost to resist the imposition of hard budget constraints. As Kornai notes, there are no demonstrations in favour of increasing efficiency at the expense of state protection.[18] The forecast for efficiency cannot therefore be a very positive one.

One can consider ways of making the link between political decision-makers, bureaucracy and state enterprises as weak as possible without changing the nominal ownership structure. One way to do this would be to make different non-private institutions the owners of state property. This could happen through investment funds and related instruments. After all, in modern capitalism ownership has been largely depersonalized. It remains to be seen whether this would be a realistic way forward for reforming economies too.

POLICIES OF TRANSITION

Like any real-life change of importance, a prospective transition from central planning to markets is plagued with contradictions. The space available permits mentioning only a few of them. One of the essential paradoxes has already been pointed out: the reform will in all probability be initiated in conditions of economic crisis, by a government weakened by social pressures and the turmoil of political change. Even the party system itself will be only in the process of formation. To be even moderately successful, however, a transition needs strong economic policies ranging from the creation of a constitutional regime to controlling the money supply, wages and prices. The concomitant democratization makes this in some respects more difficult by exposing the government to political pressures of a new kind. There may be a consensus for change in general; there cannot be a consensus for very many of the concrete changes that will inevitably lead to uneven distribution of costs and benefits.

This is true in spite of the liberal essence of the transition. In the circumstances, and given third world experiences, *laissez faire* looks like a recipe for catastrophe. After generations of state socialism, market institutions will be extremely imperfect for a long time to come. Consequently, policies will need to be institutionalist and Keynesian rather than neo-classical, whatever the doctrinal inspiration of the reformers.

In a thoughtful essay,[19] László Csaba has stressed that there are three important consequences of the fact that reforms are started in an economic crisis. The reform, since it is a consequence of poor economic performance, has the initial effect of making the crisis more open. It therefore seems to make the situation worse. The weak government will engage in counterproductive compromises which lead to numerous unintended results. And finally, because of this, any precise reform plans are bound to fail. This discussion has argued that a transition, even in the best of cases, will take decades. During this period societies will have to go through crises and upheavals. The consequences of the planned economy — low productivity, obsolete structure, spoiled environment and wasted resources — will not go away overnight. They will constrain welfare in any future economic system. Such a realistic view may be taken as the privilege of an outsider, but it does seem to have valid foundations. Still, one should not exclude the possibility that future has surprises in store. We are talking about a transition which does not have direct precedents. The East European countries are all different, and they are even now experimenting with various approaches to reform. The 'shock treatment' of Poland and the adherence of Czechoslovakia to the ranks of the reformers may well offer totally new processes to ponder upon.

NOTES

This chapter was written while the author was a visitor at the Centre for Russian and East European Studies, University of Birmingham. Financial support of the Yrjo Jahnsson Foundation is gratefully acknowledged.

1. The discussion is heavily indebted to Paul Marer, 'A Conceptual Framework of Reform in Centrally Planned Economies, with an Application to Hungary', paper presented to conference on Plan and/or Market, Vienna, 26-28 June 1989.
2. These issues are discussed in some detail in Pekka Sutela, 'Introduction', *Nordic Journal of Soviet and East European Studies*, Vol. 5, No. 1 (1988), pp. 1-9; and 'Soviet Investments and Economic Slowdown Reconsidered', *Nordic Journal of Soviet and East European Studies*, Vol. 5, No. 2 (1988), pp. 3-15.
3. Such theories are analysed in detail in Michael Ellman, *Planning Problems in the USSR* (Cambridge: Cambridge University Press, 1973) and Pekka Sutela, *Socialism, Planning and Optimality* (Helsinki: Finnish Society for Sciences and Letters, 1984).
4. There is an English translation: see Wlodzimierz Brus, *The Market in the Socialist Economy* (Oxford: Clarendon Press, 1975).
5. See Tamas Bauer, 'The Hungarian Alternative to Soviet-Type Planning', *Journal of Comparative Economics*, No. 3 (1983), pp. 304-16; Janos Kornai, 'The Hungarian Reform Process: Visions, Hopes and Reality', *Journal of Economic Literature*, 1986, No. 4, pp. 1687-1737; and Wlodzimierz Brus and Kasimierz Laski, 'Product Market and Capital Market in the Light of the Experience of the Hungarian new Economic Mechanism (NEM)', paper

presented to conference on Market Forces in Planned Economies, Moscow, 28-30 March 1989.

6. To use Tamas Bauer's phrase.

7. For more factual information see *Economic Reforms in the European Centrally Planned Economies* (New York: United Nations Economic Commission for Europe, 1989).

8. See Alexander Zinoviev, *Katastroika: Legend and Reality of Gorbachevism*, translated by Charles Janson (London and Lexington, KY: Claridge Press, 1990).

9. This is a positive, not a normative statement. It does not mean that crises would be a good thing or that every crisis would push reforms further. On the contrary, crises are very unpleasant for people who have to live through them and many, perhaps most, crises bring about conservative changes.

10. For a contrary view see Anders Åslund, *Gorbachev's Struggle for Economic Reform* (London: Pinter, 1989).

11. See Ellen Comisso, 'Market Failures and Market Socialism: Economic Problems of the Transition', *Eastern European Politics and Societies*, Vol. 3, No. 3 (1988), pp. 433-65. It is, in fact, arguable that not only are *perestroika* and *uskorenie* inconsistent, but there is also a phase when *demokratizatsiya* becomes an obstacle to *perestroika*. Discussing this, however, would take us beyond the scope of this paper.

12. 'Bulgaria: Reform Takes a Giant Step', *Eastern European Markets*, 10 March 1989.

13. See Harry Lydall, *Yugoslavia in Crisis* (Oxford: OxfordUniversity Press, 1989).

14. For a thorough theoretical discussion see Jacques H. Dreze, *Labour Management, Contracts and Capital Markets* (Oxford: Basil Blackwell, 1989).

15. See Tamas Bauer, 'The Firm Under Perestroika', *Berichte des Bundesinstituts für Ostwissenschaftliche und internationale Studien* (Cologne), 39/1989.

16. Janos Kornai, 'The Affinity Between Ownership and Coordination Mechanisms' (Helsinki: WIDER, 1989), p. 8.

17. Jan Vanous, 'Privatization in Eastern Europe: Possibilities, Problems, and the Role of Western Capital', *PlanEcon Report*, 30 September 1989.

18. Kornai, 'The Affinity Between Ownership and Coordination Mechanisms'.

19. László Csaba, 'External Implications of Economic Reform in the European Centrally Planned Economies', *Journal of Development Planning* (forthcoming).

6. The Relevance of Ideology

Rachel Walker

Such has been the momentum of change in the USSR and Eastern Europe
since Gorbachev came to power that it is scarcely an exaggeration to say that
the rest of the world is still in a state of shock. How, one asks, after
seventy-odd years can it be that Marxism-Leninism — an 'ideology' which
according to official Soviet descriptions was a monolithic hegemon — and the
system it helped to produce and reproduce should apparently have lost their
grip so quickly?

Answers to such questions are not easily come by, particularly since
epoch-making events usually defy explanation until long after their
occurrence. Nevertheless, this chapter will advance the following arguments
by way of at least partial explanation.

To put its central propositions bluntly it is possible to argue that
Marxism-Leninism never really functioned adequately as any sort of
'ideology', however one chooses to define that vexatious term. It did not
provide either the USSR or the other socialist societies with much of an
integrating identity — the sort of systemic identity that unites disparate
interests around at least some common goals, aspirations and mechanisms for
conflict resolution. It provided them with an identity of sorts, based on the
various cults of the revolution, of Lenin, and so on; but this identity was,
and in some respects remains, so ambiguous as to be almost completely
unable to organize or explain the 'actually existing' present in the socialist
societies in any coherent way. On the contrary, Marxism-Leninism functioned
largely as a mechanism of control which depended on the coercive
enforcement of conformity at whatever cost to the development of knowledge
and practice, as the Soviet authorities eventually recognized. However, once
this Stalinist mechanism of control was overtly challenged, as it now has
been, it was more or less inevitable that its power would disappear almost
immediately. In this respect there is, perhaps for the first time since Stalin

imposed his orthodoxy on the system, a real opportunity for meaningful change opening up in the system.

On the other hand, however, Marxism-Leninism did at least ensure a certain social cohesion, however artificial and enforced. Its virtual abandonment in the countries of Eastern Europe, and the rejection of its most grotesquely Stalinized forms in the USSR, has therefore left a vacuum which will be extraordinarily difficult to fill. Although the Soviet leaders have not abandoned their general commitment to socialism, nor a commitment to what Gorbachev at any rate calls 'socialist ideology', it is not clear that the new political ethos emerging in the USSR, with its emphasis on the recognition of pluralism, social diversity, tolerance — even of relative truth — can actually provide a new identity which will hold the Soviet system, let alone the so-called socialist community, together. Quite the reverse: one can argue that the Gorbachev administration made things infinitely more difficult for itself, as well as for the East European communist parties, by beginning to speak the language of tolerance, however faintly, before it had done anything constructive to support it institutionally within either Eastern Europe or the USSR. This is an indication of the power of language, in particular the language of Soviet politicians, to assist in the binding and unbinding of social relations within the socialist countries whatever the prevailing institutional bias.

Clearly, there are enormous risks in such a situation. As developments in Eastern Europe, notably the German Democratic Republic, have already demonstrated, a society begins to disintegrate rapidly into an anarchy of atomized and competing interests once it loses a sense of self. This process was already well under way by the turn of the decade. There was no indication then that any of these societies were much advanced in the construction of a new social identity — although social democracy looked to be the preferred option for many — whatever the optimism of Western 'free marketeers' on this score. It is a very moot point whether the USSR will succeed in doing so quickly enough to prevent the disintegration of the union.

CREATIVITY AND CONTROL

Contrary to first impressions, Soviet Marxism-Leninism, and its East European derivatives, have never in principle excluded creative behaviour from their understanding of action. On the contrary, the revolutionary identity associated with Marx and Lenin, and the revolutionary 'leading and guiding role' subsequently associated with the Stalinized communist parties, was precisely premised on their putative revolutionary ability to intervene creatively in the flow of history, adapting theory and practice as necessary. As Stalin remarked in his notorious *Short Course*, 'mastering' Marxist-Leninist theory meant being able to 'enrich it with the new experience of the revolutionary movement', in correspondence with 'the new historical situation'.[1] Khrushchev made the same point more often and more emphatically: 'Marxist-Leninist theory ... demands only one thing — to use revolutionary theory not dogmatically but creatively, to develop it further in the process of the practical struggle for communism.'[2] And even Brezhnev, the architect of 'stagnation', was obliged to acknowledge that

> The Marxist-Leninist party cannot fulfil its role if it does not give the necessary attention ... to the creative development of Marxist-Leninist theory.[3]

Gorbachev's own frequent calls for the 'creative approach' are therefore not only representative of a time-honoured socialist tradition, but actually constitute a rather paradoxical call to orthodoxy. As Gorbachev himself has insisted more than once, 'loyalty to the Marxist-Leninist teaching lies in its creative development'.[4]

In view of this, one would have expected the socialist countries to have been a permanent hotbed of creative development. However, of course, the very opposite has been the case. Despite constant exhortations to be 'creative', and despite successive attempts to reform the Soviet-type 'administrative–command' system, rampant creativity has not, with some exceptions, been a noticeable feature of communist party practice. What is more, the creative explosions that did occur in Eastern Europe prior to 1985, which had they been creatively and sensitively approached might have helped with the reform process within the USSR itself, were instead savagely destroyed by Soviet force.

The question we must confront, therefore, is: why? What becomes problematical from this perspective is not the fact of change in the system so much as the comparative lack of change over time — after all, the emergence of a Gorbachev, a Tito or a Khrushchev, not to mention the institution of revolutionizing processes like *perestroika*, is only to be expected. Addressed from this point of view it becomes evident that the problem has to do with power.

Creativity is by definition volatile, unpredictable, uncontrollable. It is as much the product of inspiration and spontaneity as of deliberation and controlled experiment. Crucially, it consists in breaking or manipulating the rules and established conventions of traditional practices. As a consequence creativity is generally resisted. It disrupts habit and convention. Most crucially, it disrupts, or can threaten to disrupt, the authority and power relations that are embedded in all socially communicated knowledges and practices. No community is therefore particularly accommodating to it, and certainly no political authority will be accommodating to a creative challenge that looks like being even potentially successful.

Seen in this light it immediately becomes evident that real creative action is highly antithetical to the Stalinist communist party, at both the micro- and the macro- levels, since potentially it poses a challenge to power — whether it be the power of the local party official, of the top party leadership, or of the CPSU's leadership over the fraternal parties. We are therefore presented with a major paradox. On the one hand, the possibility of generalized creativity is simultaneously intrinsic and essential to the communist party's revolutionary identity, which means that it cannot be totally abandoned; on the other hand, it is highly threatening to the party's generalized social power, which means that it must be controlled, even though controlled creativity, particularly if it is politically controlled, is something of a contradiction in terms.

It is this historical and ideological paradox that lies at the base of the Stalinist communist parties' inability to deal adequately with change in their systems, even though their leaders have constantly reiterated the obvious fact that reality, and therefore theory, can never stand still. It is also this ideological paradox that lies at the root of the disorganization and anomie of so much everyday behaviour in the socialist countries.[5] To demand creative action, on the one hand, while imposing necessarily indeterminate controls on it, on the other, is to throw people into a quandary. How should they behave in such circumstances? Political loyalty requires that they demonstrate independence of thought and action. However, the same political loyalty also demands obedience to 'the party line'. The result has been perpetual paradox and uncertainty for individuals, and the 'dogmatization' of theory and practice on the part of the communist parties. In short, the conflict between revolution and consolidation in the USSR and then by extension in Eastern Europe produced a double bind of historic proportions.[6]

It is worth pausing briefly to consider this double bind, since it is of relevance to the understanding of developments after 1985. As a system of control it was not unique to the CPSU, in so far as the other Stalinist communist parties also practised it in their own domestic politics, but it did enable the CPSU as its original progenitor to maintain its ideological and political predominance, however artificially, within the socialist common-wealth and the international communist movement, just as it enabled each of the East European communist parties to retain their 'leading role' domestically.

Taken in the abstract the double bind in question was very simple. On the one hand, it comprised a panoply of coercive instruments and relations — political, economic, legal, military — which varied in their degree of threat, both relative to each other and over time, but which nevertheless served to keep different groups within the socialist community in varying degrees of fear. On the other hand, and of central importance for our purposes, it also comprised a highly paradoxical form of communication. This simultaneously counterposed one injunction to 'good' behaviour with a contradictory injunction also to 'good behaviour', in such a way as to eliminate any possibility for unambiguous choice. Consequently, anyone attempting to fulfil the one injunction could always be punished at the discretion of the leadership for not (adequately) fulfilling the other.[7]

Thus, communists were enjoined by their leaderships to 'creatively develop Marxism-Leninism' in line with 'accumulated experience' so as to keep in touch with reality. Any failure to do so would provide ammunition for the revolutionary movement's class enemies. They were simultaneously also enjoined to 'defend the purity of Marxism-Leninism' in order to rebuff those same class enemies. At the same time, however, there was harsh condemnation of 'revisionism' and any sort of 'deviationism' from the 'agreed Marxist-Leninist line', as determined by the CPSU and corroborated by the national and international communist congresses. In addition, repression of internal and external dissidents, and attacks on them, made it abundantly clear that any 'creative development of Marxism-Leninism' that was deemed to be 'revisionist', and (to a lesser extent) any 'defence' of its 'purity' that was deemed to be too 'dogmatic', would be harshly punished by whatever means. As the preamble to the Soviet Communist Party Rules adopted in 1961 and 1986 warned:

> In creatively developing Marxism-Leninism, the CPSU decisively struggles against all manifestations of revisionism and dogmatism, which are deeply alien to revolutionary theory.[8]

The practical result was the ideological equivalent of democratic centralism:

dogmatic and formalistic repetition of 'the general party line' from the (Soviet) top down, with some allowance for local variation and local input. Since no communist could tell beforehand what the difference between 'creativity' and 'revisionism', or between 'defence' and 'dogmatism', would be, and since it was clear that 'dogmatism', if it meant constant reproduction of 'the general party line', was hardly a crime at all, then the only sure means of survival was to pay constant lip service to it. As Igor Kon put it recently in the Soviet context:

> The same deference to the authorities and fear of novelty [as in the arts] were also confirmed in science, especially in social sciences. The constant quoting of official sources and the leader's words, albeit roundly condemned, was the only defence against accusations of making heretical or unsubstantiated assertions. The attempt to re-examine any worn-out proposition was seen as revisionism. Meanwhile dogmatism, albeit rhetorically attacked, appeared a quite forgivable shortcoming and almost proof of reliability. Forbidden zones were delineated not only in the press but in our consciousness too.[9]

Thus, the CPSU leadership was able to impose its own 'creative development of Marxism-Leninism', at least in those essential particulars on which it wished absolute unanimity like the leading role of the party, not only on its own membership but also on all the other communist party leaderships who chose, or were obliged, to remain within the Soviet fold. Equally, national communist party leaderships could use the same mechanism domestically to reinforce both their own leading role and the loyalty of their own members.[10]

What gave the CPSU pre-eminence in this process, though, was the fact that it could claim 'Lenin' as its founder, and bask in the reflected glory of the first successful twentieth-century revolution. This not only endowed its arrogated leadership of the communist movement with an empirical justification, but also allowed it to rebuff any challenges to its theoretical competence by enabling it to appear as a humble 'follower' and executor of 'Lenin's behests'. By means of this Stalinist substitution, the CPSU thus appeared not as the dominant authority in the double bind but as the 'faithful follower' of a 'sacred teaching' just like everyone else. This proved to be an effective means of preventing anyone within the movement from questioning the logic of this paradoxical situation in any reasonable way: to escape it one had always to risk the possibility of retribution — as, for example, the Yugoslavs, the Czechoslovaks, the Chinese and the Albanians discovered — or remain trapped within it.[11]

The theoretical and practical consequences of all this for communist practice were devastating.

Lenin, and the revolutionary tradition generally, became grotesquely reified, and 'loyalty' to Lenin's work became a matter of dogmatic repetition of certain isolated postulates and of the constant symbolic invocation of his name.

Creativity, although clearly not eliminated, nevertheless became a dangerous business, since there could be no certainty until *after* the event that any particular party leadership, and the Soviet central leadership above all, would choose to co-opt rather than condemn whatever creative proposition had been made (from whatever quarter). This did not stop the development and flow of ideas either within the USSR or within the socialist community, but it did constrain it insofar as any debate required top-level political support to get anywhere — that famous 'window of opportunity' to which Gustafson has referred. Not that ideas necessarily disappeared if they failed to get top-level support. On the contrary, they generally stayed in subterranean circulation within the intellectual community, and therefore remained available for successive generations of party officials to absorb. Thus, innovation on the part of Soviet and East European intellectuals, not to mention the periodic upheavals within Eastern Europe, gradually expanded the universe of what it was possible to think and do within the socialist community, so that an innovator like Gorbachev, for example, had no need to start from scratch. However, such a process is agonizingly slow and pathetically inadequate to the needs of developing industrial economies. It produced an *ersatz* 'official' creativity which, because it had to rely on the furtive co-optation of ideas developed on the political periphery, was no creativity at all, but rather a 'no man's land' of constant half-measures and partial reforms. Hence the inability of these systems to reform themselves in any coherent way. Moreover, it could in any case do little to overcome the confusions of identity that consequently beset these societies.

In this respect, the Stalinist desire to master all change locked the CPSU, and its East European counterparts, into a time-warp that stunted their ability to change by constantly returning them to a revolutionary heritage which the system had either long since outgrown or which had never really belonged to them in the first place.

In the same way, the communist parties were also saddled with a conceptual Manicheism which constrained the possibilities for meaningful *realpolitik* far more successfully than any supposed 'loyalty' to Marxism or

Leninism. Stalinist 'two-campism' effectively ensured, first, that all manifestations of diversity within the 'socialist camp' would be construed as antagonistic to Soviet or communist interests and would therefore be eliminated. Second, that 'unity' would automatically connote uniform agreement with the 'general party line' as ultimately determined by the CPSU leadership. And third, that the concept of 'cooperation' would become meaningless, since enemies could not cooperate, and 'friends' did not need to do so.

The general result was the stifling of society at all levels and the development within the majority of people, including party members, of precisely the sort of apathy and 'inertia' that Gorbachev has been trying to overcome. After all, once

> someone has become convinced, through his own experience or that of others, that personal initiative is very often 'punished' or becomes a labour of Sisyphus, he chooses the path of least resistance.[12]

Thus a certain identity was enforced, based on institutions like party government, central planning, state welfarism and patriotic defense, but it bore little relation to the everyday lives of ordinary people. As Herman Diligensky, chief editor of the journal *World Economy and International Relations*, remarked:

> Social standards and values were alienated from the individual's inner world and turned from a moral imperative into formal injunctions, into 'rules of the game' which were equally absolute and rootless in that inner world.[13]

In short, the result was a painful gap between words and deeds, between official and unofficial relations, between official and unofficial identities, which could not but produce massive alienation and social dislocation.

When he came to power in March 1985, Gorbachev was therefore confronted with an ideological straitjacket. It took him and his fellow reformers two years to attempt to change the 'terms of debate'. The signs are, however, that they may have succeeded only too well.

CREATIVITY AND 'NEW THINKING'

The ideological core of 'the Gorbachev revolution' to date has been the abandonment of Stalinist Manicheism. Every aspect of the double bind just described has been challenged. The only exception has been the deification of

'Lenin', and even here the reformist critique of method has opened the way for the gradual elimination of the 'Lenin cult'.

The conceptual reversal which has underpinned the Soviet turn towards notions of pluralism, and so on, was perhaps best summarized in Gorbachev's justly renowned speech to the United Nations in December 1988. In that speech it was noticeable that the attributes of social identity which had appeared as negative or enforced under Stalinism — the notions of 'difference', 'unity', 'cooperation', and so forth — were now described as being positive. Thus, according to Gorbachev, 'Differences often acted as barriers in the past. Now they can develop into factors of rapprochement and mutual enrichment'.[14] Moreover, since 'specific interests underlie all differences between social systems, ways of life, and value preferences' there can be no disguising the need not only to acknowledge them but also to empower them and give them voice. Consequently, 'the principle of freedom of choice' for nations (but it implicitly follows for individuals as well) becomes 'a universal principle [which] knows no exceptions'. This in turn demands 'respect of others' views and stances, tolerance, the ability to learn how to coexist *while remaining different*'; it 'needs goodwill *not to see the alien as bad and hostile*'.[15]

Clearly such an open-ended conception of social differences inevitably has transforming effects on the concepts of 'unity' and 'cooperation'. In the same speech Gorbachev referred positively to the need for 'unity through variety' and to 'that kind of cooperation, that we might call creativity or co-development'. Although these were not explicitly defined, it is clear from the generality of what he said that Gorbachev intended an idea of unity and cooperation which is based on the equality, negotiation and mutual reconciliation of interests through dialogue which is aimed at 'the essence of problems, not at confrontation'.[16]

Gorbachev is by no means the first Soviet politician to have articulated such ideas, of course. It was, in fact, Khrushchev who made the first real attempt to overcome Stalinism. Indeed, some Soviet social scientists argue that the 'paradigm now referred to as new thinking' can be traced back to the twentieth congress of the CPSU in 1956, when Khrushchev made his two path-breaking speeches.[17] Certainly, the concepts of 'peaceful coexistence' and of 'different roads to socialism', articulated at that congress, prefigured the recognition that 'diversity' did not need to connote antagonism, any more than unity necessitated uniformity, and that meaningful cooperation between both friends and enemies was therefore possible. Moreover, both these concepts also owed a great deal to what was subsequently condemned as 'revisionist' critiques of socialist development. As Khrushchev acknowledged, the principles of 'peaceful coexistence' were actually developed by the Chinese Communist Party as its contribution to the founding conference of the non-aligned movement which took place in Bandung in 1955. Equally, 'different roads to socialism' owed a great deal to the thinking of the Italian Communist Party leader and theoretician Palmiro Togliatti.

Unfortunately, however, Khrushchev did not go far enough in his revision of Soviet theory, and moreover he took fright at the political consequences of the changes he did make. He did not sufficiently rethink the rather simplistic conception of class struggle which underpinned Stalinist 'two-campism'. And as a consequence his partial relaxation of it did not survive the first real manifestations of difference in Eastern Europe in 1956 and afterwards, nor did it survive the developing hostilities of the cold war. 'Different roads to socialism' and 'peaceful coexistence' remained in the CPSU's theoretical arsenal. But the first was commuted to 'socialist internationalism', in which differences among socialist countries were reduced to being reflections of the same 'common historical laws' and subordinated to the common interest of the commonwealth (as determined largely by the CPSU in both cases) — a prefiguration of the Brezhnev doctrine; and the second increasingly became 'competitive coexistence' based not so much on cooperation as on mutual crisis exploitation.

Major advances in the theory and practice of Soviet politics and foreign policy therefore awaited serious revision of the theory of class struggle which has provided much of the underpinning for the Stalinist 'bad faith model' of human relations. Such a revision has finally be given an official *imprimatur* with the advent of Gorbachev.

CLASS STRUGGLE

This theory has been fundamental to the identity and power of the CPSU. Initially it provided the CPSU with simply a set of epistemological principles for understanding the world. Under Stalin, however, it became an extremely effective political instrument for branding enemies, and as such provided the pseudo-theoretical foundation for the double bind that arose upon it, much to the detriment of its epistemological functions. Above all, it legitimated the revolutionary identity of the CPSU as the domestic and international 'vanguard' party. Any rethink of this theory therefore constitutes a highly significant development.

Gorbachev has by no means rejected the theory of class struggle outright. However, he has explicitly rejected the Stalinist uses to which it has been put, and is clearly reducing its salience for the understanding of politics. Crucially, he has explicitly condemned its political exploitation as an instrument of repression by Stalin. 'Any attempts to justify ... lawlessness by political needs, international tension or *alleged exacerbation of class struggle in the country* are wrong', he states in *Perestroika*.[18] He has also rejected the contrived 'enemy image' which has been crucial to maintaining Stalinist 'two-campism'. 'An imaginary or real enemy is needed only if one is bent on maintaining tension.'[19] In conditions of global crisis it should be possible to do civilized business even with genuine antagonists. In the same spirit, Gorbachev has abandoned 'the definition of peaceful coexistence of states with different social systems as a "specific form of class struggle"', which has been a cause of endless misunderstanding between the two superpowers in the past, and also jettisoned the pseudo-Leninist postulate that a third world war would lead to further world-wide revolution: neither of these notions appears in the revised edition of the party Programme.[20]

On the other hand, Gorbachev has not rejected the epistemological functions of the theory. In *Perestroika*, he argued that class would continue to be an objective reality in the world and that it could not, therefore, be neglected in the attempt to resolve the world's problems, although global crises such as pollution and the threat of nuclear war did set objective limits beyond which the interests of class must be subordinated to the 'universal values' of common humanity. And at the Central Committee plenum in January 1987, for example, he criticized Stalinist social theory for depicting the social structure of society 'schematically as lacking in contradictions and in the dynamism deriving from the multifarious interests of its different strata and groups'.[21]

In this respect, Gorbachev has been articulating the 'commanding heights' of a debate that has been going on for some years within both the Soviet and the East European social science communities about the nature of interests and the nature of social contradiction within socialist society, particularly in the context of the successive East European crises.[22] In general the argument has been between those, such as Richard I. Kosolapov, the former editor of the CPSU journal *Kommunist*, who have insisted on the orthodox line that differences of interest and antagonistic social contradictions cannot exist in 'developed' socialist societies like the USSR, any contradictions that do exist being 'non-antagonistic' ones, and reformist thinkers like V. S. Semenov, editor of *Voprosy filosofii*, who argue not only that differences of interest must exist within socialist societies but that social contradictions — even if they start by being 'non-antagonistic' — can rapidly become antagonistic if they are mismanaged or allowed to develop, or both, as evidenced, for example, by the Polish crisis of 1980-81, the implication often being that the same could happen in the USSR.[23]

Ironically, therefore, revision of the theory of class struggle has led to its de-politicization in ways that are finally enabling Soviet politicians and social scientists to begin coming to grips with the contradictions and antagonisms that have been plaguing socialist societies for years but which have been denied adequate recognition by Soviet politicians.

It should also be briefly noted that the same process has enabled the development of a Soviet appreciation of 'global interdependence' which, as with much else, did not begin with Gorbachev but first emerged in the mid-1970s. At that time the discussion of interdependence produced considerable tension between those who insisted on the continued importance of the 'class approach' to all problems, and the proponents of 'globalistics' who asserted that global problems required an 'all-human approach'. During Brezhnev's last years this tension was side-stepped — but not resolved — by means of the political assertion that the two approaches should be made to complement each other.[24] Gorbachev, however, is now eliminating this tension by elevating the significance of interdependence and of 'universal human values' at the global level and effectively removing class from the argument.

The implications of this 'de-Stalinization' of the theory are clearly enormous since it has enabled both a more realistic assessment of tensions and difficulties at the domestic level (where previously uniformity was always assumed), and the recognition of possible commonalities at the global level (where previously antagonistic difference was always taken for granted). However, matters do not end here since this process of revision has gone beyond the question of class struggle to address the conduct of theory and method generally.

THEORY AND METHOD

One of Gorbachev's most telling and probably most destabilizing moves has been to challenge and undermine what he has called the party's 'arrogance of omniscience', its presumption to absolute truth, which was a central spin-off of the party's putative pre-eminence in the class struggle and the central justification for its arrogated right to dictate theory and practice. He has done this in two ways.

On the one hand, Gorbachev has revoked the right of the CPSU to dictate terms within the socialist community. 'No one party holds a monopoly on truth' and 'No one has a right to claim a special position in the socialist world', as he insisted back in 1987.[25] He has also argued that 'Socialism does not and cannot have any "model" that everyone must measure up to', and even suggested that all those notorious occasions for enforcing the 'general party line' — such as the 'binding international conferences' of previous years — should now be consigned to the past.[26] This constituted an early repudiation of the so-called Brezhnev doctrine which paved the way for much of the subsequent disintegration in Eastern Europe.

On the other hand, he has also revoked the right of communist party officials to preside over the bureaucratic control of theory and method. Instead of simply condemning 'dogmatism' as a bureaucratic deformation, as his predecessors did, Gorbachev has increasingly spelled out the errors of method that have helped to produce it. Two interrelated problems appear to be particularly crucial to the argument.

First, Gorbachev has remarked on the dogmatic reification of theory, and its consequent alienation from reality, as products of Stalinism which have had much to do with subsequent deformations in the development of the socialist societies. For example, in his speech to the January 1987 Central Committee plenum, he argued that under Stalinism 'vital debate and creative thinking disappeared from theory and the social sciences, and authoritarian evaluations and opinions became unquestionable truths that could only be commented upon'. As a consequence, the 'theoretical concepts of socialism in many respects remained at the level of the 1930s and 1940s, when society was resolving entirely different tasks'. Worse still, certain practical forms of social organization were 'absolutized' and 'dogmatized' as though they were unchanging and essential characteristics of socialism. As a consequence, theory had chronically failed to move with the times, with disastrous practical results.[27]

Second, Gorbachev has associated this destruction of theory with the dogmatic deformation of Lenin's theoretical work. According to Gorbachev, the 'creative development' of Leninism does *not* mean copying his decisions:

'we cannot copy, literally repeat the approaches of the past', since this would be the 'worst type of talmudism and dogmatism'.[28] What it does mean is learning to use Lenin's method, which consists in mastering 'the art of specific analysis of a specific situation'.[29] This in turn means that 'new, unorthodox approaches' to life are both possible and necessary, since reality never stands still. According to Gorbachev's reading, therefore, Leninism presupposes diversity of approach and a 'pluralism of opinion'.[30]

Of course, it has been common practice for a new general secretary to reinterpret the 'Leninist heritage' to suit his purposes. Until now, however, this process has consisted entirely in the replacement of one set of injunctions taken out of context with another set. Now is the first time that a general secretary has sought to go beyond this to propose such an open and plastic reading of the 'Leninist method'. Taken to its logical conclusion, of course, such an interpretation will inevitably move beyond the rather narrow confines of historical Leninism all too soon, since to reduce the Leninist method simply to Lenin's startling ability to engage with reality is in principle to lift all political and theoretical restrictions entirely. On the other hand, of course, it might also presage an attempt to return to a genuine Lenin, to the extent that the Stalinist idol — 'the Santa Claus image'[31] — is debunked and the real historical Lenin is recuperated, warts and all. There are certainly signs that this may be under way.[32]

In either case, however, one result is likely to be the eventual relativization of Lenin and the consequent elimination of the CPSU's most symbolic legitimating device (apart from the revolution itself).

The other likely result is a major crisis of identity for the CPSU, which is clearly apparent in preparations for the Twenty-Eighth Congress in 1990. The process is bound to be fraught, since Gorbachev has systematically undermined every single element of the party's Stalinist identity, without replacing any of the old certainties with new ones. Unfortunately for the conservatives, however, no matter how much they might balk at the steady haemorrhaging of the old rules, the fact that the Soviet population more or less rejected the party at the very first opportunity clearly indicates that its identity and role have been at the top of the 'real' political agenda for a long time. Gorbachev or no Gorbachev, the problem has to be confronted, although the experience of Eastern Europe suggests that there are no easy solutions.

SOCIALISM AND THE QUESTION OF IDENTITY

Similar considerations apply to the identity of 'socialism'. Perhaps one of the most startling consequences of all these developments is that it has become less and less easy for anyone to grasp in what socialist society, once freed from all historical deformations, should actually consist.

Of course, it would be distinctly contradictory to expect anyone to have a set of ready prescriptions for the 'new' socialism, since this is precisely the sort of political behaviour that reformers have been castigating. However, it is difficult to resist the conclusion that no one knows what socialism is when Gorbachev himself has argued that Soviet theorists have to clarify 'what exactly socialism is and by what methods it can and must be built, renewed, perfected', and that they must determine the criteria for establishing 'What is genuinely socialist and what is foreign to the very idea of socialism'.[33] And when Eastern Europe is so clearly in disarray on the subject.

In some respects this is probably all to the good, since it irretrievably and explicitly opens up the USSR to the examination and possible adoption of all sorts of new ideas. Such frankly acknowledged uncertainty can only unleash whatever creative potential there is in the system. However, this process threatens to spell an end to the federal union, just as similar processes spelled the end of the socialist commonwealth, and for similar reasons.

As I intimated at the outset, Marxism-Leninism never provided the Soviet type of society with an integrating identity because it could not do so. To begin with it was never more than an instrument of Stalinism: a name coined by Stalin to disguise the fact that the invention of the 'general party line' was largely his, and that this 'line' would be an instrument for general political control, not a medium for revolutionary democratic action. As such, Marxism-Leninism was not about *winning* hearts and minds to produce new organic solidarities of whatever form, but about controlling, moulding and exploiting those that already existed at the time. This means that the old organic solidarities of nation, religion, blood and soil were neither totally transformed nor totally eradicated, although these changes also occurred, through their becoming overlaid by, or syncretically combined with, official categories like 'socialism'. To the extent that such categories obtained a purchase on ordinary lives, therefore, they did so through the medium of local cultures and identities and through the medium of individual material interests, not *vice versa*.

Official agnosticism from the vanguard of vanguard parties concerning the nature and identity of socialism and of Marxism-Leninism therefore came as a double shock to the general system. To challenge the Marxist-Leninist double bind and remove its political controls was to confront all these societies with the fact that they had no integrating ideology, no coherent, organic and unifying ethos. All they had were the old solidarities, notably the nationalisms, which had never disappeared and most of which run along quite different cultural and geographical fault lines from those which define the existing states. Moreover, in beginning to speak the language of difference and tolerance in such a situation, however faintly, without simultaneously — or, better still, previously — providing adequate political mechanisms for the articulation, aggregation and conciliation of interests and for general discussions of what the good life might be, the reformers not only enabled but even forced these old organic solidarities to reassert themselves. The result has been the rapid, in some cases catastrophic, disintegration of state power in Eastern Europe and its threatened disintegration in the USSR. As Paul Lewis so percipiently remarked (quoting Wolin) *à propos* of the Polish situation back in 1983-84:

> contemporary experience ... 'exposed the meaning of meaninglessness to be power without right'. In that case the delegitimation of the party-state was such that state power was not so much undermined or challenged as felt to be irrelevant. ... such sentiments could prove to have far-reaching consequences if they surface again in Eastern Europe.[34]

The nation-building in which the other half of Europe, including the USSR, is now fundamentally engaged requires the re-establishment of a 'power with right', of a state with legitimacy. Ironically, therefore, it might be argued that 'ideology', defined as creating and maintaining the basic ethos and identity of system, will actually become truly important, not to say vitally necessary, in these countries for the first time in years.

NOTES

1. *History of the Communist Party of the Soviet Union (Bolsheviks): Short Course*, authorized edition, 1938 (Moscow: Foreign Languages Publishing House, 1945), p. 356.
2. Nikita Khrushchev, 'Central Committee Report to the 20th Party Congress', *Stenograficheskii otchet*, I, Moscow: Gos. izdatel'stvo, 14 February 1956, pp. 113-14.
3. Leonid Brezhnev, 'Report of the Central Committee of the Communist Party of the Soviet Union', in *XXVI s"ezd Kommunisticheskoi partii Sovetskogo Soyuza: Stenograficheskii otchet* (Moscow: Politizdat, 1981), Vol. I, p. 96.

4. Mikhail Gorbachev, 'The Political Report of the Central Committee of the CPSU to the XVII Congress of the Communist Party of the Soviet Union', *Pravda*, 26 February 1986, p. 9.

5. For Soviet discussion of these problems see, for example, the following in the English edition of the Soviet journal *Social Sciences*: Igor Kon, 'The Psychology of Social Inertia', Vol. XX, No. 1 (1989); Igor Kondakov, 'Spiritual Culture: Old and New Thinking', ibid.; Igor Dedkov, 'Literature and the New Thinking', Vol. XIX, No. 4 (1988); Herman Diligensky, 'Spiritual and Psychological Uplift in Soviet Society', ibid.

6. For a fuller analysis of the concept of the 'double bind', see Rachel Walker, 'Marxism-Leninism as Discourse: The Politics of the Empty Signifier and the Double Bind', *British Journal of Political Science*, Vol. 19 (1989), pp. 161-89.

7. See Michael E. Urban, 'Conceptualizing Political Power in the USSR: Patterns of Binding and Bonding', *Studies in Comparative Communism*, Vol. 18 (1985), pp. 207-26, for a useful discussion of the structure of a double bind.

8. See Graeme Gill, *The Rules of the Communist Party of the Soviet Union* (London: Macmillan, 1988), pp. 205 and 229.

9. Kon, 'The Psychology of Social Inertia', p. 63. This article originally appeared in the leading party journal *Kommunist*, 1988, No. 1.

10. See, for example, Ray Taras, *Ideology in a Socialist State: Poland, 1956-1983* (Cambridge: Cambridge University Press, 1984).

11. And, of course, the fear of retribution can be as bad as the retribution itself: not for nothing were the Polish events of 1980-81 called a 'self-limiting revolution'.

12. Kon, 'The Psychology of Social Inertia', p. 64.

13. Diligensky, 'Spiritual and Psychological Uplift in Soviet Society', p. 87.

14. *Pravda*, 8 December 1988.

15. Ibid.; emphasis added.

16. Ibid.

17. See, for example, Kondakov, 'Spiritual Culture: Old and New Thinking', p. 85.

18. Mikhail Gorbachev, *Perestroika: New Thinking for Our Country and the World* (London: Collins, 1987), p. 106; emphasis added.

19. Ibid., pp. 216-17; emphasis added.

20. Ibid., pp. 147-8.

21. Mikhail Gorbachev, in *Pravda*, 28 January 1987.

22. See, for example, Ronald J. Hill, *Soviet Politics, Political Science and Reform* (Oxford: Martin Robertson, 1980); Stephen Shenfield, *The Nuclear Predicament: Explorations in Soviet Ideology*, Chatham House Paper 37 (London: Routledge & Kegan Paul, 1987); Jacques Rupnik, 'Soviet Adaptation to Change in Eastern Europe', Journal of Communist Studies, Vol. 2, No. 3 (1986); Alfred B. Evans, 'The Polish Crisis in the 1980s and Adaptation in Soviet Ideology', ibid.

23. Rupnik, *op. cit.*, p. 256.

24. Shenfield, *op. cit.*.

25. Mikhail Gorbachev, in *Pravda*, 11 April, 1987; see also David S. Mason, 'Glasnost, perestroika and Eastern Europe', *International Affairs*, Vol. 64 (1988), pp. 431-48 (p. 436).

26. *Pravda*, 3 November, 1987.
27. Mikhail Gorbachev, in *Pravda*, 28 January 1987.
28. *Pravda*, 11 May 1988.
29. Quoted in Archie Brown, 'Ideology and Political Culture', in Seweryn Bialer (ed.), *Politics, Society and Nationality Inside Gorbachev's Russia* (Boulder, CO, and London: Westview, 1989), p. 16.
30. *Pravda*, 11 May 1988.
31. 'Forward to Lenin', *New Times*, 1989, No. 17 (25 April — 1 May), p. 24.
32. See Thomas Sherlock, 'Politics and History under Gorbachev', *Problems of Communism*, May- August 1988; this contrasts with the debunking of Lenin by, among others, Yu. N. Afanas'ev.
33. *Pravda*, 11 May 1988.
34. Paul G. Lewis (ed.), *Eastern Europe: Political Crisis and Legitimation* (London: Croom Helm, 1984), p. 202.

7. The Advent of a *Rechtsstaat*

Theodor Schweisfurth

The restructuring of Eastern Europe entails a whole range of elements in the identity of the modern nation. Rebuilding the economy is a fundamental goal — and, in a number of cases, was the prime motivating factor — followed closely by political reform, to some extent seen as a means of winning the support of populations for uncomfortable economic measures. And a central element in the political reform is the adaptation of the legal system and the framework of legislation, to meet the new conditions in which the communist party forgoes its political monopoly in favour of what is more clearly recognizable as a *political* role. The behaviour of individual citizens and groups is to be regulated according to different principles from those of expediency subordinated to the needs of a permanently ruling party of communists.

This chapter considers the development of a particular conceptual approach to the question of the rule of law in the countries of 'socialist' Eastern Europe, with the adoption of the notion of a 'law-governed state', commonly referred to in legal literature by the German term *Rechtsstaat*. The discussion concentrates on the development of this principle in the Soviet Union, Poland and Hungary; however, it should be observed that the changes elsewhere in the region portend similar developments in other countries, so that the experience related here may be generalized. Our discussion follows the following broad structure: first, a discussion of what has happened — how was the concept of the socialist Rechtsstaat placed on the political agenda of the countries concerned?; secondly, we examine who initiated the introduction of this concept — who were the principal sponsors of the concept? thirdly, what were the motives of those who raised this issue? and finally, what are the implications of this development for the evolution of the system?

THE INTRODUCTION OF THE CONCEPT

The Soviet Union

The promulgation of a 'socialist Rechtsstaat' (in Russian, *sotsialisticheskoe pravovoe gosudarstvo*) was announced on 7 May 1988. At a meeting with leaders of the mass media, ideological institutions and the creative unions, Mikhail Gorbachev asserted: 'We must complete the creation of a socialist Rechtsstaat'.[1] As soon became clear, this was a preliminary quotation from the 'Theses of the CPSU Central Committee to the Nineteenth All-Union Party Conference', presumably already agreed by the Politburo, formally accepted by the Central Committee on 23 May 1988, and published in the press four days later.[2] Thesis 4 read as follows:

> Objective analysis of what has been accomplished during the past three years in the economy, in the social sphere and in culture, and consideration of problems that have arisen in the course of *perestroika* led to recognition of the necessity of reforming the political system of Soviet society. The aim of this reform is to include the broad masses of workers into the direction of all the affairs of state and society and to complete the formation of the socialist Rechtsstaat.

Thesis 8 opened with the demand that 'the process of consistent democratization of Soviet society must complete the creation of the socialist Rechtsstaat as the form of the organization and execution of political power that corresponds completely with socialism and socialist democracy'.

The nineteenth party conference convened in the last week of June 1988. At that conference the demand for the creation of a socialist Rechtsstaat was made part of the party's programme for legal policy. Among the various resolutions adopted by conference was one 'On the course of the realization of the decisions of the XXVII Congress of the CPSU and the tasks of deepening *perestroika*', point 4 of which declared that the reform of the political system 'in the last resort has as its goal the completion of the establishment of the socialist Rechtsstaat'. A second resolution, 'On legal reform', observed that 'significant measures have been carried out to secure *perestroika* legally. But these measures have to be regarded as only the beginning of the great work that is connected with the construction of a socialist Rechtsstaat'.[3]

The CPSU's declaration that reform of the political system in general and legal reform in particular aims at the establishment of a socialist Rechtsstaat was a further sensation in the altogether surprising course of *perestroika*.

Never before in the history of the Soviet Union had its political leadership envisaged the evolution of the Soviet system towards a Rechtsstaat. Indeed, the term 'Rechtsstaat' had always been regarded as bourgeois through and through, one of the ideological inventions of the bourgeoisie to defend existing property relations.[4] What a turn-about in legal–political thinking must have occurred when a deputy minister of justice of the USSR could in June 1988 exclaim, 'For me it was a festive occasion when the thesis of the Rechtsstaat was proclaimed!'[5]

The following question arose immediately: what is the concept of the 'socialist Rechtsstaat' that the supporters of *perestroika* have in mind? Does the term 'Rechtsstaat' suggest the acceptance of substantial elements of the idea of the Rechtsstaat as it has been developed, mainly in German constitutional thought, since the early nineteenth century? After all, the Russian phrase *pravovoe gosudarstvo* is none other than a literal translation of 'a specific German coinage of words'.[6] Or does the proclamation of a *socialist* Rechtsstaat portend something different from the ideas that arose in bourgeois legal thinking?

An answer to these questions can be deduced by analysing the documents produced and adopted by the Nineteenth CPSU Conference: that is, through analysis of all seven conference resolutions, together with the discussions of legal reform surrounding the conference. The results of such an analysis may be formulated as follows:[7]

1. The idea of the socialist Rechtsstaat combines the element of *constitutionality*, that is, a hierarchy of norms with the constitution at its peak, and the element of the *rule of law*, that is, the principle that the legislator is bound by the constitution, and the executive, the judiciary and the party also are bound by the constitution and by statutes. One component of this second element — the principle of legality of administrative power and the judiciary in the sense of the supremacy of the law (in Russian, *verkhovenstvo zakona*) — is considered to be 'the most characteristic' element, 'the highest principle' of the socialist Rechtsstaat. During the discussions of legal reform, it has also been said that the legal position of the individual can be determined only by statute,[8] hence the so-called reservation of the statute is also an element of the socialist Rechtsstaat.

2. The idea of the socialist Rechtsstaat, secondly, encompasses a guarantee of the basic rights of the individual, according to which the fundamental relationship between the citizen and the state is adjusted *by law*. Here not only are social rights emphasized, but in the same manner the basic political

rights and the fundamental rights of individual freedom, together with basic duties. The guarantees of the basic rights are not only the so-called material ones: also significant for the socialist Rechtsstaat is the development of judicial protection and other 'legal' or juridical guarantees of basic rights.

3. The idea of the socialist Rechtsstaat comprises as further elements the institutionalization of procedures for the control of norms, in order to guarantee the hierarchy of norms, the independence of the judiciary, and the guarantees of basic rights in the judicial process.

4. The idea of the socialist Rechtsstaat comprises, fourthly, the separation of power between the party and the state, meaning that the party shall not exercise the functions of the state directly. The separation of powers *within* the state is also an element of the socialist Rechtsstaat insofar as the separation between the judiciary and executive power is concerned. The imposition of separation of powers at the level of the individual — meaning the prohibition of the combination of an office in the state administration with a mandate in the representative organ that controls that particular administrative body — is also regarded as characteristic of the socialist Rechtsstaat. However, the principle of unity of state power (as opposed to the 'bourgeois' separation of powers, long derided in Soviet theory) is upheld, and is manifest in the competence accorded top the elected representative organs, the Soviets of People's Deputies.

5. The idea of the socialist Rechtsstaat, finally, has also an international dimension. An additional basic attitude of the Rechtsstaat is compliance with the rules of international law, and the domestic legal order must be in accord with international legal obligations: 'The socialist Rechtsstaat is also an international-law state'.[9]

If we summarize all these elements of the socialist Rechtsstaat we come to the conclusion that they accord with many elements of the so-called formal Rechtsstaat, a concept structured mainly in German constitutional thought. However, the concept of the socialist Rechtsstaat also contains the idea of the Rechtsstaat in the material sense, bearing in mind that the socialist Rechtsstaat aims at 'the highest possible guarantee of the basic rights and liberties of the Soviet man'.

As noted above, the resolutions of the Nineteenth Party Conference of June-July 1988 represent nothing other than the CPSU's programme for legal policy. We may now ask what has been done to turn this programme into legally valid rules of Soviet domestic law. In fact, a number of acts were already taken before the nineteenth Conference.

For example, the old 1970 regulations concerning entry and exit permits were supplemented by a new regulation on 28 August 1986 concerning entry and exit on personal affairs. This regulation does not guarantee to Soviet citizens completely free exit and entry, and it can be regarded as simply a victory of the principle of *glasnost*, since the relevant rules — hitherto secret — were now made public.[10]

Similarly, on 30 June 1987 a 'statute under Article 58, Paragraph 2' of the USSR constitution of 1977 was promulgated under the title, 'Statute on the judicial procedure for complaints against illegal acts of state servants that infringe the rights of citizens'.[11] Although the constitution provided for the enactment of such a law, it was never issued during the 'period of stagnation' under Leonid Brezhnev. The new statute makes a small improvement to the procedural position of citizens subject to illegal acts by the executive organs, by opening the ordinary courts to citizens seeking redress for illegal administrative acts, and limits these to the actions of *individual* state servants. However, since the majority of administrative acts are corporate decisions, against which the aggrieved citizen remains without redress, since the statute failed to introduce general judicial control over the executive, the measure has been vehemently criticized as 'stillborn' and 'undemocratic'.[12] The Nineteenth Party Conference reflected the deficiencies in the statute and called for an improvement in the practice of this law's application.[13]

Another example is a decree (*ukaz*) of the USSR Supreme Soviet Presidium, dated 5 January 1988, which sanctioned the 'Regulation [*polozhenie*] on the conditions and the procedure of psychiatric assistance'.[14] In cases of committal for psychiatric treatment, this measure introduces the possibility of judicial control in favour of the citizen concerned.[15]

The process continued following the party conference, with, for instance, on 28 July 1988, two further decrees: 'On the procedure for organizing and holding meetings, manifestations, processions and demonstrations in the USSR',[16] which implemented Article 50 of the 1977 constitution, and 'On the duties and rights of the interior troops of the USSR Ministry of Internal Affairs in the maintenance of public order'.[17] This was the first legal regulation of these matters. During the Soviet debate over these decrees, both were criticized for the vagueness of some of their provisions, although some deputies praised them as steps towards the formation of the socialist Rechtsstaat.[18] In comparison with the previously unregulated situation, when there were no legal barriers to arbitrary executive action, both decrees should be regarded as remarkable attempts to secure law and order. However, neither decree guarantees judicial remedies.

A major package of reforms introduced in the wake of the party conference involved changes to the USSR Constitution, adopted on 1 December 1988 following barely a month's public discussion. How far did these changes reflect the programmatic ideas of a socialist Rechtsstaat?[19]

The first novelty that deserves attention is Article 125, which establishes a Constitutional Review Committee as a procedural device to guarantee the hierarchy of norms. That article is correctly seen as 'a concrete embodiment of the idea to erect the Rechtsstaat'.[20] The principle of the priority of the constitution and the priority of statutes was already stipulated in Article 1973 of the original 1977 constitution, but in practice lawmaking scarcely conformed to this provision. Henceforth, the Constitutional Review Committee is to examine the constitutionality of statutes and regulations and the lawfulness of regulations. It is not competent, however, to abrogate unconstitutional statutes and regulations, or regulations that contravene statutes: it can only draw up advisory opinions and present them to the law-making organ 'in order to abolish the ascertained infringement'. The ascertainment of unconstitutionality or unlawfulness in the Committee's advisory opinion leads, however, to the suspension of the act under review. In its Spring 1989 session, the Congress of People's Deputies — the highest representative organ, newly introduced by the constitutional changes of December 1988 — established all the organs provided for by the amended constitution save one: the Constitutional Review Committee. There was a lively debate in the congress as to whether the Committee could be established prior to the enactment of a 'Statute on constitutional review in the USSR', which is provided for by Article 125, paragraph 3, of the constitution. The congress elected a special commission to draft such a statute, and the establishment of the Review Committee was postponed until the Autumn 1989 session of the Congress.[21]

Certain new provisions of the revised constitution have had an impact on the problem of separation of power *within* the Soviet state. In spring 1990, constitutional revisions tackled the problem of the separation of powers between the party and the state: Article 6, which established the special position of the communist party in the political system and in society at large, came under fire in the autumn of 1989, when other socialist countries were dropping this provision from their fundamental law, and was amended on 14 March. The constitution continues to uphold the principle of the concentration of powers within the soviets, since Article 93 remained unchanged. However, the constitutional revision of 1988 attempted to bring this hitherto purely decorative article into greater conformity with reality. In the context of our discussion, of particular importance is Article 113, paragraph 7, which aims at depriving the bureaucracy of some of its power by establishing a parliamentary prerogative to enact law in certain matters that were previously regulated by the Council of Ministers.[22]

In addition to these, further new provisions displayed in their gestation the idea of separation of powers within the state. Thus, Article 96, paragraph 4 (taken together with Article 11 of the new law on elections to the Congress of People's Deputies) forbids certain high members of the executive to serve as deputies of the soviet that elected them.

The constitutional revisions clearly intend a strict separation of powers between the judiciary, on the one hand, and the executive, legislative and party, on the other. The revised Articles 152 and 155 strengthen the independence of the courts. All professional judges are now elected for a ten-year period of office, and 'any interference' in the work of judges is impermissible. This provision is directed against the practice of 'telephone law', whereby judges were privately given 'recommendations' by party or state executive officials. The constitutional provisions concerning the independence of the judiciary have subsequently been elaborated in the 'Statute on the status of judges in the USSR', adopted on 4 August 1989 and due to come into force on 1 December 1989.[23]

The process of establishing a socialist Rechtsstaat in the Soviet Union has therefore been proceeding steadily, although not necessarily as rapidly or as thoroughly as some would wish. However, set against the background of lack of legislative provision in many areas of public life and administration, the steps adopted so far represent a considerable advance.

Poland

The advent of a Rechtsstaat began much earlier in Poland than in the Soviet Union. Since the beginning of 1980 several institutional reforms were introduced which, seen together, shape the picture of the Polish socialist Rechtsstaat. The most important of these institutional reforms are as follows.

First, a law of 31 January 1980 revised the Code of Administrative Procedure and established the Central Administrative Court in Warsaw, with several branch offices the provinces.[24] This law improved the procedural position of citizens in seeking redress for illegal acts of the executive, although it failed to introduce a general clause to open the court for all actions seeking such redress. Article 196 of the Code of Administrative Procedure contains a list of twenty branches of administrative activity against which action may be taken for illegal acts; these supposedly cover approximately 95 per cent of all fields of administrative activity.[25] Next, an amendment to Articles 33a and 33b of the Polish constitution, introduced on 25 March 1982, provided for the establishment of a State Tribunal and a Constitutional Court.[26] The importance of the State Tribunal, competent to decide on the responsibilities of high-ranking state officials, was vitiated by the enactment shortly afterwards of an amnesty.[27]

According to Article 33a of the Polish constitution and the 'Statute on the Constitutional Court', adopted on 29 April 1985,[28] the Constitutional Court is a procedural mechanism to guarantee the hierarchy of norms. It checks the constitutionality of statutes and regulations and the lawfulness of regulations. It may advise the Sejm (parliament) of unconstitutional statutes, and the Sejm must respond by amending or repealing the offending legislation, or by formally rejecting the Court's judgement (on a two-thirds majority). The Court's powers to annul lesser legislation are considerably greater. The Polish Constitutional Court could develop a very significant role: between November 1986 and December 1988 it took seventeen decisions on norm control procedures.[29]

On the basis of a law of 15 July 1987, a new institution to supervise the observance of civil rights and liberties was established: the Commissioner [*Rzecznik*] for Citizens' Rights, whose functions appear comparable with those of the 'Ombudsman' appointed in a number of West European states in recent decades.[30] In performing his functions the Commissioner is independent of other state agencies and is responsible only to the Sejm, by which he is elected. His function is to safeguard citizens' rights and liberties as determined by the Polish constitution and by other provisions of the law, and he acts on the basis of information given by citizens concerning infringements of their rights and freedoms. In seeking redress for an infringement of a citizen's rights, the Commissioner may issue a recommendation to the relevant agency, lodge a motion with its superior body, or demand civil or administrative proceedings. The Commissioner's bureau has been overwhelmed with complaints since it began to operate on 1 January 1988: over 50,000 in the first eleven months.[31]

Recent political events in Poland give added impulse to the formation of the Polish Rechtsstaat. Even before the collapse of the communist government of the Polish United Workers' Party, a number of ideas were already under discussion, within the party itself or in the 'Round Table' discussions with Solidarity in the Spring of 1989. At the tenth plenum of the PUWP Central Committee in December 1988 and January 1989, such principles as separation of powers, the Rechtsstaat, pluralism and constructive opposition were supported as potential future aims. The Round Table talks, held from 6 February to 5 April 1989, led to a general agreement on reforming the political system according to such principles as separation of powers, independence of the judiciary, and the priority of the concept of the sovereignty of the people over that of the leading role of the party.

The new Prime Minister, Tadeusz Mazowiecki, when first announcing the new government, suggested the realization of such basic principles as the state bound by law, pluralism and freedom of opinion. An early task of the new Sejm was the enactment of a new law on political parties. However, the main task with respect to the formation of the Polish Rechtsstaat is the formulation of a new constitution, ideally for adoption on 3 May 1991 — the two-hundredth anniversary of the first Polish constitution (of 3 May 1791). The commission on law-making of the new Senate favoured instead the preliminary adoption of a 'provisional constitution', in order quickly to transform the decisions of the Round Table conference into constitutional law, with particular reference to a number of amendments of symbolic significance, such as the elimination of Article 3 of the existing constitution (relating to the leading role of the party and its permanent coalition with other parties of the bloc).[32] Twenty-three communist deputies moved an amendment to this effect in September 1989,[33] and the article was deleted on 29 December.[34]

Quite clearly, the establishment of a Rechtsstaat in Poland, in place of the Stalinist inheritance, is proceeding steadily, and in the light of the formation of a government not dominated by communists, it is questionable whether talk should be of a *socialist* Rechtsstaat. Similar considerations apply to Poland's neighbours, including Hungary.

Hungary

Before 1988-89, when the movement to reform the Hungarian political system got into its stride, only a very few institutions could be seen that might be regarded as elements of a socialist Rechtsstaat. After the 'events' of October 1956, a new Code of Administrative Procedures introduced to citizens the possibility of taking action in the courts against illegal administrative acts. As in Poland, the scope of this right was limited by the principle of enumeration; the list of matters in which recourse to the courts was possible was enlarged in 1981.[35]

In 1984, a new body for norm control procedures was established, the Constitutional Law Council,[36] conceived as a subsidiary organ of parliament. If the Council deems a statute of parliament or a decree of its Presidential Council to be unconstitutional, it passes its 'declaration of opinion' to the chairman or the Presidential Council of parliament. The Law on the Constitutional Law Council is silent about how the parliament shall deal further with this opinion. As in Poland, the Constitutional Law Council has power to suspend the application of unconstitutional or unlawful regulations. The establishment of the Constitutional Law Council was welcomed by Hungarian specialists, who expected an enrichment of constitutional life.[37] But in the time since then, this institution has lost the sympathy of Hungarian constitutionalists, and it is certain to be abolished when a fully-fledged Hungarian Rechtsstaat is established in the course of the current political reforms.

The principal vehicle for the establishment of a Rechtsstaat in Hungary will be a new constitution, originally planned for the spring of 1990. However, a postponement of this was inevitable, since in September 1989 a new sequence of reform steps was agreed upon in the 'Delta talks'. To begin with, the parliament was to enact a number of 'constitutional statutes': a revision of the constitution currently in force with respect to the constitutional aims, and a prohibition of intervention by force and by the supreme military command; a law introducing a constitutional court as an independent judicial body, to replace the Constitutional Law Council; a law on political parties, an electoral law, a penal code, and a code on penal procedure. Later, the adoption of a new constitution by referendum will be the crowning act in the establishment of the Hungarian Rechtsstaat.[38]

That the Hungarian reformers are determined to establish a Rechtsstaat in their country was in evidence with the publication of the 'Guidelines for the conception of the Constitution of Hungary' in February 1989,[38] which outlined current Hungarian ideas of the Rechtsstaat.

If constitutionality (a hierarchy of norms, with the constitution at its pinnacle) is one element of the Rechtsstaat, a prerequisite is the legal character of the constitution itself. The guidelines therefore suggest that the new constitution should stress that it is a legal and not merely a political document, and that it contains legal rules and not simply political goals. The new Hungarian constitution shall not be a 'declaratory' constitution, as its predecessor was, but in reality the basic law of the country, to which all other legislation is subordinated. The hierarchy of norms shall be guaranteed in the future by special machinery, the Constitutional Court, to be established as an independent body and not as a subsidiary organ of the parliament. The relationship between the decision-making power of the Court and the sovereignty of the parliament will presumably be regulated in a manner similar to that in Poland: that is, the validity of a statute declared unconstitutional by judgement of the Court can be upheld only by a two-thirds majority vote in parliament.

It is intended that the separation of powers shall be introduced in a stringent and twofold manner. There will be a strict demarcation between state power and the power of the parties. A constitutional provision that asserts the leading role of one party (as the current constitution did at Article 3, in favour of the 'Marxist-Leninist' party) is, of course, inconsistent with a multi-party system such as is being introduced, and was in fact deleted from the constitution in October 1989. The classic system of the separation of powers within the state is also to be formulated in the text of the new constitution, 'as the normative principle for the exercise of state power'.

The Hungarian Rechtsstaat is also to be a Rechtsstaat in the material sense of the concept. A catalogue of basic rights and duties of citizens is to form the first section of the new constitution. The basic rights shall be directly applicable, and the 'interests of society' shall no longer be a general barrier to their exercise by individuals. Procedural guarantees against infringements of basic rights shall be introduced, among them recourse to international machinery, as provided, for example, in the Optional Protocol to the UN Covenant on Civil and Political Rights, to which Hungary recently acceded.[40]

It therefore seems clear that, as in Poland, the course of reform in Hungary is moving steadily and logically towards the establishment of a Rechtsstaat, with significant steps already taken during 1989 and further developments mapped out for early in the new decade.

THE REFORMERS

Who initiated these reforms? Who are the principal sponsors of the concept of the Rechtsstaat in these socialist countries? Study reveals that the processes of initiating the idea and applying it to the practical formation of a Rechtsstaat varies.

In *Poland*, it was not the ruling communist party (the Polish United Workers' Party) that decided to change the existing legal-constitutional order into a system with the qualities of a Rechtsstaat. Rather, the party was pressed by political forces from within Polish society, in the direction of reforms and developments of the legal system, amounting eventually to the formation of a Rechtsstaat. It is certainly no exaggeration to suggest that the Polish community of legal scholars played (and continues to play) a prime role in the long process of building up a Rechtsstaat in their country. In the conditions of relatively substantial freedom of opinion, it was possible to discuss in the professional legal literature various problems associated with different elements of a Rechtsstaat. Such technical discussions influenced the thinking of politically relevant groups and decision-makers, and culminated in the adoption of new laws and statutes, some of which were recorded above. Politically vital pressure came, of course, from the Solidarity movement — an obvious comment when we look into the various 'social agreements' of the year 1980. For example, the Gdansk agreement between the governmental commission and the plant strike committee of 31 August 1980 contained points pertinent to some elements of a Rechtsstaat.[41] Presumably not so much of its own accord, but rather in a spirit of joining the mainstream of the new efforts to restructure the political system, represented by what had hitherto been the opposition, the PUWP endorsed the idea of a Rechtsstaat at its tenth Central Committee plenum in January 1989.

In the *Soviet Union* the idea of the socialist Rechtsstaat was promulgated and gained ground from precisely the opposite side of the power structure. It was the leadership of the party itself that took the initiative in declaring the construction of a socialist Rechtsstaat as the final aim of political reform. The thesis that the socialist Rechtsstaat should correspond completely with socialism and socialist democracy came as a considerable surprise to the politically aware Soviet public. This is true especially of the country's legal scholars and professional lawyers as a whole. For, despite their advocacy of many specific reformist measures over several decades, they were quite taken aback — not to say upset — at the thought that a constitutional concept hitherto condemned as intrinsically bourgeois should now become the leading idea for the reform of the Soviet political system. Nevertheless, legal scholars and other participants in the public debate over political reform quickly overcame their perplexity and joined ranks with the party in discussing what the nature of the Rechtsstaat in the Soviet Union should be:

they were, of course, more familiar than the lay public with the theory of the Rechtsstaat. After the Nineteenth Party Conference in 1988, and the revision of the constitution later in the year, the discussion is in full swing — in newspapers, in scholarly journals, and in the Supreme Soviet. The viability and acceptance of the party's leading role in this matter is demonstrated by the fact that we do not now find opponents in principle to the idea of the Rechtsstaat in published opinion. Whether, and to what extent, the idea of building a socialist Rechtsstaat is supported — or even understood — by the mass of the population is difficult to assess.

In *Hungary* the development parallels that of the Soviet Union. When, at the end of the Kádár era in May 1988, the reformist wing of the Hungarian Socialist Workers' Party (HSWP) came to the fore, it was the leadership of the party that initiated the transformation of the authoritarian political system into a pluralist and democratic one and announced the formation of a Rechtsstaat in Hungary. The current impression is that the aim of the party to transform the constitutional system into a Rechtsstaat in the formal and material sense is supported by a majority consensus in the Hungarian population.

EXPLANATIONS

Why has all this happened? What are the motives of those who are pressing for the establishment of the Rechtsstaat in these Eastern European countries?

In Poland, where the formation of a Rechtsstaat was initiated 'from below', the original motive was to improve the legal position of individuals *vis-à-vis* state power and, with the establishment of the Constitutional Court, to stress the normative character of the constitution, on the one hand, and to strengthen the Sejm in relation to the executive, on the other. These were relatively limited aims, not based on an all-embracing programme of radical political overhaul. But such broad programmes have been or are being formulated in the Soviet Union and Hungary, and following the political developments of the summer of 1989 in Poland the scope of reform there has been widened considerably. The words of the Hungarian Minister of Justice, Kálmán Kulcsár, sum up the position: the processes of disintegration of the authoritarian system, and of the unfolding of a pluralist democratic political system, are taking place 'in different ways and by producing different phenomena, but, as a result of the identical basic socio-economic contents of these processes, the essence is the same'.[42]

The motives for the acceptance by the reformers of a legal-political programme aimed at the transformation of the existing constitutional and legal order into an order with the qualities of a Rechtsstaat can be easily understood if we look, from the perspective of the concept of the Rechtsstaat, at the main features of the authoritarian system.

There is good reason to denote this system as an 'administrative-command system', as Gorbachev has done. In this system, it is the executive power that plays first violin, an executive that is duplex, comprising the state bureaucracy and the bureaucracy of the ruling communist party. It is in the bureaucracy and not (as the constitutions allege) in the representative bodies that state power is concentrated. The bureaucracy does not simply fulfil its proper task, namely administration, but has usurped the power to legislate and has directed the judiciary. The administrative-command system not only led to the deformation of socialist ideas in general, and steered the economy at the end of the first stage of modernization into the blind alley of stagnation, but it also led to a deformation of the legal culture, and in fact prevented the development of a high legal culture.

In the adminstrative-command system the constitution is treated mainly as a political rather than legal document. Only the constitutional provisions relating to the state organs and state organization are more or less in harmony with reality. The basic rights of the citizens are regarded by the bureaucracy as not directly applicable: instead, sub-constitutional norms determine their proper content, and the general barrier against exercising them — 'the interests of society' — is defined by the bureaucracy. The interests of individuals and of groups of individuals are neglected under the ideological presupposition of the identity of interests of all social categories and the absence of antagonistic contradictions. The infrequency of the sessions of the representative bodies prevents them from exercising their constitutional competence to legislate. That competence is thus transferred to the presidiums or executive committees of the representative bodies, which must be regarded in this context as part of the bureaucratic system; however, law-making is mainly exercised by the administration in the form of various governmental or ministerial regulations, orders, instructions, etc. This led to a reversal of the hierarchy of norms, whereby it is not the constitution that enjoys the 'highest legal validity' but the ministerial regulations, which in practice often over-rule the constitution as well as statutes.

The executive tends to exercise its law-making power to a considerable extent. It desires to regulate social activity in every field, and as far as possible in detail. This tendency leads to the phenomenon of 'over-regulation', and a far-reaching channelling of all social activities.

The judiciary is directed by the bureaucracy mainly by using two means of influence: it guides the recruitment of judges to short (five-year) periods in office, and it interferes with their decision making by giving 'recommendations' in cases it regards as important.

From individual citizens, economic entities and social organizations, the bureaucracy demands behaviour according to the principles of 'socialist legality' — which in practice means that they must obey all the rules set mainly by the bureaucracy. The underlying principle of legality in the administrative-command system is the authoritarian maxim that everything is forbidden that is not expressly permitted.

These features of the administrative-command system lead to a number of legal-sociological consequences. On the one hand, the phenomenon of over-regulation causes the strangulation of social activity and apathy; and on the other it produces the phenomenon of 'legal nihilism'. If the satisfaction of individual or group interests is made virtually impossible by a dense network of regulations, some of the citizens respond by simply not obeying the legal rules. And such behaviour is enhanced when citizens realize that 'socialist legality' is treated by the bureaucracy as a one-sided principle, a postulate addressed only to the citizens but not to the bureaucracy itself. When the executive frames its regulations without taking the constitution and the statutes into account, it is quite incomprehensible that the citizens should obey the rules. Thus, unconstitutional and unlawful behaviour — or, in one word, *arbitrariness* on the part of the state produces non-compliance with the law on the part of the citizens. The legal order in various of its parts thereby loses its efficacy.

Perestroika, or restructuring, began with the reform of the economic system. In Hungary, the reforms were for a long time restricted to the field of economics. In the Soviet Union, in the remarkably short period of approximately two years, the reformers perceived that it was impossible to overcome the stagnation in the economy without a reform of the political system.[43] And the reform of the political system had to be in its core a 'revolution of the law', as Gorbachev has said.[44] The label of this revolution, and its content, is the construction of the socialist Rechtsstaat.

The construction of the Rechtsstaat is the medicine to overcome the central defects of the administrative-command system. It is not accidental that the priority of the law (*verkhovenstvo zakona*) is regarded as 'the most characteristic element' of the socialist Rechtsstaat. The enforcement of this principle by means of a special machinery to examine the constitutionality and lawfulness of regulations, together with the strengthening of the control functions and the statute-enacting activities of the representative bodies, destroys the power of the bureaucracy in one of its important aspects: law-making. The judicial control of adminstrative acts, along with the realization of the principle of judicial independence, aims at the abolition of arbitrariness in administrative behaviour.

The guarantee of civil rights and liberties is also directed against arbitrary administrative behaviour and will stimulate the activities of citizens in all sectors of public life. To make use of the directly applicable civil rights and liberties guaranteed by the constitution will overcome a phenomenon which in Marx's analysis was a characteristic of capitalist society and which was reproduced in the administrative-command system: the alienation of the human being from the means of production, from the result of its labour, and from the institutions of the state. The new maxim for the citizen's range of activities is now 'all is permitted that is not expressly forbidden'.

TRADITIONS AND THE FUTURE

That the advent of a Rechtsstaat within the group of socialist states of Eastern Europe began in Poland is certainly due to the traditions of legal culture in that country, and is rooted also in the legal thinking of the resurrected republic, and of the Austrian and Prussian legal cultures during the time of the partition of Poland. The Hungarian constitution of 1949, which was based on the Soviet constitution of 1936, broke the continuity with the previous constitutional development of the country, as the Hungarian Minister of Justice, Kulcsár, said: the task of the reconstruction of the continuity of Hungarian constitutional development is now the integration of the Hungarian legal culture into 'the mainstream of European constitutional development'.[45] The Soviet Union cannot refer to similar traditions. It has been argued with reason that it is impossible to speak now of the 'completion' of the Rechtsstaat in the Soviet Union because 'our state in the whole history of its existence has never been for one day a Rechtsstaat in the proper sense of that word'.[46] Therefore, in supporting the construction of a Rechtsstaat in the Soviet Union, its partisans refer to what they call 'the general human values which shaped during the thousand-year process of development of the humanistic idea and which concentrate the rich historical experience of the growing of social progress, and of freedom and equality of the human being'.[47]

Conscious of the lack of an appropriate tradition and of the deformation of the legal order caused by the administrative-command system, the institutional development of a Rechtsstaat in the Soviet Union is coupled with a comprehensive educational programme. This programme is intended to make not only lawyers but every citizen understand what the ideas of the Rechtsstaat are, in order to build up a 'high legal culture' as a characteristic feature of the new political system.

A comparative view of the developments in Poland, the Soviet Union and Hungary suggests that the tradition of the legal culture is not the decisive but a supporting force for the formation of a Rechtsstaat in thecountries of Eastern Europe. Decisive is the resolve to destroy the administrative-command system, because it has proved its inability to manage the further development of the economy and to satisfy the interests of the various groups in society.

The formation of a Rechtsstaat in the countries of Eastern Europe is a task that cannot be resolved within one or two years. But if it is resolved successfully, the historical consequences will amount to the end of the conflict between opposing systems.

NOTES

1. 'Through democratization to a new stature of socialism', *Pravda*, 11 May 1988.
2. *Izvestiya*, 27 May 1988.
3. *Pravda*, 5 May 1988.
4. See F.C. Schroeder, 'Rechtsstaat und sozialistische Gesetzlichkeit', *Aus Politik und Zeitgeschichte*, 1980, No. 3.
5. M.P. Vyshinskii, in a discussion entitled 'The Rechtsstaat: how shall it be?', *Literaturnaya gazeta* (*Lit. gaz.*), 8 June 1988.
6. 'Eine spezifisch deutsche Wortprägung': see K. Stern, *Das Staatsrecht der Bundesrepublik Deutschland*, Bd. 1 (Munich, 1977), p. 602.
7. For the details, see T. Schweisfurth, 'Die Sowjetunion im Aufbruch zum sozialistischen Rechtsstaat', in *Staat und Völkerrechtsordnung: Festschrift für Karl Doehring*, Hrsg. von K. Hailbronner, G. Rees, T. Stein (Beiträge zum ausländischen öffentlichen Recht und Völkerrecht, 98) (Berlin, etc., 1989), pp. 903-21.
8. *Izvestiya*, 23 September 1987.
9. V.S. Vereshchetin and R.A. Myullerson, 'Novoe myshlenie i mezhdunarodnoe pravo' (New thinking and international law), *Sovetskoe gosudarstvo i pravo* (*SGP*), 1988, No. 3, p. 4.

The Advent of a Rechtsstaat

111

10. *Sobranie postanovlenii pravitel'stva SSSR (SPP)*, 1986, No. 31, pos. 163. For an analysis of the new regulation see E. Paetzold, 'Die Novelle von 1986: Liberalisierung der sowjetischen Ein- und Ausreisebestimmungen?', *WGO: Monatshefte für osteuropäisches Recht*, 1987, pp. 125 *et seq.*

11. *Vedomosti Verkhovnogo Soveta SSSR (VVS SSSR)*, 1987, No. 26, pos. 388.

12. See, for example, A.M. Yakovlev, department head in the Institute of State and Law of the USSR Academy of Sciences, in *Lit. gaz.*, 8 June 1987; V.M. Savitskii, department head in the same institute, in *Sovetskaya yustitsiya*, 1989, No. 5, p. 6.

13. See point 5 of the resolution 'On the struggle against bureaucratism'.

14. *VVS SSSR*, 1988, No. 2, pos. 19.

15. See O. Luchterhand, 'Die psychiatrische Zwangsbehandlung in der UdSSR nach altem und neuem Recht', in *WGO*, 1988, pp. 151 et seq.

16. *VVS SSSR*, 1988, No. 31, pos. 504. This decree was supplemented by republican rules concerning the criminal responsibility for breaches of the rules of the law on demonstrations: see, for example, for the RSFSR, *VVS RSFSR*, 1988, No. 31, pos. 1005.

17. *VVS SSSR*, 1988, No. 31, pos. 505.

18. See *Izvestiya*, 31 October 1988.

19. See the revised text of the constitution in *VVS SSSR*, 1988, No. 49, pos. 727.

20. See L.V. Lazarev and A.Ya. Sliva, 'Konstitutstionnaya reforma — pervyi etap' (Constitutional reform: the first stage), *SGP*, 1989, No. 3, p. 13.

21. See the verbatim record of the debate in *Izvestiya*, 10 June 1989.

22. These matters are as follows: property relations; the organization and administration of the economy and the socio-cultural set-up; budgeting and finance; wages and price-fixing; taxation; environmental protection and the use of natural resources; and the procedures for the realization of constitutional rights, liberties and duties of citizens.

23. *Vedomosti S"ezda narodnykh deputatov SSSR i Verkhovnogo Soveta SSSR*, 1989, No. 9, pos. 223.

24. *Dziennik Ustaw*, 1980, No. 4, pos. 98.

25. Bernhard Bytomski, 'Einführung des Hauptvertaltungsgerichts in der Volksrepublik Polen', *WGO*, 1980, pp. 55 *et seq.*

26. *Dziennik Ustaw*, 1982, No. 11, pos. 83.

27. Kazimierz Dzialocha, 'Der neue Staatsgerichtshof in Polen', *Osteuropa Recht*, 1982, pp. 202 *et seq.*

28. *Dziennik Ustaw*, 1985, No. 22, pos. 98.

29. Rudolf Machacek and Zdzislaw Czescejko-Sochacki, 'Die Verfassungsgerichtsbarkeit in der Volksrepublik Polen', in *EuGRZ*, 1989, pp. 269 *et seq.*

30. *Dziennik Ustaw*, 1987, No. 21.

31. Anna Kamicka, 'Rzecznik Praw Obywatelskikh (Pierwsze doswiadczeniya i perspektiwy organizacyjne)' (The Commissioner for Civil Rights Protection: Initial Experience and Organizational Prospects), in *Panstwo i prawo*, 1988, No. 12, pp. 37 *et seq.*

32. Klaus Ziemer, 'Auf dem Weg zum Systemwandel in Polen', *Osteuropa*, 1989.

33. *Frankfurter Allgemeine Zeitung*, 20 September 1989.

34. Simultaneously, the crown was restored to the traditional symbol on the country's emblem of the white eagle, and the state reverted to its pre-war title of Republic of Poland.
35. Klaus-Jürgen Kuss, 'Gerichtliche Verwaltungskontrolle in den sozialistischen Staaten', *Osteuropa*, 1987, p. 256.
36. By Law I/1984, *Magyar Közlöny*, 26 April 1984.
37. Antal Adám, 'Die Entwicklungstendenzen der Verfassung und der Verfassungs-mässigkeit in Ungarn', in *Jahrbuch des öffentlichen Rechts der Gegenwart*, NF/Band 34 (1985), pp. 567 *et seq.*
38. The Hungarian Minister of Justice, Kálmán Kulcsár, to the *Frankfurter Allgemeine Zeitung*, 21 September 1989.
39. *Magyar Hirlap*, 23 February 1989.
40. Kathrin Sitzler, 'Ungarns politische Reformen im Spiegel der neuen Verfassungskonzeption', in *Aus Politik und Zeitgeschichte: Beilage zur Wochenzeitung das Parlament*, B23/89, pp. 29 *et seq.*
41. Leszek Garlicki, 'Gedanken zum Inhalt der gesellschaftlichen Vereinbarung in Polen', in *Osteuropa Recht*, 1982, pp. 149 *et seq.*
42. Kálmán Kulcsár, 'Constitutional State, Constitutionalism, Human Rights in the Transformation of the Hungarian Political System' (unpublished paper presented to a conference on constitutional law, Budapest, 25-27 April 1989), p. 4.
43. See T. Schweisfurth, 'Perestrojka durch Staatsrecht', in *Zeitschrift für ausländisches öffentliches Recht und Völkerrecht*, 1989, No. 4.
44. Interview in *Der Spiegel*, 1988, No. 43 (24 October), p. 26.
45. See note 38.
46. *Literaturnaya gazeta*, 8 June 1988.
47. V. Kudryavtsev and Ye. Lukasheva, 'Sotsialisticheskoe pravovoe gosudarstvo' (The Socialist Rechtsstaat), *Kommunist*, 1988, No. 11, p. 44.

8. Religion and Politics in a Time of *Glasnost*

Krzysztof Pomian

To speak about relations between religion and politics in Eastern Europe was for a very long time tantamount to describing the implementation of a programme aimed at the extirpation of the former by the latter as embodied in the communist party apparatus and its secular arms (political police, censorship, state agencies administering education and culture, etc.). The measures taken to achieve this included the outlawing of religious orders and religious instruction; the prohibition of massive public manifestations of religious sentiments (pilgrimages, processions and other such ceremonies) and of religious literature (including the Bible); the dismantling of ecclesiastical institutions and the submission of what remained to state control exerted by the security services; the persecution of members of the clergy and lay believers who resisted (through long-term imprisonment, torture and execution), and the enrolment in satellite organizations of those who surrendered and accepted collaboration; the closure of places of worship together with the confiscation or even destruction of buildings, works of art, libraries and archives; and the compulsory atheism and official anti-religious propaganda.

Although broadly sketched out, this was indeed the state of religious affairs after 1917 in what was to become in 1922 the Soviet Union,[1] and since the late 1940s or early 1950s in the 'people's democracies'.[2] Nevertheless, the differences among countries were always significant, Poland being as a rule the least repressive, even during the heyday of militant Stalinism, and the first to re-establish, after 1956, a real, even if limited, religious liberty. There were also in every country periods of greater and of lesser intensity of anti-religious measures. For example, in the USSR the churches were opened during Second World War and the authorities tolerated religious marriages,

baptisms and some participation in services. By contrast, during Khrushchev's and Brezhnev's periods in power the struggle against religion reached
a peak.

The present situation regarding religion in 'post-communist' East
European countries is more sharply varied than it has been in the recent past.
In Poland complete religious freedom has been a reality since 1978, the
communist party's attitude towards the Church having changed, in the
climate of growing discontent, even before the election of Pope John Paul
II.[3] And during the 1980s the Polish Episcopate became the first partner of
the communist leadership and the most important independent political
institution of the country — more important even than Solidarity. To be
sure, some traces of the Stalinist past have not yet been erased. But now,
after the re-establishment of diplomatic relations between Poland and the
Holy See and the liquidation by the new prime minister of the Office for
Religious Affairs, a former stronghold of the communist party and of the
political police, this can be expected very soon.

In Hungary religious freedom, reintroduced later than in Poland, was also,
until very recently, more limited.[4] Now Hungary, too, has re-established
diplomatic relations with the Holy See and is repealing the last remnants of
the legislation dating from the Stalin era. In Czechoslovakia, where despite
little change in the legal status of the Roman Catholic Church, the communist
leadership's religious policy was already showing signs of evolution —
massive religious gatherings were being tolerated, some bishoprics had been
provided with bishops and several parishes with priests, and negotiations with
the Vatican were in progress[5] — in February 1990, for the first time since
the communist takeover forty-two years earlier, all dioceses were provided
with bishops and the new president, Václav Havel, inaugurated his term in
office with an invitation to the Pope to visit the country: this visit took place
on 21-22 April 1990.[6]

But the most spectacular, even sensational, changes have occurred during
recent years in the Soviet Union: in Lithuania, where the Catholic Church has
been able to renew its ties with Rome and to celebrate its religious
ceremonies attended by tens of thousands of believers,[7] and in Russia itself
where the millennium of the Baptism illustrated the new position of the
Orthodox Church.[8] Gorbachev's visit to the Vatican in 1989 has added a new
impetus to this development, followed in the spring of 1990 by the exchange
of ambassadors. For the first time in its history, the Soviet Union is becoming
a country where the churches and small religious denominations are no

longer persecuted by the state. A similar evolution was accomplished by the end of 1989 in Bulgaria and Romania, as it had been earlier in Yugoslavia and the GDR. Only Albania still claims to be a country 'liberated' from religion, and there are signs in mid-1990 of possible relaxation in this field in that country, too.[9]

Until very recently, the question of the influence of religion on the current policies of the communist parties and on the long-term evolution of the communist regimes was generally considered irrelevant. The Polish case was inconsistent with such thinking and was therefore treated as an exception to be explained by the peculiar character of Polish history. But the events of 1989 have shown that the Catholic Church played an important, if not crucial, role in the peaceful overthrow of the communist regime in Czechoslovakia, and that the Lutheran Church did the same in the GDR. The question of the political influence of churches and of religious ideas must therefore be raised not only with respect to Poland but in the majority of East European countries. Indeed, it may be one of the most important questions for drawing possible scenarios for the internal transformation in any one of these countries, the Soviet Union included. This chapter attempts to argue the validity of such a belief.

CARTOGRAPHY OF PRESENT RELIGIOUS CONFLICTS

Let us first consider certain religious conflicts which are much older than communist power itself, any open expression of which the communists tried to repress over the past forty years. For a long time they did this with such efficiency that these conflicts were sometimes considered in the West as finally settled. We now have plenty of proof that this idyllic vision was simply false. If we travel either in the European part of the Soviet Union or in Eastern Europe, from the south-east towards the north-west, we meet pogroms of Armenians in Azerbaijan, anti-Abkhazian manifestations in Georgia,[10] the Albanian revolt against the Serbs in Kosovo, the tension between Bosnians on one side and Serbs *cum* Croats on the other in Bosnia-Herzegovina,[11] and the persecution of Turks by Bulgarians. All these openly or latently violent events have a common denominator, namely the religious conflict between Muslims and Christians.

In all these cases the religious conflict is superimposed on a national one which has almost everywhere a territorial and sometimes also a linguistic dimension. But the religious conflict has a dynamic of its own fuelled today by, among other things, the revival of Islamic fundamentalism. This acts everywhere as a powerful factor which reinforces in every concerned nation the feeling of a threat to its future existence on its historical territory — this is what the conflict in Nagorny Karabakh is about, as is the conflict in Kosovo — and therefore the feeling of self-identity which expresses itself in the tendency towards separatism. As such, it is one of the most powerful centrifugal forces which undermine the cohesion of the federal state in both the Soviet Union and Yugoslavia.

At the same time, in the Soviet Union the revival of Islamic fundamentalism pushes towards the creation of an alliance of small Christian nations, such as the Armenians and Georgians, with the Russians, the former feeling themselves unable to resist independently the pressure of Islam. Such an alliance cannot, however, become a reality without a negative effect on Russian — Islamic relations. Hence Soviet power, which is essentially Russian power, is obliged to practise a policy of neutrality between Christians and Muslims, with the risk of increasing discontent on both sides and therefore of a strengthening of those centrifugal tendencies it is trying to weaken. Nevertheless the Muslim — Christian conflict does not seem to be dangerous for the Soviet Union in the short term. That is not the case in Yugoslavia, where it may contribute either to the disintegration of the country or to the appearance of a military regime aiming to preserve its unity.

If we continue our journey in the same direction, from the south-east to the north-west, we cross the second major religious frontier of Central and Eastern Europe which separates Greek from Roman Christianity, the Orthodox from the Catholic Church. It is manifest in Yugoslavia where Serbs are Orthodox while Croatians and Slovenes are Catholics; this religious divergence goes together with opposing cultural and even political orientations, the Orthodox being attracted to Russia while the Catholics turn towards the West.[12] The same frontier goes through Romania where, as in Yugoslavia, it partly coincides with frontiers between different nationalities. And it is present also in Poland where small Ukrainian and Belorussian minorities profess the Orthodox creed. In the Soviet Union, on the other hand, the Ukraine and Belorussia are predominantly Orthodox with minorities attached to Catholicism, and the same is true to a much greater degree of Russia, while the Baltic countries are part of Western Christianity: Catholic for Lithuania, Protestant for Latvia and Estonia.

The frontier between the Catholic and the Orthodox variants of Christianity appears to be a peaceful one. But this peace is a recent phenomenon, produced by Soviet persecution of both, and partly artificial because of a persistent resentment on the part of the Orthodox Church, with its traditional distrust of the Papacy. Moreover, there is still at least one important object of strife: the future of the Uniate Church. Created at the end of the sixteenth century under the protection of the Polish kingdom, this Church recognizes the authority of the Pope (and is therefore a part of the Catholic Church) while preserving its own liturgy. Savagely persecuted by the tsarist authorities following the partition of Poland, it survived in Galicia, which was included in the Austrian Empire and which after 1918 became the eastern territory of the Polish Republic. When this area was incorporated into the Soviet Union, the Uniate Church was officially integrated into the Orthodox Church; opponents of this decision were persecuted.

Since 1945 the official Soviet point of view, and that of the Orthodox Church which agreed with it on this subject, was that the Uniate Church no longer existed in the territory of the Ukraine. But according to the Uniates themselves their Church is still there and it must be legalized to achieve religious freedom in the USSR. There are moreover some four million participants in underground liturgical celebrations of the Uniate Church, who now publicly demand legal recognition from the Soviet authorities, with all the consequences such a measure would entail (restitution of ecclesiastical property, opening of seminaries, and the possibility of communication with Rome, among others). The problem of the Uniate Church therefore creates tensions at the local level between its adherents and the Orthodox Church. It also influences the relations between Rome and the Moscow Patriarchate, and between Rome and the Kremlin. It is probably now the most important obstruction to some form of reconciliation between Catholicism and Orthodoxy.[13]

There are two more religious frontiers through Central and Eastern Europe. The first separates Catholics from Protestants, the second Christians from Jews. The first is important in Romania, Hungary and Czechoslovakia, and it almost coincides with that between Poland and the GDR. Today, with the development of the ecumenical movement and following the rehabilitation by the Papacy of Jan Hus and even of Martin Luther, this frontier no longer generates conflicts. The second is much more malignant despite the extermination of the Central and East European Jewry by the Nazis and the emigration of the few who escaped the *final solution* after the outburst of official anti-semitism in the last years of Stalin's rule, and later, in Poland in 1967-69. Experience has shown that anti-semitism does not need Jews in order to reproduce itself: it creates them. This being so, anti-semitism remains a powerful force in post-communist countries even if its true constituency is very difficult to assess. It is a component of different authoritarian, nationalistic and xenophobic associations and movements like *Grunwald* in Poland or *Pamyat* in Russia which are important for our subject because they present themselves as defenders of tradition and therefore also of the religion conceived as its core. When thinking about religion and politics in post-communist countries, one also has to take into account such a phenomenon, which may, unfortunately, one day become a truly influential one.[14]

Among several consequences which follow from what has been said so far, the one to be stressed is that which affirms the importance of the link between religion and national identity. In the majority of cases briefly noted above, the frontier of two religions separates two different nations and therefore the religious conflict is also a national one or, to be more precise, the present conflict of two nationalities is rooted, among other causes, in an old conflict of two confessions. It is true that all nations have religious minorities, but in Eastern Europe the latter are either statistically insignificant, as in Poland where they amount to less than five per cent of population, or they are at the same time national minorities, as in Romania. It seems that there are only two important exceptions to this rule: the frontier between Catholics and Protestants which divides Hungarians as it divides Czechs, and the frontier between Uniates and Orthodox which divides Ukrainians.

RELIGION AND NATIONAL IDENTITY

The existence of a strong link between religious and national identity does not mean that the two overlap. National tradition everywhere has two opposed faces: one religious, the other anti-clerical, or even free-thinking if not openly atheistic. In order to understand the different issues in the struggle against religion in different countries subjected to communist rule, several factors must be taken into account, one of the most important of which is the strength of national religious traditions in comparison with the strength of national secular traditions (anti-clerical, free thinking, atheistic, and so on). The latter are of two kinds: traditions of the state which struggled to impose its authority over the Church on its territory in order to use it as a tool of its politics, and traditions of intelligentsias which struggled to emancipate themselves from ecclesiastical surveillance which, in the countries where the Church was controlled by the state, was also exerted by the state bureaucracy, the state censorship and state police. These two kinds of secular tradition are present in all the countries of Eastern Europe, but in different proportions in each. In Russia and in what was to become the Prussian part of Germany, the state was victorious in its confrontation with the Church. In the former, the Moscow Patriarchate was reduced in the course of the seventeenth century to the position of a state agency for religious affairs; in the eighteenth century the Church was definitely put in the service of the state, while the tsar was becoming the object of a deification which persisted until the revolution.[15] All dissent on theological and ecclesiological subjects was therefore identified as a revolt against the state and pitilessly repressed. This notwithstanding, the Old Believers who rejected the submission of the Church to the state and also different millenarian sects had numerous followers among Russian peasants. Moreover, the opposition of popular faith to the creed of the official Church was an important dimension of the conflict between the peasantry and the social elite in Russia. After the revolution, with the Church completely controlled and manipulated by a state that was now openly atheistic and anti-religious, the sects which always preserved some audience, particularly in the countryside, made possible the survival of religion in Russia. And perhaps its future revival too, because the secular tradition of the intelligentsia has been perverted by the communists, who represented themselves as its heirs and used it in order to establish their legitimacy, to show they had roots in the Russian past.[16]

In Prussia, a country born out of the conversion to Lutheranism, in the first quarter of the sixteenth century, of the Crucifers who had originally been a military and religious order, ecclesiastical authorities were from the very beginning submitted to and controlled by the prince's court and later also by the state bureaucracy as in all other Lutheran countries. As the Western tradition separates temporal and spiritual powers, this control of the Church by the Prussian State was never comparable to what it was in Russia whose Christianity originated in Byzantium, which did not recognize such a separation of powers. The distinction between the official and the popular religion was, however, present in Prussia, as everywhere in Lutheran Germany, the latter having taken the form of pietism. With the appearance in the nineteenth century of the unified Germany as a multi-confessional country and the progress there of civil liberties, state control of the Church was seriously weakened. But the tradition of state intervention in religious affairs survived and was inherited by the German Democratic Republic.

Despite apparent similarities between Russia and Prussia there were nevertheless important differences concerning the relationship of religious affiliation to the national one. In Russia the two were officially identified. A conversion of a Catholic or of a Uniate to Orthodoxy was, in the Russian part of Poland or in the Ukraine, the first step towards Russification,[17] while a conversion of a Russian to Catholicism was considered almost as high treason. In Prussia, on the contrary, the German national identity was not connected to any definite Christian denomination. Moreover, Prussia never knew of the antagonism between the popular and the official religion, which was peculiar to Russia. At least, while in Germany the distinction was implemented between private beliefs and the public space which has to be religiously neutral, the secular tradition of the Russian intelligentsia indissolubly tied in with its struggle against tsardom, never recognized the validity of such a distinction. Rather, it made of atheism a religion *sui generis*, an anti-religious religion as compulsory as was the religion itself.

In all other countries of Eastern Europe the national state, if it ever existed, and if it ever managed to impose its authority on the local Church, was sooner or later destroyed by foreign invasion: in the Balkans, in Moldavia and Wallachia (which are at present parts of Romania) and in Hungary (with the exception of Transylvania) by the Turks in fourteenth to sixteenth centuries (hence the presence of Muslims in Yugoslavia and Bulgaria); in Bohemia and Moravia, lands of the Czechs, by the Habsburgs in the seventeenth century; and in Poland by a coalition of Russia, Prussia and Austria at the end of the eighteenth. Lack of space precludes detailed discussion of so many different cases here, but a few words are required on three of them: that of Orthodox countries conquered by the Turks, that of Bohemia and Moravia, and that of Poland.

The Turks ruled in Hungary until the end of the seventeenth century, for 170 years. In the Balkans, however, they ruled for almost five centuries, until the second half of the nineteenth century, when Serbia, Romania, Bulgaria and Montenegro became independent while Bosnia was annexed by Austria; Albania became independent at the beginning of the twentieth century. During all this historical epoch a Serb or a Bulgarian who converted himself to Islam was regarded as becomimg a Turk because the Turkish identity, until the Young Turks' revolution, was in fact determined by the religious criterion to a greater extent than by the ethnic one: a convert to Islam adopted also the Turkish language, the Turkish costume and the Turkish mores.[18] To remain a Bulgarian, a Romanian or a Serb, therefore, one had to remain faithful to the Orthodox Church: the religious affiliation was effectively tantamount to the national one. This helps to explain the absence of a deeply rooted secular tradition either on the part of the intelligentsia or on the part of the state, both being recent phenomena in the countries with a Turkish past.

In the kingdom of Bohemia, of which Moravia was a part, after the Hussite reformation of the fifteenth century, the Catholic ecclesiastical organization virtually collapsed; for two centuries the dominant religion was a national religion, Utraquism, and the kings of Bohemia were obliged by oath to respect the religious freedom of their subjects. When this agreement was broken by the Habsburgs at the beginning of the seventeenth century Catholicism was reimposed upon the Czechs by the use of intimidation and even force, and the ecclesiastical organization was rebuilt in the seventeenth and eighteenth centuries, although it never attained influence equalling what it had in other Catholic countries. As a result of this history, Roman Catholicism was perceived by the Czechs, and particularly since the nineteenth century by the Czech nationalist intelligentsia, as an alien creed whose history meant the defeat of Czech independence. The early industrialization and urbanization of Bohemia and Moravia resulted in secularization making rapid advances, which deeply penetrated the Czech culture and the Czech national self-consciousness.[19]

In Poland the course of history was almost exactly the opposite. The spread of the Reformation, which initially seemed irresistible, was stopped at the end of the sixteenth century and later the trend was reversed. The Polish nobility became, in the course of the seventeenth century, almost exclusively Catholic. And the Polish crown, whose principal enemies were Protestants (Swedes, Prussians), Orthodox (Cossacks, Russians) or Muslims (Turks), identified itself from the end of the sixteenth century more and more with the Catholic cause. When Poland was destroyed as an independent state and divided between three powers, one of which was Orthodox and another Protestant, the Catholic Church became the only institution common to the nation as a whole and therefore the symbol of Polish national identity and an essential factor acting towards an unification of the country. Hence the very strong connection of Polishness with Roman Catholicism.[20]

THE RETURN OF THE PAST

These old histories have direct relevance to the present. For one of the most amazing features of the present in post-communist countries is the spectacular return of the past we are now witnessing. Thus, the map of religious conflicts sketched at the beginning of this chapter is in its broad characteristics the same as half a century ago. And it is intelligible only if one goes back to the Reformation, the Turkish conquest, the establishment of Jews, and the Byzantine Empire. The lesson taught by it is that forty years of the communist regime were not enough to erase a thousand years of previous history and to build up a new man in a new cultural environment. This is perhaps a trivial lesson. But it is nevertheless worth learning by all those who believe that the present can be understood without taking into account the past, sometimes even the very distant past.

History explains, moreover, the reception of the Soviet model of relations between politics and religion which was imposed upon the countries of Eastern Europe after the seizure of power by communist parties backed by the Soviet army. For it shows that this was a Russian communist model; that it was rooted in the Russian past with its submission of the Church to the state and its absence of the distinction between private beliefs and the religiously neutral public space; and that it was rooted too in the history of European ideologies, particularly in the Marxist tradition and in its antecedents. Its reception in any country into which it was imported depended therefore upon the attitude towards Russia dominant in the country concerned and upon the level of secularization of that country's intelligentsia, that is, its sensitivity to arguments borrowed from the repertory of the Enlightenment.

The first factor divided the countries of Eastern Europe in two groups. The first was composed of the Orthodox ones and the other of those which are part of Latin Christianity, the former having been as a rule Russophiles (with the exception of Romania because of its territorial dispute with Russia) while the latter were as a rule rather Russophobes (with the exception of Bohemia and Moravia). The Russophilia of Orthodox countries resulted not only from their community of religion with Russia but also from the aid the latter accorded them during their struggle against the Turkish domination, while it repressed the national upheavals in Hungary and Poland. By contrast, the levelof secularization was lower in Orthodox countries than in Catholic and Protestant ones which passed through the Renaissance, the

Reformation and the Enlightenment. But it was the dominant attitude towards Russia, even though now Soviet Russia, that determined the reception of the Soviet model in general.

All nations of the area under study perceived, albeit with varying intensity, the struggle of communists against religion as a repudiation of a component of the national identity so essential that without it this identity could no longer be the same. And indeed in the beginning the communists tried to establish their legitimacy not on the basis of traditional national values but on the revolutionary past, on the social justice they claimed to have established, and on a vision of future happiness. For some time such claims were accepted and the communists ruled not only by mass terror, but also by their success in winning an important popular following, very different in the various countries, but everywhere massive, particularly among the youth.

Now, from what has been said it can be understood why this following was greatest in Bulgaria, the most Russophile of the countries of the area, and the lowest in Poland, simultaneously the most Russophobe amongst them and the least secularized. In the hierarchy of diminishing Russophobia Poland was followed by Hungary, Romania, the GDR and Czechoslovakia, the latter, or rather Bohemia and Moravia only, being also the most secularized country of the area, perhaps with the GDR. (I leave aside Yugoslavia and Albania: the first because its precocious break with the USSR gave to its communist party a legitimacy which it maintained for long time; the second because of its uniqueness as the only country of the area where Islam was the dominant religion.)

The hope awakened by peace and by the first years of post-war recovery quickly dissipated itself, and the following that communists obtained after having realized the agrarian reform and taken initial measures of modernization, began to give way to manifestations of discontent provoked by the deteriorating living conditions and by the growing intensity of attacks of the communist regime upon national traditions, religion included. In the GDR and in Czechoslovakia the protest of workers in the early 1950s was directed principally against the politics of industrialization and the accompanying terror. Even during the Prague Spring of 1968 national requirements played only a secondary role and the religious ones were almost absent. Both were, by contrast, among the most important driving forces of the Hungarian revolution of 1956 and of peaceful Polish upheavals in the same year and later, in 1980-81.

With the progressive decay of the communist ideology and particularly with the disappearance in the 1960s and the 1970s of its capacity to mobilize people to work, appeals to patriotic feeling acquired an increasing importance in the official propaganda. The communist parties called more and more upon national traditions and tried to present themselves as heirs of great national heroes and of political movements of the past, in order to replace the revolutionary legitimacy with a nationalistic one supposed to be more effective. The use of anti-semitism by the Polish communist party in March 1968; the chauvinistic politics of Ceausescu with its compulsory Romanianization of Hungarians in Transylvania; the introduction by the GDR into its pantheon of Frederick the Great and of Bismarck; the toleration if not the protection granted in Russia to the anti-semitic and xenophobic organization Pamyat; the persecution of Turks in Bulgaria in order to transform it into a monoethnic country; the revival of claims of Serbia to exert a dominant role in Yugoslavia.[21] All these facts are only the most spectacular examples of the dramatic search by the communist parties of Eastern Europe for a new legitimacy rooted in the past: in the traditional national myths and in traditional national hatred.

COMMUNISTS, CHURCHES AND LEGITIMACY

Even such measures, however, were not enough when the economy went bankrupt and with it the pretension of having realized social justice; when nobody believed any more in a radiant future; when the deep crisis of the legitimacy of the communist regime manifested itself in a drastic fall in productivity, in the decay of social discipline and in the increasing number of pathological phenomena; and when it diminished the governability and opened the way to the growth of a political opposition whose capacity to mobilize people against the regime became a real threat to the power of the communist party. Yet the massive terror could not be used as a treatment for this general political disease. For such a terror needs executants strongly committed to the communist ideology. The erosion of this commitment, which after 1956 was slowly replaced by a superficial bureaucratic obedience, deprived communist regimes of their previous power to apply repression on a mass scale.

At this point, achieved by Poland a dozen years ago, by Hungary some years later, and only quite recently by the Soviet Union and other East European countries, the attitude towards religion began to change. First of all, the discovery is made by the communist establishment that religion is not simply a relic of times past but a present-day phenomenon, and one in full expansion at that. And in fact, in all communist countries an increase in the number of believers practising religious observance could be seen, as attested by growing participation in services, in pilgrimages and other religious gatherings, and by the growing number of baptisms, religious marriages and religious funerals and of *samizdat* publications of religious content in the countries where religious literature could not be published openly, and of members of religious associations where they were legal or at least tolerated. Czechoslovakia — or rather, that part inhabited by Czechs — is a particularly significant illustration of this phenomenon simply by virtue of its having been the most secularized country of Eastern Europe.[22]

Once the defeat of decades of anti-religious policies was admitted, several symptoms could be seen of a new attitude towards religion and its institutions on the part of communist parties, characterized in particular, in every country where it was manifest, by an acknowledgement of their positive role in the nation's history. The selective treatment of the national past, which was amputated according to the criteria of the communist doctrine, has given way to acceptance of it almost in its entirety. Any communist party which was changing its attitude towards religion was trying among other things to operate its own integration into the national history and therefore into the national future, and thereby to acquire a new legitimacy. But, deep as it was, this change was not enough to achieve such an ambitious objective.

Deprived of any legitimacy, the communist parties of Eastern Europe have also been deprived since the spring of 1989 of their most powerful ally, the only force that was able to maintain their rule against the will of the populations, namely, the fear of Soviet intervention, made improbable after the Soviet army's retreat from Afghanistan. As the national security and armed forces — Yugoslavia excluded — were useless without Soviet backing, the East European communist parties had no choice but to leave power when they could no longer govern their respective countries because of strong popular demonstrations directed against themselves. For all of them, that was the beginning of the disintegration.

With the exception of the Soviet Union (plus, of course, Albania), communist parties no longer possess a monopoly of power in an East European country. The free elections in the spring and early summer of 1990 either eliminated these parties from parliaments completely, or greatly reduced their importance.[23] Everywhere the transition seems to be under way from a centrally planned to a market economy, and from totalitarian or authoritarian regimes to democracy, declared by almost all political currents, including former communists, to be the system they wish to implem·nt. In this new situation, what is the role of the Churches likely to be?

The answer obviously depends on the religion they profess. But all of them, their differences notwithstanding, will very probably exert a stabilizing influence on the process of institutional change, trying to prevent recourse to violence and attempting to organize dialogue between competing forces. Whatever their choice, it will be all the more important that in each country new political parties, newly created or reborn, will probably be in the beginning very numerous and too weak to control their constituencies. The Churches, by contrast, are strong. They profit from their virtually monopolistic position and from their deep roots in the national tradition. For some time to come, the precise period varying from country to country, the Church's blessing may be a significant advantage for a political party or an individual politician, since the Churches are perceived as holders of legitimacy.

In Orthodox countries the Churches' political role may manifest itself particularly in the attitude they choose with respect to the cleavage between traditionalists and Westernizers. In the past, Orthodox Churches have been rather strongly anti-Western. Will this attitude survive? And with what strength? These are important questions for the future of Orthodox countries, because the answers may orientate cultural, political and even political development for years to come. In Catholic countries, the Church's political role may be even more important, especially in the short run. In Poland, the Church already openly intervenes in politics, where it is represented by a newly created rightist political party. In Hungary and Czechoslovakia, where the behaviour of the Church will certainly be less triumphalistic and more cautious, it may nevertheless be impossible in the near future to implement any measure that opposes the Church's positions. Everywhere the state, extremely weakened by communist rule, reduced almost to ruins, and in need of rebuilding from its very foundations, is faced with a Church or Churches more powerful than ever and invested for years to come with popular faith and support. The interplay of these two protagonists in the crucial period of establishing the new legal order and new institutional structures may determine the social and political regime and the cultural life of the East European countries for a long time to come.

NOTES

1. The persecutions of the Church in the USSR are now described, sometimes in detail, in the Soviet press: see as a recent example L. Annenskii and O. Mikhalkov, 'Imena ili psevdonimy' (Names or pseudonyms), *Literaturnaya gazeta*, 25 October 1989.

2. See Bogdan Cywinski, 'Ogniem Probowane. Z dziejow najnowszych Kosciola katolickiego w Europe srodkowo-wschodniej' (Trial by Fire: A Recent History of the Catholic Church in Central and Eastern Europe), in *Korzenie tozsamosci* (Roots of Identity) (Rome, 1982). This volume deals with a period preceding the imposition of communist power on the countries of the area; the second volume will deal with the period following 1945. See aslso Jerzy Kloczowski, in *Histoire religieuse de la Pologne* (Paris, 1987), pp. 497ff.

3. See Krzysztof Pomian, 'Religione e politica in Polonia', in G. Ruggieri (ed.), *Una nuova pace costantiniana? Religione e politica negli anni '80* (Casale Monferrato, 1985), pp. 114-58; or the abridged French version 'Religion et politique en Pologne', *Vingtième siècle: Revue d'histoire*, 1986, No. 10, pp. 83-101.

4. See Francis Crnu, 'La Hongrie entre la Faucille et le Goupillon', *Le Monde*, 19 August 1988.

5. See Sylvie Kaufmann, 'Le lent retour de la religion au quotidien', *Le Monde*, 28 September 1988; and on the nomination by the Vatican of three new bishops in Czechslovakia: *Le Monde*, 28 July 1989.

6. See Henri Tincq, 'Les Eglises de l'Est sortent du silence', *Le Monde*, 10 February 1990.

7. See E. Zagiell, 'Kronika litewska' (Lithuanian Chronicle), *Kultura*, 1988, No. 11, pp. 121-4, and No. 12, pp. 120-2.

8. See Bernard Guetta, 'Après les babouchkas, le temps des petits-fils', *Le Monde*, 2 June 1988; an interview with the archbishop of Omsk and Tyumen on the Orthodox Church in Siberia, *Moskovskie novosti*, 27 December 1988; correspondence on the visit of the archbishop of Paris, Cardinal Lustiger, to Soviet Catholics, *Le Monde*, 3 and 5 May 1989; Henri Tincq, 'En URSS, la lente remontée de catacombes', *ibid.*, 10 August 1989.

9. On the recent religious situation in Albania, Czechoslovakia, the GDR, Hungary, Poland, Romania and Yugoslavia, see the special issue, 'Religion et politique en Europe du Centre-Est', *L'Autre Europe*, Nos 21-2 (1989).

10. On the Caucasus, see Georges Charachidzé, 'L'Empire et Babel: Les minorités dans la perestroika', *Le Genre Humain*, 1989, No. 20, pp. 9-36.

11. See Paul Yankovitch, 'Qui sont les musulmans de Bosnie-Herzégovine?', *Le Monde*, 8 October 1987.

12. See Istvan Deak, 'A Conglomerate Country', *The New York Review of Books*, 7 November 1985.

13. Henri Tincq, 'Les tribulations des catholiques d'Ukraine', *Le Monde*, 8 June 1988. In May and July 1989, Uniates demonstrated in Moscow seeking the legalization of their Church: see *Libération*, 29 May 1989, and *Le Monde*, 28 July 1989.

14. On anti-semitism in the Soviet press, including *Nash sovremennik* and *Literaturnaya Rossiya*, see *Oktyabr'*, 1989, No. 10, pp. 198-202.

15. See V.M. Zhivov and B.A. Uspenskii: 'Tsar i Bog: Semioticheskie aspekty sakralizatsii monarkha v Rossii' (Tsar and God: Semiotical Aspects of the Sacralization of the Monarch in Russia), in B.A. Uspenskii (ed.), *Yazyki kultury i problemy perevodimosti* (Languages of Culture and Problems of Translatability) (Moscow, 1987), pp. 47-153.

16. See 'Le Christianisme russe entre millénarisme d'hier et soif spirituelle d'aujourd'hui', special issue of *Cahiers du monde russe et soviétique*, Vol. XXIX, Nos 3-4 (1988).

17. See Daniel Beauvois, *Le noble, le serf et le revizor: La noblesse polonaise entre le tsarisme et les masses ukrainiennes (1831-1863)* (Paris, 1985).

18. See Bernard Lewis, *Islam et laicité: La naissance de la Turquie moderne* (Paris, 1988), pp. 288ff.

19. See Joseph Macek, *Jan Hus et les traditions hussites (XVe-XIXe siècles)* (Paris, 1973).

20. See Norman Davies, *God's Playground: A History of Poland*, 2 vols (Oxford: Oxford University Press, 1981).

21. See Patrice Claude, 'La grande fête du nationalisme serbe', *Le Monde*, 30 June 1989.

22. See Marie-Elisabeth Ducreux, 'Entre le Catholicisme et le Protestantisme: les Tchèques', *Le Débat*, No. 59 (1990; forthcoming).

23. The case of Bulgaria is unclear following the former communists' electoral victory in 1990; similar uncertainty remains in Romania following the election of the National Salvation Front under Ion Iliescu, and its behaviour in office.

9. Nationalist Challenges to State Integrity

Kristian Gerner and Kerstin Nyström

Nationalism has never been dead in the USSR and Eastern Europe: what was new in the late 1980s was that it became legitimate. A new future seemed to be in the making both for the subject peoples of the Soviet Union and for the vassal states in Central and Eastern Europe. Or was it, perhaps, a return to patterns of the past? As Joseph Rotschild put it: '... political patterns in the 1980s look more continuous with those of the 1930s than seemed conceivable in the midst of the revolutionary decades of the 1940s and 1950s'.[1]

This can be read as a recognition of the resilience of national political traditions, in which nationalism occupied a central position. In a more general sense, the perception of the past, in terms of facts, myths and unrealized ambitions, tends to define views of the future. As a consequence of Gorbachev's breaking out of stagnation in the Soviet Union, two different dreams appeared to become realistic.

Gorbachev's own dream was evidently to restore imperial might and glory to Moscow and its Soviet empire. In his first years in power, Gorbachev recalled traditions from the imperial Russian state of Peter the Great and later tsars. He even used the expression 'Russia' when referring to the Soviet Union.[2] Among the non-Russian subjects in the Soviet Union and the bloc Gorbachev's open admittance that Soviet economic and ethnic policies had been wrong for decades, and his recognition of the serious weaknesses in the Soviet economic and political system, seriously impaired the legitimacy of the empire and called to life old dreams of national self-determination and liberation from the Soviet yoke.

Prior to the obvious decline of Soviet power and the ascendancy of Gorbachev, the strong anti-Russian nationalism in the non-Russian Soviet republics and throughout Eastern Europe had not been taken seriously by

West European politicians, businessmen and mass media. Outside the circles of sovietologists, the dreams of East Europeans were definitely not represented in Western scenarios for the future. Intellectuals, politicians and businessmen in Western Europe did not regard the Russian rulers as imperialist oppressors. The Soviet Union was treated as a legitimate state. Without much reflection, Russian dominance over and deep interference in the national life of a number of previously sovereign countries in Eastern Europe was taken for granted. With the exception of events when national resistance to Soviet power could be interpreted more as a wish to establish democracy in a Western sense than as an expression of virulent ethnic nationalism, namely in Hungary in 1956, in Czechoslovakia in 1968, and in Poland in 1980-81, non-Russian nationalism seemed to be politically illegitimate, whereas Russian chauvinism was not recognized as such.

Communist dictatorship was certainly resented in broad circles, but the Western image of the Soviet empire was one of quiet and order, of the final solution of the national question. Although a number of sovietologists pointed to ethnic nationalism in the Soviet west and in Eastern Europe as a potentially destabilizing factor,[3] the general public, the political parties and capital in the West did not seem to take cognizance of this fact. The suppression of national conflicts by force was misinterpreted as their solution. However, once the pressure decreased and political forces could emerge on the public scene in the USSR and Eastern Europe, politics became ethnicized and the ethnic question became politicized. Within a single year, 1988, a number of economic, ecological, social and cultural conflicts in the Soviet Union became defined according to ethnic characteristics and cleavages. At the same time, national contradictions were sharpened in and between some of the Eastern European states, especially in the Balkans.

NATIONALISTS OF ALL COUNTRIES, UNITE!

This ironic slogan is from a Russian scholar who gave a lecture to a conference in May 1989 which was devoted to national problems in the Soviet Union.[4] He highlighted the point that nationalism as an international phenomenon is in a sense contradictory. The positive evaluation of one's peers is often combined with disdain for or suspicion of one's neighbours. From a Russian perspective, however, one might imagine the menacing scenario of a union of non-Russian nationalists and nations against one common enemy — the Russians. This was one of many ambiguities of the situation in the late 1980s. It must be stressed that the issue is complicated. Nationalism is compatible with any political ideology. It cannot be considered to be inherently 'good' or 'bad'. However, as was the case with the Spring of Nations in 1848 and the creation of the successor states in Europe in 1918-20, what might evoke sympathy and even support in the West was and is a nationalism which embodies demands for democracy and for freedom of expression and organization, and respect for other nations. In a recent analysis of developments in Eastern Europe, Timothy Garton Ash indicated four principal dimensions behind the current politicization process: the resurgence of nationalism, of religion, of civil society, and of private enterprise. Regarding the first dimension, nationalism, he observes:

> The first may be called a popular rediscovery of the national past: a widespread and passionate interest in history, prewar national traditions, forgotten authors, ethnic minorities past and present ... and regional ties. ... To subsume all this under the label 'nationalism' would be crass oversimplification. Much of it is simply the quest for what is regarded in the West as a 'normal' cultural continuity: and identification with national symbols, traditions and even myths, is as benign in moderation as it is dangerous in excess. The lack of 'normal' access to the national past was a form of deprivation; the recovery of it is a form of emancipation. ... But does the recultivation of tradition necessarily conduce to the democracy of the living? What about the authentic, national un- or antidemocratic traditions? And cannot nationalism act — or be used — as a substitute for democracy?[5]

Garton Ash's discussion of 'nationalism' points to the multi-dimensionality of the concept with regard to both content and carriers. As for the latter aspect, it seems necessary to differentiate three levels. Nationalism may be an ideological instrument of rulers, used as a means to mobilize the majority against internal minorities and alleged threats from the outside. The Romanian nationalism of Ceausescu, the Serbian nationalism of Milosevic, and the Bulgarian nationalism of Zhivkov all belong to this category. In contrast, nationalism may be an instrument of oppositional intellectuals in their endeavour to mobilize the masses into political action against rulers who are perceived to be both dictatorial and ethnically foreign, or at least to be agents of a foreign power. The nationalism of Polish and Hungarian intellectuals exemplifies this variety, which combines nationalism with democracy. Finally, there is the rather unreflective and emotional ethnic nationalism, into which most people are socialized in the family and in everyday life, especially in ethnically mixed societies, where there is a certain division of labour and unequal distribution of political power among different ethnic groups. The popular sentiments against the Russians all over the Soviet bloc are expressions of this kind of nationalism. It is obvious that when nationalism was legitimized in political life, as happened through Gorbachev's *glasnost* and democratization campaigns, all three varieties came into play. The situation became as loaded with political risks as were similar processes in earlier stages of European history, at the turn of the twentieth century and in the inter-war period.

However, a further aspect must be discussed regarding the relationship between tradition and nationalism. As soon as history is evoked, the constructivist aspect of the matter should be stressed. 'History' is never a matter of any innate self-evident identification with an unambiguous, certain past among an ethnic group in its totality. 'History' is rather the result of conscious attempts by rulers or intellectuals to create a common basis for a collective identity of an ethnic group. In the Soviet Union and Eastern Europe, the communist dictatorship and the absence of political opposition in a Western sense often turned intellectuals into political spokesmen for their ethnic brethren. When they regained the ability to act politically in the late 1980s, primarily in the USSR, Poland and Hungary, they relied on historiography and myths, much as their predecessors in 1848 and during the First World War had done, 'to fill the need to bolster up a newly urgent sense of national identity'.[6]

Past events and processes are converted into historical facts and interpreted as guidelines for contemporary politics by being perceived and connected with each other by the necessarily selective, socially conditioned human mind. Once constructed and imbued with emotions, history helps in moulding the individual's perceptions of reality. In the 1980s, the official Soviet and communist interpretations of history and views of the future were exchanged for ethnically or nationalistically defined perspectives on both the past and the future. The relativism inherent in this kind of politicization of history has been formulated by Hayden White:

> ... it is not a matter of choosing between objectivity and distortion, but rather between different strategies of constituting 'reality' in thought so as to deal with it in different ways, each of which has its own ethical implications.[7]

We must add: and ethno-political implications. In the USSR and Eastern Europe the new interpretation of the significance of the past meant that the Marxist class approach to history and politics was superseded by an ethnic nationalist perspective; that the tradition of 'democratic centralism' — that is, communist dictatorship — was re-interpreted as a perversion and was exchanged for stress on the positive heritage of political pluralism in, for example, the Baltic republics, Hungary and Poland. Last but not least, the tradition of individual human rights, a heritage from the European Enlightenment, was evoked instead of the collectivism hailed by totalitarian (or at least authoritarian) Leninism and Stalinism.

'Patriotism' and 'socialist internationalism' were key terms in the political language of communism. The words were used to denote the allegedly good, progressive way of collective identification with the state and its rulers in communist-ruled countries. In early 1989, the slogan 'Proletarians of all countries, unite!', could still be read as part of the masthead of the communist party dailies in the USSR and Eastern Europe. 'Patriotism' thus meant working-class identification with the Fatherland, and 'socialist internationalism' referred to solidarity with the class brethren in other communist states. The message was that the Russian-dominated Soviet Union should be venerated by all citizens in the country, regardless of ethnic origin, and by all manual workers in the world. In the same communist language, 'bourgeois' or 'petty bourgeois' nationalism was the favourite term to denote the allegedly bad, reactionary identification with specific historical traditions, linguistic communities and religious groups and institutions. Identification on the basis of ethnicity was condemned as a violation of the principle of class solidarity, as a capitalist ideological device to deceive the workers and divert their interest from the class struggle.

The communist phraseology outlined above obscured reality rather than describing it. In practice, a Russian nationalism of sorts was promoted in the Soviet Union from the late 1920s onwards, whereas all other expressions of ethnic identification — Ukrainian, Jewish, Turkish and so on — were condemned as 'bourgeois' and suppressed.[8] However, even though the mendacious propaganda was consciously fabricated in the ideological department of the CPSU, it seems that the Soviet rulers became prisoners of their own propaganda.[9] They did not reckon with the rather obvious fact that beneath the calm surface the psychological alienation of most non-Russians from communism, the Soviet Union and the camp of socialist states was preserved, not to say reinforced.

Ethnic nationalism has been an ideological and political factor in the communist states of Eastern Europe ever since Khrushchev's de-Stalinization campaign in the late 1950s. The search for political legitimacy through an appeal to national sentiments was a vital necessity for the communist rulers of Eastern European states once the Stalinist model was exposed as an aberration. Early examples were Gomulka's return to the political scene in Poland in 1956 and Imre Nagy's attempt to dismantle the Stalinist system in Hungary in the same year. Later examples are the Czechoslovak Prague Spring of 1968, with its open allusions to the national political heritage of Jan Hus, Tomás Masaryk and Eduard Benes, plus the emergence of Ceausescu's 'Dacian' and Zhivkov's 'Thracian' mythologies in Romania and Bulgaria and the harsh treatment of the Magyar and German, and Turkish and Gypsy minorities in the various countries in the 1970s and 1980s. However, Moscow's interventions in Hungary in 1956 and in Czechoslovakia in 1968, together with its repeated pressure on Poland in 1956 and 1980-81, made vassal-state nationalism seem more or less politically insignificant as a challenge to the established order.

In 1988, the evaluation had to change. Moscow was beleaguered by an array of nationalist challenges, from Estonia to Tadzhikistan within the USSR and in different ways in the states in Eastern Europe. However, with few exceptions, the separate national movements were rather poorly coordinated. Moreover, not all of them were primarily anti-Russian: the conflicts between Azeris and Armenians and Georgians and between different Turkish peoples in Central Asia, and also those between Hungary and some of its neighbours, were evidence of the variety in the animosities. The slogan 'nationalists in all countries, unite' was less a working political slogan than an ironic twist of the official 'proletarian' counterpart. The new caption was real, however, in the sense that it denoted the basis for political mobilization under *glasnost*. Class struggle was superseded by national emotions and contradictions as the basis for political action.

TIMING AND CHARACTERISTICS

Why did the nationalist challenges occur in 1988, although national tensions had been a fact for decades? Why was there an ethnic and nationalist rather than a social and political mobilization once political action became possible?

Perestroika was originally aimed at improvement of the economic system, and *glasnost* was obviously regarded by the Soviet leaders as a necessary precondition for the economic reform programme to be implemented. *Perestroika* and *glasnost* were geared towards political mobilization of the apathetic Soviet people in order to save the Soviet Union from further economic slowdown and a possible relegation to the status of a second-rate power. However, these policies were not a simple invention by a skilful politician but rather a necessary outcome of social processes. In the 1980s, the communist command economies and single-party political systems were rapidly approaching the end of the road. This road was not taking them towards realization of the communist utopia or to a kind of welfare state, but to catastrophe. Gorbachev and his advisers were more or less forced to act by the force of circumstances.

In the course of the 1980s, destruction of the natural environment, in particular, went so far in different parts of the USSR and Eastern Europe as to make huge areas perfectly unhealthy to live in. In Estonia and Latvia, Belorussia, the Ukraine, Moldavia, Siberia and Soviet Central Asia, and in Poland, Czechoslovakia and the GDR, pollution of water and the air, the destruction of forests and salination and erosion of the soil took on alarming proportions. The Aral Sea dwindled in area, its fishing fleet marooned, destroying a people's traditional way of life. The upper Danube valley in Hungary was threatened by a planned Austrian-Czechoslovak-Hungarian joint hydroelectric power project. Because of contamination with poisonous chemicals and other pollutants and exposure to the exhausts from the burning of low quality coal, millions of people fell ill and came under direct threat of an early death. The survival of whole nations, such as the Estonians and the Karakalpaks, or certain regions, such as Silesia in Poland, northern Moravia and Silesia in Czechoslovakia, and Kohtla-Järve and Maardu in Estonia, seemed to be at stake. Individuals could not escape into privacy and isolation, because their own lives and those of their children were in danger. The multitude and magnitude of the different environmental catastrophes did not allow for the 'solution' of emigration. Since there was no possibility of individual or collective exit as a solution to the problems, use of a political voice became a necessity.[10] *Glasnost* and democratization in the USSR and the withering away of communist power in Eastern Europe made this a real option.

It was obvious that the individual voice could not accomplish any changes in the policies of the state. Collective action was the key to success. But in what form, and with whom? On the basis of what collective identity? Certainly not through the communist parties that bore the main responsibility for the catastrophic state of affairs. Although spurred by Gorbachev's campaigns of *glasnost* and 'democratization', politicization soon slipped out of the communist party's control in different Soviet republics and in Eastern

Europe. Politics were called to life, as intended, but took the form of 'bourgeois' nationalism, which was unforeseen. This particular form of politicization was related both to tradition and to the international environment of the Soviet state and bloc. Social, cultural, economic and ecological issues were linked to the individual's identification with a certain ethnic group and territory, that is, to the history and culture of a distinct nation. In addition to this came the impact of contemporary Western society. The global information revolution and the expanding commercial contacts with the West under Brezhnev eroded the ideological walls established by Stalin. Intellectuals were able to acquire information about the standard of living in Western society and, moreover, they learned from the examples of the peace and environmental movements in the West about organization from below. They also learned that regionalism and cultivation of the national culture were legitimate political undertakings in a Europe which prided itself on increasing voluntary integration. The West European model seemed to be a viable alternative to the barren Soviet federation and CMEA.

The outcome of the revival of national traditions and increased contacts with the West was the emergence of alternative political cultures in the Soviet republics and the East European states, bearing the imprint of both sources of inspiration. For the western Soviet republics, plus Hungary and Poland, the year 1988 saw a return to Europe in a double sense: to their own 'European' — as distinct from Russian and Soviet — heritage, and to contemporary European reality. It was not an abstract Europe, however, but the Europe with the traditions of 1848 and 1918-20, the Europe of movements for national self-determination and of sovereign national states, the Europe that once had dissolved and buried four continental empires in which ethnic inequality had been a basic trait: Austria-Hungary, Germany, Russia and Turkey.

VARIETIES OF NATIONALISM

There were three different sets of nationalist challenges to the established order in Eastern Europe. The first concerned the Soviet Union, where the challenge from the non-Russians was against Russian dominance, communism, and the Soviet state as such. This was a challenge from within and a menace to the survival of the existing system and the integrity of the state. The second challenge concerned the Warsaw Pact states, where the issues were Soviet–Russian dominance, internal communism and demands for increased autonomy for the national states. This was primarily a challenge to the remaining communist power-holders within the respective states and a menace to the cohesion of the Soviet bloc. The third challenge concerns Yugoslavia, where the structural position of the Serbs is reminiscent of that of the Russians in the Soviet Union, and the grievances of other nations bear a similar character. The challenge is both to the survival of the state and to the political system as such. The main difference from the other two cases lies in the fact that non-aligned Yugoslavia was not a member of the Warsaw Pact and thus not directly linked to the question of the viability of the Soviet empire, as the other two cases are.

The revelations about the miserable record and actual state of 'real socialism' in the Soviet Union, the core of the socialist system, indicated an admission by the rulers themselves that communism as practised is inferior to the Western system in certain basic respects. The system began to lose even the appearances of legitimacy. Moreover, the democratization drive in the USSR itself made Soviet resistance to democratization in the vassal states an increasingly irrelevant argument. The chronic crisis of legitimation deepened for the allied regimes. They could no longer argue that communist party rule was in the best interests of the nation, and they could not even insist that they, the local communist leadership, were the lesser evil, as the only alternative to direct Russian rule. What had seemed to be a plausible implicit argument behind General Jaruzelski's repression of the Polish democratic movement on 13 December 1981 — the threat of direct Soviet intervention — had lost all credibility on 3 July 1989, when Vadim Zagladin, a spokesman for the CPSU Central Committee, declared that the Soviet Union was prepared to have relations with any Polish government elected by the people, including even a government established by the Solidarity movement — precisely the movement which in 1981 had been condemned as a threat to socialist Poland and to the Warsaw Pact's cohesion.[11]

In East European countries, nationalism meant that the ruling communist parties and the democratic opposition endorsed the *glasnost* and democratization policies of Gorbachev in the USSR and drew the conclusion that the way was open for a return to 'normal' political life, that is, to some kind of Western-style democratic system. The stress was on national consensus to revive politics and on a peaceful distancing from the Soviet Union and the Soviet model by rulers and opposition alike.[12] Only in Romania was this kind of coalition ruled out, and until the violent overthrow of Ceausescu in December 1989 nationalism continued to mean centrally directed persecution and even the expulsion of tens of thousands of the Hungarian minority, accompanied by the promotion of xenophobia.

The nationalist challenge in Eastern Europe to the cohesion of the Soviet bloc thus had two different sides. All but one East European state pointed towards reunion with Western Europe and a farewell to communism and the Soviet Union, and the option for Romania was a retrenchment into the very Stalinism which the Soviet leader deemed it necessary to dismantle for the socialist system to survive at all. In the first case, the challenge implied dissolution of the bloc but the survival of its parts. In the second case it raised the prospect of stubborn local leaders leading their country to economic breakdown and social cataclysms that would threaten political stability and be a potential danger for Soviet security. The Romanian people took matters into their own hands in December 1989, and the Ceausescu regime collapsed in a matter of days — not without a bitter struggle, but with the blessing of Moscow.

The Yugoslav case mirrored both alternatives: dissolution and survival, or persistence on the road to common disaster.

THE YUGOSLAV MODEL

Yugoslavia is a federation, but the federation is not as ephemeral as its Soviet counterpart, because modern Yugoslavia is not the simple outcome of a thousand years of Serbian domination in the same way as the Soviet Union is the direct continuation of the Russian empire. Moreover, in contrast to the six Warsaw Pact states, Yugoslavia has been a fully sovereign state since the Second World War.

Yugoslavia is of special interest for a comparative analysis of present developments in the European communist states because in a certain way the conflicts maturing both in the Soviet Union and in Eastern Europe in the late 1980s were prefigured decades earlier in Yugoslavia. After the break with Moscow in 1948 and the politically motivated striving to establish an alternative model for a communist society, three basic conflicts set their mark on Yugoslav society: the conflict over which economic principle should be adhered to; the issue of political power; and the question of ethnic relations. The conflicts are connected with each other through a network of feedback loops.

The conflict over the economy is the 'classic' one of central command *versus* decentralized market relations. The political conflict is two-dimensional, over democracy *versus* one-party rule, and, regarding the latter, over the status of the republican communist parties in relation to the *Savez Komunista Jugoslavije*, the federal party organization: so far, the political conflict has boiled down to the question of whether the state shall be centrally ruled or a federation of autonomous republics. The national conflicts concern the right to protect and promote specific regional and ethnic cultures rather than being obliged to adhere to a Yugoslav culture, which because of demographic factors and political traditions has been dominated by Serbs.

In the 1980s, the most serious of all the social conflicts in Yugoslavia turned out to be the national conflict between Serbia and its autonomous republic Kosovo, which has a majority of ethnic Albanians. In 1968, the first demonstrations for political autonomy for Kosovo took place. This was granted through the new Yugoslav constitution of 1974 which gave economic and cultural decision-making power to the republics. Within Serbia, Kosovo and Vojvodina (with a sizeable Hungarian minority) were given almost the same national rights as the six federal republics. The only right denied to them was the right to leave the federation.

However, at the same time as economic and cultural decentralization progressed, the League of Communists of Yugoslavia became more centralized, which meant increased central control over the republican parties. The result was that the republican party leaders came under cross-pressure between the party leadership in Belgrade and the demands emanating from the local population. The awkwardness of the communist definition of political reality as one-party rule became glaringly evident when Yugoslavia's economic crisis worsened in the early 1980s. The gap between the more and less developed republics widened but there was no political preparation for the question of whether a federal state could comprise both market and command economies, or republics ruled by a party with a monopoly of political power as well as republics governed by democratically elected governments. In this situation, ethnic tensions grew and nationalism became the politically mobilizing force. The identity of Yugoslavia was at stake. At the end of the 1980s, the one institution expressing its unequivocal support for the established federal structure of Yugoslavia was the armed forces. This stance could not replace politics, however.

The introduction of political democracy was the solution preferred by Slovenes and Croats, in the form of a genuine multi-party system. In 1989, Slovenia already had several different political parties of a socialist and liberal orientation and also independent action groups, for example local Greens. In Croatia, the existence of a sizeable Serbian minority (11.6 per cent of a total population of 4,601,000 in 1981) made matters somewhat more complicated.[13] However, in both republics there was a conscious, explicit allusion to the political traditions of the time of the Habsburgs and the practice of fighting out political struggles in legal and constitutional forms, regardless of ethnic and cultural characteristics. The idea of a Rechtsstaat and of a civil society emerged as alternatives to communist dictatorship. At the same time, the implication was that the qualities in question had never been part of the political culture of Orthodox Serbia.

In Serbia, the proposed solution to the crisis of legitimacy is nationalism. The Serbian party leader Slobodan Milosevic led his compatriots in a veritable crusade against Kosovo and Vojvodina with the goal of regaining total Serbian control over the two autonomous provinces. The task was accomplished in the spring of 1989 with the help of direct intervention in the parties of Kosovo and Vojvodina and various kinds of manipulation, all under the impact of Serbian mass demonstrations in Belgrade. The 1974 constitution was revised. A direct consequence of the increased Serbian control over Kosovo was that Albanian dissidents were prevented from expressing their views in the local mass media and had to publish in the Croat and Slovenian press. Slovene public opinion, in particular, sided with the Albanians, not because of any cultural affinity but obviously because Serbian nationalism was perceived as a menace to Slovene strivings for increased autonomy.

In the summer of 1989, the Serbian Communist Party and the Serbian Orthodox Church carried through a joint celebration of the six-hundredth anniversary of the Battle of Kosovo, on 28 June. Hundreds of thousands of Serbs gathered on the historic field, while the Albanians stayed at home; contrary to what might have been feared, the celebrations did not lead to violent clashes between Serbs and Albanians. In January 1990, however, new outbursts of ethnic violence in Kosovo and Serbian nationalist demonstrations in Belgrade showed that the conflict over Kosovo is profound and will remain a destabilizing factor for years to come.

The Yugoslav case has a number of special traits which cannot be dwelt upon in this context. Its 'model' importance is as follows. The command economy has failed completely. Not even the erstwhile ideological pride of socialist Yugoslavia, the workers' councils and self-management in the factories, could save it. Once economic centralization was abandoned, regional differences showed themselves. Instead of identification with the federal state of Yugoslavia, people identified along traditional lines with their region, language and religion, that is, with their cultural heritage. The Catholic western and the Eastern Orthodox and Turkish halves drifted apart. Whereas Slovenia and Croatia looked to Central Europe, giving vent to a nationalism that turned its back on Yugoslavia and concentrated on the well-being of their own nation, Serbia retained its traditional strivings for hegemony, for transforming Yugoslavia into a Greater Serbia. And whereas Slovenia and Croatia opted for political pluralism and democracy, Serbia persisted too long with one-party rule under its charismatic populist leader Slobodan Milosevic. Within Yugoslavia, nationalism has thus proved to mean many different things: for Croats and Slovenes, a means of mobilization of the people for the market economy and political pluralism, for Albanians an expression of identity in the face of Serbian great power pressures, and for Serbs, the realization of great power dreams and a wish to extend their power. The myth of the Habsburg civilization stands against the myth of the Byzantine culture, traditions of pluralism and muddling through against traditions of despotism and radicalism.

THE BALTIC MODEL

In the Soviet Union, the Baltic states — since the 1940s reduced to the status of 'union republics' — have displayed the most deep-going, consistent and massive nationalist challenge to Soviet rule. It is legitimate to concentrate the discussion of developments within the USSR on these republics, because they can be considered to be models for developments in Belorussia, the Ukraine and Moldavia, and also in the Transcaucasian region.

In the Baltic republics, Moscow's economic policy, implemented through the ministerial command system, which gave the centre control over more than ninety per cent of the economy, has led to substantial pollution of the natural environment and to a heavy influx of ethnic Russians. In 1987-88 new threats were emerging at the same time as the policies of *glasnost* and democratization created possibilities for expression.

In Estonia plans for considerably increased phosphate mining became known, threatening serious pollution. In Latvia, where the Gulf of Riga had already become heavily polluted, the issue in 1988 was a planned hydroelectric power plant on the Daugava, involving the flooding of historic sites. In Lithuania, the main concern was with the nuclear power station at

Ignalina, which had two reactors in operation and a third under construction. Common to all three republics was the fact that the products from the power stations, mines and factories would exceed local needs. At the price of increased damage to the natural environment and further pressure on the national cultures through immigration of Russian labour, Estonia, Latvia and Lithuania would give the already despised Russia fertilizers for its backward agriculture and energy for its highly inefficient industry. Central policies were regarded as colonial exploitation of occupied territories.

While *glasnost* and democratization were necessary conditions for stimulating nationalism, concern for the natural environment and resentment against the local Russians were precipitating factors. Memories of political traditions from the inter-war period and examples from Western Europe, Poland and Hungary helped shape the organizational forms of opposition. In 1988, Popular or National Fronts were established in the Baltic republics, in which ethnic nationalism was the focal point. As in Poland's Solidarity movement and in several of the Hungarian independent groups, communist party members took part in the Baltic Popular Fronts. The local Russian communist and non-communists organized themselves in so called Interfronts to defend their position, thereby establishing national polarization as the decisive political cleavage.

The crucial aspect of the ethnicization of politics in the Baltic republics was that the Soviet Union was externalized and treated more or less as a foreign power. The question of national sovereignty and independence naturally became central, and was accompanied by a number of political demands. These included re-negotiation of the treaty of union, implying acknowledgement that the incorporation into the USSR in 1940 had been an illegal act; the introduction of republican citizenship; the establishment of a democratic political system; republican control of the economy and of all decisions affecting the state of the natural environment; privatization of agriculture; and other measures to secure national autonomy.

In 1988 and 1989 there was a tug-of-war between the Balts and Moscow regarding most of the issues of contention. Because of the lack of traditions of rule by law in the Soviet Union and the unclear relationship between all-union and republican legislative bodies, the picture was far from clear. The main conclusion to be drawn, however, is that what mattered was not constitutions and laws, but political actions. The political struggle continued into 1990, when contested elections boosted the position of the separatists: the dismemberment of the Soviet Union seemed to come steadily closer.

THE HUNGARIAN MODEL

Hungary's national question is different from that of the other states in the Soviet bloc because it primarily concerns not conditions inside Hungary but the relations with the Hungarian minorities in neighbouring Czechoslovakia, Romania, the Soviet Union and Yugoslavia (the Hungarian minority in Austria does not seem to be a political issue). Because of Hungary's record of irredentism in the inter-war period and its status as a defeated former ally of Hitler's Germany, the question of the minorities abroad was taboo during the immediate post-war decades. During the 1970s and 1980s, however, in pace with the development of market relations and increasing political pluralism within the country, contrasted with the deplorable situation of the Hungarian minorities in Romania, Czechoslovakia and the Soviet Union, the national question increasingly became a cause of concern for Hungarian intellectuals. In particular, the two million Hungarians in Romania under Ceausescu were subject to oppression and persecutions so grave that both Hungarian and Western observers have found it valid to speak of a cultural genocide.[14]

The principal features in the revival of state nationalism in Hungary were the opening up of the country to massive Western influence following the introduction of market elements in the economy and the comparatively liberal central policy in the past two decades; a reappraisal of the history of the nation, combined with concern for the fate of ethnic brethren in Transylvania and Slovakia; and disquiet about environmental issues.

The new generation of communist leaders chose to meet the challenge and to endorse some of the basic demands of the opposition. Cases in point were official criticism in international human rights forums of Romania's oppressive policies against the Hungarian minority and the decision to postpone further work on the Nagymaros-Gabcikovo hydroelectric power project on the Danube. Independent political movements working for democracy, for environmental protection and for improvements in the position of the Hungarians in Romania and Slovakia gained momentum in May 1988 when János Kádár, the symbol of the communist past, was dismissed as party leader and a representative of the post-1956 generation, Karoly Grosz, took his place. During the following months, the party leadership was purged of conservatives at the same time as the independent groups flourished and new political parties were founded or formed anew. The triumph of a national Hungarian over a Soviet communist perspective on life and politics was symbolized by the solemn re-burial in Budapest of Imre

Nagy on 16 June 1989 and the official acknowledgement two weeks later that his execution in 1958 had been illegal. The symbolism of the event was underlined by the fact that Kádár died on the very same day as the verdict against Nagy was declared illegal, on 6 July 1989. In October, the ruling party was reformed and it promised democratic elections, which were held in April 1990, and in which the former communists fared poorly. In the new Hungarian republic, nationalism rather than socialism will be the basis for politics.

CONCLUSION: DOING AWAY WITH FIFTY YEARS OF HISTORY

The main effect of the resurgence of ethnic nationalism in the Soviet Union and Yugoslavia and of state nationalism in the other East European countries in the late 1980s was that the fifty years of history since the beginning of the Second World War were eliminated from the collective self-image of the peoples involved. On a symbolic level this was manifested by the revival of the pre-war national flags in the Baltic and Yugoslav republics and by the reintroduction of the state heraldic emblem in Hungary and the crown to the eagle in Poland. There was clearly an ideological need to create a past that would legitimate present political goals. What happened was reminiscent of both the 'ideology of silence' used by the Russians to eliminate the fact of Mongol rule from their historical chronicles,[15] and the attitude towards the 150 years of Turkish occupation in Hungary.[16] Now Soviet power and communism were treated in a similar way: as a parenthesis and as a reactionary interlude, without any intrinsic value for the future.

The different nationalists did not unite. However, there was an international dimension to the national challenge to the Soviet system. Everywhere in the bloc, politics were ethnicized, and there were mutual influences and chain reactions. The Baltic states and Hungary acted as catalysts. In the Soviet Union, attempts to establish popular fronts spread to Belorussia, the Ukraine, Moldavia, Transcaucasia and Central Asia. In Eastern Europe economic reforms and movement towards political pluralism and democracy in the name of the nation served as a positive reference for the opposition and for the reformists in the communist party.

The democratically inclined and market-oriented ethnic nationalisms in Croatia and Slovenia stand in sharp contrast to the one-party and centralist state nationalism in Serbia. Together the two lines bear witness to the fact that once communism's failure is recognized and history is evoked to fill the ideological void, nationalism is bound to become central in political life, regardless whether it is linked to democratic or to despotic strivings. The national challenges to communist rule in the late 1980s marked the beginning of the post-Soviet era in East European history. The Balts' rejection of the legacy of the Molotov–Ribbentrop pact of 1939 was a symbolic gesture which expressed the wish to obliterate the traces of fifty years of history and to win a second chance to fulfil the dreams of national self-determination.

NOTES

1. Joseph Rotschild, *Return to Diversity: A Political History of East Central Europe since World War II* (New York: Oxford University Press, 1989), pp. 222-3.
2. See Kristian Gerner, 'Nationalities and Minorities in the Soviet Union and Eastern Europe', *Nordic Journal of Soviet and East European Studies*, Vol. 4, No. 2 (1987), pp. 5-30, and the examples quoted there.
3. See Hélène Carrère d'Encausse, *L'Empire éclaté: La Révolte des Nations en U.R.S.S.* (Paris: Flammarion, 1978).
4. Lecture by Aleksei Klyuchevski, 'Nationalism in Yakutia', Seventh Sakharov Congress, organized by the Second World Center, Amsterdam, 11 May 1989.
5. Timothy Garton Ash, 'The Opposition', *The New York Review of Books*, 13 October 1988, p. 3.
6. Denys Hay, *Europe: The Emergence of an Idea* (Edinburgh: Edinburgh University Press, 1968), p. xxi; see also Z.A.B. Zeman, *Pursued by a Bear: The Making of Eastern Europe* (London: Chatto & Windus, 1989), pp. 20, 82-3.
7. Hayden White, *Tropics of Discourse: Essays in Cultural Criticism* (Baltimore: Johns Hopkins University Press, 1978), p. 22.
8. See Gerhard Simon, *Nationalismus und Nationalitätenpolitik in der Sowjetunion: Von der totalitären Diktatur zur nachstalinschen Gesellschaft* (Baden-Baden: Nomos, 1986).
9. See the admission by M. Gorbachev, 'O perestroike i kadrovoi politike partii', *Kommunist*, 1987, No. 3, pp. 28-9.
10. See further Stefan Hedlund, 'Exit, Voice and Loyalty — Soviet Style', *Coexistence*, Vol. 26 (1989), pp. 179-208.
11. *Svenska Dagbladet* (Stockholm) (TT-Reuter), 4 July 1989. For an analysis of the Soviet official attitude in 1981, see Kristian Gerner, *The Soviet Union and Central Europe in the Postwar Era: A Study in Precarious Security* (Aldershot: Gower, 1985), pp. 62-70.
12. Timothy Garton Ash, 'Revolution: the Springtime of Two Nations', *The New York Review of Books*, 15 June 1989, pp. 3-10.
13. Kerstin Nyström, 'The Serbs in Croatia: a Dual Identity', *Nordic Journal of Soviet and East European Studies*, Vol. 4, No. 3 (1987), pp. 31-52.
14. See, for example, 'A Declaration of the Ecumenical Council of Churches in Hungary' and Jean Guiscard, 'Transylvania through French Eyes', *The New*

Hungarian Quarterly, Vol. 30, No. 113 (1989), pp. 99, 108. The anti-Hungarian violence in Transylvania in March 1990 indicates that Romanian nationalism, although manipulated by the Ceausescu regime, had a firm basis in popular attitudes.

15. See Charles Halperin, *Russia and the Golden Horde* (Bloomington, IN: Indiana University Press, 1985).

16. See Jenö Szucs, *Nation und Geschichte: Studien* (Budapest: Corvina Kiadó, 1981), pp. 56-8.

10. The Changing Meaning of Security in Europe

Godfried van Benthem van den Bergh

One of the characters in the 'Peanuts' strip cartoon cannot do without his security blanket. Something similar can be said of the Soviet Union in the post-war period, after the Red Army rolled out a blanket over what came to be called Eastern Europe.[1] The way in which it was used led to the peculiar kind of hostile interdependence between West and East in Europe, which was institutionalized in NATO and the Warsaw Treaty Organization (WTO, or Warsaw Pact) and fortified by the global great power rivalry between the United States and the Soviet Union. Until it actually happened, no one believed that the Soviet Union would ever voluntarily let its security blanket go.

The liberation of Eastern Europe from Soviet domination, made possible by the 'new thinking' in the Soviet Union (and by its new policies), has ended the symmetrical relationship between the two alliances in Europe. That relationship was based on nuclear deterrence and on a clear demarcation of vital interests, as best expressed in the mutual recognition of the division of Germany into two member-states of hostile alliances. These foundations of European security have now been eroded. The meaning of security in Europe is changing fundamentally, even though there still exist elements of continuity, such as nuclear deterrence. The aim of this essay is to examine the implications of that transformation. However, this calls first for a description of the main elements of the old security structure.

SECURITY IN POST-WAR EUROPE

In the bipolar context, 'security' increasingly meant the stability of mutual expectations of peaceful conduct. Being secure implies that one has to fear neither an attack from an opponent (where there is only one, the security calculus is relatively simple) nor a crisis so serious that it may run out of control. The inherent uncertainty of international politics implies that security can never be absolute. In Europe, however, it was guaranteed fairly well or to a high degree, depending on the criteria of assessment. But even though differences of opinion remained, as manifested clearly enough during the INF debate, they ranged with but few exceptions on a narrow band at the right end of the insecurity–security continuum. Political arguments became more and more dominant, even though they often took the guise of military and strategic ones (such as 'coupling'). Europe in the age of nuclear weapons and bipolarity was in face quite safe. The basis of European security had but one serious weak spot: the Warsaw Pact was based on force and oppression, on a blanket that began to rot away. It can also be said that European security was procured at the expense of the peoples of the East. Still, it was difficult to deny that the prevention of nuclear war should have been (and remains) the first priority.

European security is thus based on nuclear deterrence. But what exactly does that mean? In the public discussion about the requirements of deterrence, the term is usually defined as a military posture sufficient to deter the opponent from an attack under all conceivable circumstances. It is thus seen as one-sided, although mutual, in the sense that both the opponents maintain such postures and deter each other. Notions such as limited nuclear options, flexible response, escalation dominance and protracted nuclear war capabilities are all part of this universe of discourse. In terms of actual conduct, however, it is the danger of nuclear war, as the possible result of the unintended interweaving of moves and counter-moves by the opposing parties, that deters them both. The rivals can never be certain that a military confrontation between them can be kept under control. There is always present a risk of escalation, even in a low-key political crisis turning serious. Given the possible and likely destructive consequences of a nuclear war (mutual assured destruction, or MAD), there can no longer be any reasonable political or military goal for which it is worth taking the risk of initiating a serious crisis. The opposing sides are no longer deterred by each other but by a common danger, a shared risk. It is therefore more realistic to speak of common deterrence than of mutual deterrence.[2]

If that is so, it also means that conventional weapons became 'nuclearized' and have lost their specific character. Conventional military postures were therefore left with but one important function: to ensure the possibility of escalation. Conventional superiority or strategies for conventional war no longer possess any strategic meaning — only the meaning of a political symbol that has still been attributed to them. That this is the case has become quite clear following the changes within the Soviet Union.

Although a necessary condition, common nuclear deterrence was not the only pillar of stability in Europe, a position that has not changed. Their political base was quite different, yet the existence of the two alliances made possible a clear delimitation of vital interests. They also fulfilled pacifying functions, each in its own domain.[3] The other side of the coin was, again, that the rivals — and in this case the Soviet Union in particular benefited — did not have to fear a military response from their opponent if they intervened in the domestic affairs of one of their allies (or vassal states). But the alliances as such were a source of stability. That was strengthened even more by arms control and confidence-building agreements and negotiations, especially in the context of the CSCE (or Helsinki) process.

The only obstacle to stabilizing such security arrangements even further was, on both sides, the pre-nuclear approach to military strategy and conventional weapons. Because the Soviet Union maintained a military posture geared to an offensive strategy, intending to fight outside its own borders in the event of war, its conventional superiority was seen by NATO as a threat.[4] In the same way, new weapons technology coupled with designs such as SDI (President Reagan's Strategic Defense Initiative, popularly known as 'Star Wars') and FOFA (Follow-On Force Attack strategy) were considered a threat by the Soviet Union. But such thinking in terms of scenarios for pre-nuclear war could not really undermine the stability that was assured by the mutual expectations of peaceful conduct engendered by common deterrence and détente in Europe. Before the unexpected events of 1989 did away with the post-war order, therefore, it was not at all far-fetched to envisage as both desirable and possible a gradual rapprochement between the alliances, and their transformation into politically more symmetrical security communities with much smaller military postures, through both conventional and nuclear arms control, and tied together by agreements for both crisis prevention and crisis management. To think in terms of security communities implies that the security function is no longer fulfilled by the individual members of an alliance but by the community as such, led by a great power.[5] This implies that military conflicts between the members of the community have been excluded, even if they have not become unthinkable. But such symmetry would have been possible only through a far-reaching democratization of the Warsaw Pact. Again, that was the fundamental weakness of what appeared in all other respects to be a realistic conception. Now that the liberation of Eastern Europe from Soviet domination has unexpectedly come about, this view of the future was shown to have been less realistic than it appeared. The bipolar security structure is quickly disappearing and the security conceptions attached to it have to change.

THE CHANGING MEANING OF THREAT AND INSECURITY IN EUROPE

Insecurity is usually perceived in terms of threat. In international politics a threat cannot be defined through an estimate of the opponent's likely conduct: it has to be determined by the security dilemma which states face because of the anarchical nature of their relations.[6] Unlike politics within states, relations between states are not regulated by an authority that through its monopoly of the means of violence can force them to settle their conflicts peacefully. States can therefore never be certain that they will not be attacked or forced to submit to the will of another state, unless they possess the means to defend themselves or have powerful allies. In that perspective, a nation cannot derive the requirements for its security simply by interpreting the present intentions of the opponent: they have to be based also on the development of the nation's own capabilities. This becomes a security dilemma, because a nation's own capabilities will be the basis of the opponent's assessment of the level of threat. That can lead to an arms race and to decreasing security for both parties, as the danger of the unintended escalation of crises and military clashes will grow. Arms control then becomes necessary for stabilizing the military postures of the rival powers.[7]

The security dilemma also forces opponents to define the threat which they face in terms of worst-case scenarios. In the bipolar structure the threat was seen as a surprise attack.[8] Security could be obtained only through possessing the ability to resist such an attack successfully, which required among other things the matching of all the opponent's weapon systems, both current and future. This led to a preoccupation with the military balance and the development of military technology, with military hardware and its role in war scenarios. It was not sufficiently understood that common deterrence and the absolute character of the nuclear balance had done away with the security dilemma.[9] Anything beyond the 'assured destruction' level of the nuclear arsenals (although that can be defined in different ways) was meaningless.

Not only that, but common deterrence did away with any incentive to attack, and even with an incentive to take a political or military initiative that could conceivably risk escalating into nuclear war. But until recently, pre-nuclear conceptions of the meaning of military power remained politically important and continued to determine strategies and to justify large conventional and nuclear capabilities.

What do these considerations imply for the future? The Soviet Union, either within its present borders or even after the secession of all its non-Slavic parts, is likely to remain a great power.[10] That the Soviet Union will fall apart is far from certain. Even the Baltic states, most recently incorporated, may eventually settle for a separate autonomous status within the union rather than full independence. The Soviet Union will probably remain the only great power in Europe, unless the European Community develops into a federal state, which now appears to have become even more unlikely than it already was. But for the continuation of a nuclear balance in Europe, the other European states will remain confronted with uncertairty and therefore with a security dilemma. A 'common European home' thus cannot remain stable and durably peaceful without common deterrence. But that can be maintained with much smaller nuclear arsenals and greatly diminished conventional military postures. Without common deterrence, it is impossible to exclude conventional arms races and even recourse to biological and chemical weapons.

What, then, about the worst case of the surprise attack? The Pentagon has already withdrawn its airborne nuclear war command. The warning time of an impending Soviet attack is now estimated at forty days, which removes the spectre of a genuine surprise attack. That notion was in any case based on the purported Soviet capacity to pursue an offensive strategy, which can no longer be workable given that Eastern Europe has been lost for that purpose; whether it ever was a real option is doubtful. Gorbachev has already replaced traditional Soviet strategy with the criterion of reasonable sufficiency for territorial defence.

If the threat that existed has now been removed, what is the worst case now? What is the main threat to European security in the future?

It is frequently argued that there exists a real possibility of a reaction against Gorbachev's reform policies in the form of an alliance between Russian nationalists, party conservatives and the military. Although at the moment this seems far-fetched, it can still be asked whether such a regime would turn again to expansionist policies and a military build-up. That does not appear at all probable. Retrenchment is much more likely, as such a regime would either have to keep the Soviet Union together in the face of continuing separatist pressures (and it seems quite likely that terrorist movements will build up in Azerbaijan), or reorganize what remained of the union after a number of secessions. Neither could a regime ruled by an alliance between conservatives and Russian nationalists make it rain pennies from heaven: it would therefore have to cope with a population even more dissatisfied, frustrated and apathetic than under Gorbachev. It would thus have to be an inward-looking dictatorship, although it might still remain concerned with preserving the Soviet Union's great power role. However, that could be achieved only by continuing the now evolving pattern of relationships with the West and by remaining 'respectable'. Arms control would become more difficult and its pace slower; but as long as the military establishment was involved in such a regime, common deterrence would hold because the Soviet military are well aware of the danger of nuclear war and the risks of escalation. The Soviet leadership would then also have to take into account the fact that Eastern Europe can no longer be considered as its own military and strategic preserve in which it can freely intervene without provoking a reaction from the West. Politically the Berlin Wall is no longer there, borders have become more or less open again, and most Soviet troops will be withdrawn in the near future. Expansionism to reconquer what has just been lost would be precluded by common deterrence. Adverse political developments in the Soviet Union therefore do not justify continuation of the perception of the 'threat' in the old form. The fear that such a regime will raise in the rest of Europe and the United States will be more dangerous than its real potential will justify: from the perspective of military strategy, it is much less of a danger than is often asserted.

Worst-case scenarios thus cannot be derived from a return to the past, but from the increasing difficulty of containing unintended crises arising from conflicts either between or within states, or from a combination of these.[11] The liberation of Eastern Europe not only makes the unification of the Federal Republic of Germany (FRG) and the German Democratic Republic (GDR) a certainty, but it could also revive territorial claims and ethnic nationalism and rivalries. Combined with the difficulties of attaining rapid economic reform and development, these may lead to and be used by right-wing populist regimes developing conflict-prone foreign policies. If such regimes are no longer part of an alliance — as is quite possible given the disintegration of the Warsaw Pact — they might not be restrained by common deterrence either.

That, then, seems to be the worst case, and it could develop in the future from events that are at present impossible to foresee. Security in Europe will require the containment of nationalism instead of the containment of the Soviet Union and communism. The unification of a democratic Germany, embedded in the EC and NATO, will be far less threatening than frustrated nationalism of the right-wing *Republikaner* kind in both the FRG and the GDR. What a united Germany in fact can and will do is less dangerous than the fear which it inspires, since that leads to patronizing attitudes and statements that make Germans feel discriminated against. Hence, a worst-case scenario cannot be derived from Germany unity as such, but rather from spiralling nationalism.

A large-scale war in Europe does not in any case seem likely, and can be prevented by the security arrangements to be discussed below. But local or civil-military confrontations or wars cannot be excluded. New political instabilities may also lead to political and economic disintegration — posing such problems as how to accommodate large numbers of either refugees or migrants (or both) — rather than to increasing cooperation and supranationalism.

Security will therefore have to be more broadly defined than in military-strategic terms. It will have to include not only international political and economic relations, but also domestic political and economic developments. Nationalist movements thrive on both collective humiliation and widespread personal economic insecurity. Security will have therefore to include the development of viable political and economic institutions to regulate and shape the interdependence among all European states. There will also have to be continuity in terms of the role of the great powers, NATO (possibly modified), and a transformed Warsaw Pact in maintaining common deterrence and in conflict management.

In the future, the nature of interdependency, especially the degree of asymmetry (a 'new colonialism'), power balancing and institutional arrangements may well become more important than the role of military power. But such a transformation of security arrangements will be a precarious process.

CHANGING SECURITY ARRANGEMENTS

The uncertainties about the future of Europe are so great that specific scenarios are already obsolete when they are published. The only approach possible is to attempt to itemize the relevant aspects of the problem of European security in the future.[12] I shall discuss the following aspects: military alliances, capabilities and strategies; new balancing considerations; economic and ecological interdependencies; and institutional arrangements. Some overlap among the different sections cannot be avoided.

Military alliances, capabilities and strategies

The pace of events in the past year or so has been so fast that there is so far no satisfactory analysis available of what has made them possible. One interpretation of conventional wisdom holds that a combination of Western determination and economic necessity forced Gorbachev to retreat and accommodate. But the Soviet economy was in decline or stagnation for quite some time without weakening the competitiveness of Soviet military power. It was in fact argued in the West that the Soviet Union's military power was still increasing.[13] Even the technological gap between the rival powers was not becoming greater. It can thus be argued that Gorbachev acted as much out of choice as of necessity. Of course, the Soviet economic system worked very badly and frustrated the aspirations of the majority of the Soviet population; but that had already been the case for many years. The question, then, is how Gorbachev could combine domestic reforms with such a complete turnabout in Soviet foreign and defence policy instead of simply promoting détente within the existing bipolar structure. Would that not just as well have provided him with the favourable conditions he needed for economic reforms?

Gorbachev's motives have never been revealed, but one necessary condition for his decisions is clear enough. If the military-strategic equation were still what it had been in pre-nuclear times, a great power like the Soviet Union, with a hostile alliance on its borders (not to mention China as a rival on the other side) would necessarily have continued to feel acutely threatened. Only the expectation of peaceful relations induced by common deterrence can explain the relaxed manner in which Gorbachev gave up the traditional Soviet strategy and posture and the country's control over Eastern Europe.[14] Until recently that was generally considered to be the indispensable and immutable sphere of influence of a great power engaged in a struggle for dominance with its rival, the United States.

Just as common deterrence made possible the new foreign policy of the Soviet Union and the liberation of Eastern Europe, it will remain a necessary guarantee for the peaceful management of the drastic political and economic transformations still to be expected. A return to pre-nuclear conditions could again give military power the same function that it had before the Second World War. The security dilemma would be reinstated and expectations of war revived. This leads to the inescapable conclusion that the security of Europe in the future demands that the basis for common nuclear deterrence should be preserved. What does this imply?

At the moment, the basis for such deterrence comprises the American and Soviet nuclear arsenals, to which the British and French capabilities are added. Nuclear weapons not only fulfil the function of preventing war, but are also integrated in war-waging strategies such as that of flexible response (by compensating for conventional inferiority; allowing coupling; facilitating escalation dominance, and so forth). If the logic of common deterrence is accepted, that second function is (and in fact already was) no longer necessary. Now that the worst case of a consciously planned Soviet attack has manifestly disappeared, that is surely the case. What will be needed in future, therefore, is a guarantee both for peaceful conduct in general, and for preventing the spread of local or civil wars. To keep intact the danger of escalation to nuclear war requires the preservation of only a relatively small number of invulnerable nuclear weapons. Their range should not be too small, so as to avoid making potential targets too geographically specific, as they are at present. A considerable part of the current nuclear arsenals of both alliances fails to fulfil this condition. A second condition would be that the risk of escalation to *general* nuclear war must be maintained. That rules out the French and British nuclear forces, whether separately or in combination, as the basis of common deterrence. American nuclear weapons in the context of NATO must remain in Europe. A European nuclear force is not an attractive alternative, since it would imply German participation and aggravate the problem of dealing with a unified FRG and GDR. It is also impossible so long as a federal European state has not been formed, a development that is extremely unlikely in the foreseeable future, given the difficulties even of establishing a monetary union and the persistent rivalry among the former great powers in Europe.

Until very recently it remained Soviet policy to advocate the abolition of nuclear weapons, and thus to denuclearize Europe.[15] That would, of course, have meant military superiority for the Soviet Union in Europe, at least in numerical terms. However, in a speech before the European parliament in June 1989, Gorbachev declared that the Soviet Union was prepared to have the two alliances examine and perhaps agree on the possibility of a minimal nuclear deterrent capability. That would indeed be the best manner in which to ensure the preservation of common deterrence as a political tool, rather than as part of a one-sided deterrent capability. Negotiated minimal nuclear postures for common deterrence will also be the only way of ensuring the legitimacy of nuclear weapons in public opinion. That is all the more urgent because unilateral modernization of land-based nuclear weapons in Western Europe has become impossible in the light of the new position of Germany and the public mood. The alternative could be stand-off weapons on airplanes or cruise missiles on ships; but these, if unilaterally introduced within the framework of NATO, would come uncomfortably close to infringing the INF treaty, if not constituting an actual infringement of it, and would also be unacceptable to public opinion.

Negotiated common deterrence will therefore be the best way to preserve the war-prevention and political stabilization functions of nuclear weapons, while at the same time reducing the risk of an unintended nuclear war. It will also guarantee the continued involvement of the United States in Europe's new security arrangements. That will then be possible at greatly reduced cost, as neither a minimal nuclear posture nor common deterrence as such require large numbers of American troops. A continued US presence in Europe will thereby become much easier to maintain. The United States has re-emphasized that it will remain involved in guaranteeing European security. It also wants closer economic ties with the EC, now that Japan is seen as the United States' strongest economic rival. It appears also that America's turn towards the Pacific rim is less definite than was assumed a few years ago. Partly because of the creation of the Single European Market in 1992, partly for its real economic achievements and increasing competitiveness, Europe has once again become more attractive for the United States. Neither does it wish to be left out of the new opportunities that the liberation of Eastern Europe may present. Finally, NATO remains politically important for the United States, since it provides it with the leadership role needed for its own survival as a great power.

Commonly agreed common deterrence can therefore survive. It will have to be accompanied by a reassessment of current strategies. The Soviet Union has already engaged in such a reassessment, although it is not yet clear what its defensive strategy will mean in terms of capabilities.[16] What is clear, however, is that the strategy of flexible response, no matter what its meaning may have been, has become obsolete with the disappearance of the kind of threat towards which it was directed. In fact, the most important purpose of conventional military postures already was to assure the risk of escalation. It should now be recognized that it no longer makes sense to prepare for a large-scale conventional war as one of the possible steps on the escalation ladder.

It is difficult to indicate precisely the required level of conventional military capability, since this will be assessed according to perceptions of the opponent's capabilities. However, it goes without saying that the liberation of Eastern Europe has made forward defence obsolete. So what might replace it?

The most reasonable criterion for a new strategy and conventional posture — and one that could be unilaterally applied — would be the capacity to put up meaningful resistance, sufficient to avoid being overrun immediately. That would not necessitate nuclear escalation, but would leave open that possibility, thus balancing the requirements of deterrence and crisis- or confrontation-management. This criterion will demand restructuring of conventional forces in the direction of smaller and more mobile units, armed with lighter and perhaps more advanced weapons. Such a development would also make such units more suitable for peace-keeping operations, either within Europe or outside. The difficult question remains whether and to what extent such a development would be compatible with military integration in NATO.

Such a transformation of NATO strategy and posture would make it possible to continue with conventional disarmament after the Conventional Forces in Europe (CFE) negotiations have been successfully concluded. Those negotiations, however, may well be bypassed by the rapid withdrawal of Soviet troops demanded by non-communist governments in Eastern Europe. Nevertheless, conventional disarmament negotiations remain politically important, not least for maintaining the cohesion of NATO. A scramble for arms reduction is already beginning; but to proceed further, conventional disarmament must be tied to an agreement about the nuclear capabilities guaranteeing common deterrence.

The greatest difficulty is how to reconcile the symmetrical relationship needed for common deterrence with the inescapable asymmetry between Western and Eastern institutions resulting from the liberation of Eastern Europe. With respect to troop withdrawals, symmetry is impossible as it would seriously undermine the cohesion of NATO to no good purpose. It is thus not even in the interests of the Soviet Union. Measures and relations aimed at symmetry belong to the disappearing bipolar structure. New criteria, such as 'reasonable sufficiency' or 'capacity for meaningful resistance', must now be specified.

This will all take time. That, however, has one important advantage: it can facilitate the reorientation of military establishments and the conversion of arms production.[17] Military establishments have a professional propensity to think in terms of pre-nuclear worst-case scenarios. That is understandable, because in pre-nuclear times the security dilemma did require worst-case thinking. It belongs in a sense to the professional code of the military, which will not easily accept that there can no longer be any need for the kind of overall strategy that guided their efforts in the past. Reorientation of the role of the military will be painful, even though the preservation of common deterrence and new tasks such as verification, peace keeping, crisis prevention and crisis management are challenging enough. Nevertheless, too rapid and drastic changes in security arrangements may have adverse results: they may lead to conservative populism, to military involvement in politics (especially in the Soviet Union), and to the spread of unnecessary fears among the population. The function of alliances and military capabilities will in any case remain crucial for preserving common deterrence and mutual expectations of peaceful conduct.

New kinds of power balancing

After 1945 the balance of power in Europe was primarily determined by the rivalry between the great powers. One result of the Second World War was to make Europe subject to an externally imposed bipolar order. The European great powers had been pushed back to a second-rank position. They found some compensation for that humiliating decline in the process of European integration, but because of its slow progress, the transfer of their own nationalism to 'Europe' had to remain embryonic. The three former great powers — Britain, France and Germany — continued to engage in competition for leadership of the EC and for privileged relations with the United States. Power rivalries and power balancing have thus never been absent from Europe, although their nature and form have changed and will do so even more in the future. The European balance can no longer be seen as bipolar and based primarily on the two 'bloc' organizations and on military and strategic considerations. The balance will become — in fact, it already is

— a combination of bipolar and multipolar relations. As such, it will probably acquire two new components: a unified Germany, and five or more very different 'East European' states, each of which has to find its own political form and identity.

As for the development of relations between the FRG and the GDR, full unification and integration will take a little time. However, the pressures for unity — including, notably, the consequences of the large number of GDR citizens migrating westwards — are such that it is necessary to examine the likely consequences, and one particular aspect of unification must be discussed. Gorbachev has accepted that unification cannot be prevented; but it is clear that the Soviet Union will accept with complete equanimity the total merging of the GDR into the FRG, with the implication of its incorporation into the EC and NATO through the simple enlargement of a member-state. In its former security perspective, that was inconceivable. But NATO membership itself will change in meaning, as its military functions becomes subordinate to its political role, and its strategy and posture are transformed. Now that the Soviet Union has lost its control over Eastern Europe, it can hope to retain some influence only if the Warsaw Pact, too, is transformed into a new political and economic, rather than military, organization, on the basis of voluntary participation by sovereign states. A unified Germany could come in as the power to be balanced by the Soviet Union and provide a role for such an organization. It should also be borne in mind that 'neutrality' (like demilitarization or Finlandization) has lost the meaning it had in the bipolar structure. A neutral Germany means only that it could go it alone, which would not be an attractive prospect for anyone, including Germany itself.

Power balancing itself also is not what it used to be in pre-nuclear times. The unification of Germany under Bismarck upset the power balance in Europe to such an extent that it can even be said to have led to the First World War. There is, of course, no reason to expect a repeat of that: the FRG is solidly democratic and has no great power ambitions, seeing its role within the context of the EC and NATO. Yet it is already the largest economic power within the EC, and the combination of the economic potential of the FRG and the GDR will boost Germany's weight, although without placing it in control of the EC, where its power can be balanced by changing coalitions of other member-states. However, that economic power will be both welcomed and feared in Eastern Europe, which will again find itself in between Germany and the Soviet Union, still frequently perceived as

Russia. Both those powers have in the past incorporated portions of Eastern European countries' territory, and border issues remain extremely sensitive, particularly for Poland. For that reason, the concept of 'reunification' has already been forsworn by both German governments, since the prefix 're' carries an association of the borders of 1937. Power balancing therefore remains important, if only for psychological reasons.

The freely elected governments of the Eastern European states will undoubtedly regard the preservation of the two 'blocs' as anathema, yet from a power-balancing perspective they have a clear interest in the continued involvement of the United States in Europe and in the political and military integration of Germany into NATO. For that reason they may also come to see it in their interest to preserve an institutional relationship with the Soviet Union. They will never consent to having Soviet troops on their territory again once these have been withdrawn, and they will also wish to reconstitute their complete sovereignty. Nevertheless, the maintenance of friendly relations and a reasonable degree of mutual trust with the Soviet Union could be necessary for them, as it was for Finland during the bipolar period. From the classical perspective of great power rivalry, it can be argued that the Soviet Union has 'lost' Eastern Europe, a valuable asset. To accept Gorbachev's decisions requires an understanding of the changed meaning of military power in the nuclear age: not everyone in the Soviet Union may share that understanding.

In any case, it will not be in any European state's interest to deny the Soviet Union a leading role in an 'Eastern' organization, even though that might remain largely symbolic. An isolated great power on the border of a greater Europe, excluded from the European home for which it pleaded, would feel humiliated and possibly revengeful. Revanchist noises coming from the Soviet Union would be dangerous, as they could create fear and perhaps a rush to new defensive measures in the rest of Europe. In any new European security arrangement, therefore, there should remain room for a leading role for the Soviet Union, in order to preserve both common deterrence and political cooperation. Such a policy conforms to the traditional rule of balance of power politics, that one should help to rebuild a defeated opponent rather than destroy him completely. After the First World War that rule was broken, which greatly facilitated the rise of national socialism.

Other balancing considerations also call for a new kind of cooperative relations between Eastern Europe and the Soviet Union — perhaps a transformed Comecon. The Eastern European states will be unable to raise their economies quickly to match Western Europe, yet they will not wish to become economic colonies of the West, even though they will undoubtedly need at least a special relationship with the EC. Here, too, relations with the Soviet Union may come to have a balancing function, especially after the unification of Germany. Justified or not, and despite whatever assurances Germany may give, fears may well be raised about the durability of existing borders, something an alliance of 'sovereign states' with the Soviet Union might help to alleviate.

Cooperation among the Eastern European countries themselves — perhaps including Yugoslavia, but probably not now the GDR, given how its relations with the FRG are developing — may also become necessary, for economic reasons and for purposes of maintaining the balance. If not, they will each not only have to face the overwhelming economic power of the West, but also be forced to compete with one another for favourable monetary, trade and investment conditions and opportunities. Their economic situation, despite considerable differences among them, appears to be so weak that if they are not stimulated to cooperate — as Western Europe was at the time of the Marshall Plan — they will not be able to move towards the kind of economic self-reliance that their future political stability (and eventual membership of the EC) requires. Whether this will remain compatible with membership of a revamped Comecon is uncertain.

It is clear that the disappearance of the post-war bipolar structure and the declining importance of military power, so long as common deterrence is preserved, render much more complex the task of power balancing. Political leadership, economic power and overlapping institutional arrangements now become more diversified balancing tools. Moreover, it is also clear that the concept of 'balance of power' in its pre-nuclear meaning is inappropriate, because common deterrence has replaced it (and has been more successful as a policy), and power balancing now takes place within a much tighter network of international and supranational institutions.

Economic and ecological interdependencies

Economic interdependencies in themselves can contribute equally to peace and to war.[18] They may lead to cooperation between states to deal with common interests, but they may also lead to bitter rivalry. In the past, late industrializing countries such as Germany, Japan and Italy developed fierce nationalism to mobilize and discipline their populations. For a brief period national communism fulfilled the same function.

In the recent past, parliamentary democracies have been quite successful both in their economic performance and in the way they deal with international economic interdependencies. Although the cold war and the development of NATO as a security community was at first a favourable, if not indispensable, condition, the more or less supranational economic integration of Europe acquired its own dynamic. Recently the sudden imminence of German unification has led to attempts to speed up the development of the EC — through such proposals as moves to monetary union, strengthening the powers of the European parliament, and reinforcing European political cooperation — as means of more firmly binding Germany into a European framework. This may well be counter-productive, since it indicates a lack of trust in Germany's political loyalties. Moreover, it fails to take into account the strength of Germany's existing economic, cultural and political interdependencies with the EC — and with NATO, for that matter.

It may be submitted that the development of the EC is a function of the development of stronger and more intensive interdependencies, rather than the other way round. The ideology of European federalism may inspire plans for moving forward with 'Europe' (hitherto always identified with Western Europe), but usually to little avail. The stagnation of the 1970s and early 1980s could not have been overcome without the fight against the declining competitive position of Western Europe *vis-à-vis* Japan and the United States. Common policies can cement the members of the EC together even more tightly. However, both common policies and the original political finality of the EC will now have to take into account the political position and the economic condition of the East European states, and to some extent of the Soviet Union. The East European economies are still more dependent upon the Soviet Union and one another than on Western Europe. There is no sound reason not to admit them eventually to full membership of the EC, but the necessary reorientation of their economies will take time. The main task before the EC is therefore to help them in such a manner that their dependence on the EC does not become one-sided, probably by actively stimulating institutional cooperation among them, and perhaps by reorienting the CMEA. As their full membership of the EC will be impossible for quite some time and their economic development probably slower than expected, disappointment with the West is not unlikely, nor is reaction in the form of authoritarian nationalism. A concern with the nature of the development of interdependencies is therefore at least as important as new institutional arrangements.

As to ecological interdependencies, their importance and trans-European nature has been made even clearer by the shock of Chernobyl than by the effects of acid rain. The Soviet Union and Eastern Europe also lag behind in environmental policies, although their urgency is now recognized by populations and governments alike. Although more adequate national policies will remain crucial, the European (and global) level of legislation and policy making will become more and more important. With respect to the ecological issue, there seems to be no reason not to start as soon as possible with the creation of a European agency for environmental protection, which would include all the European states participating in the CSCE; the US and Canada could be invited to attend as observers. Ecological interdependencies of their very nature lend themselves to regulation and coordination by a greater European organization. The urgency of dealing more adequately with ecological interdependencies also bears security implications, since such a European agency could develop stronger ties between its member-states.

Institutional arrangements

Institutions are often seen as ends in themselves. The model of the federal state is then projected on the international arena, as in pleas for a united Europe or for world government by the United Nations. Yet in seeking new institutional arrangements for handling relations within Europe, a range of issues arise. For one thing, the boundaries of 'Europe' are uncertain: does it include Turkey? And what about Siberia — an exceptionally significant appendage of European Russia? Yet for political, economic, ecological and security reasons, the Soviet Union has to be seen as part of Europe, and this must be reflected in any plans for security arrangements for greater Europe. The Soviet concept of a common European home, vague though it remains, is an example of such thinking, as are proposals for the complete dissolution of the two 'blocs' and their replacement by a pan-European security organization. As noted above, such proposals presuppose the development of a whole of Europe into a security community, as a group of states in which war has become impossible and inconceivable. It seems very difficult to argue that this can indeed be the case in the short term. The Soviet Union will remain a great power in the foreseeable future; Germany may become one; local or civil wars may erupt.

In all of this, we must bear in mind that new institutions cannot rely on magic: they must have a basis in real interdependencies and security problems. For that reason, an all-embracing European security organization will not be feasible: common deterrence will have to remain.

This conclusion implies that West European federalism, and even the search for a separate West European defence identity, should be seen as relics of the past. They will hinder rather than help the search for new security arrangements. It is now more than ever necessary to overcome nationalism, including its projection on to larger entities such as (Western) Europe. That does not imply abandoning the further development of the EC into a supranational organization with common social, economic and monetary policies. It does mean, however, that the desirability of such a development will also have to be regarded in the light of its consequences for security and for Eastern Europe.

Nevertheless, Western organizations such as NATO and the EC will continue to have perhaps the most important security functions in Europe, as argued above. The involvement of the US will remain necessary, in order to preserve common deterrence and fulfil balancing functions, for Eastern Europe as well. The strong and continuing need for NATO implies that it is not clear why the new situation should call for reinforcing the Western European Union, as has been suggested. NATO should continue to be the main political security organization in the West, even though its military strategy and posture will have to be transformed. If that is done, there is no need for Europe to take over when a sizeable number of US troops are withdrawn. European political cooperation in the framework of the EC will be sufficient to supplement the role of NATO, if this is needed.

The EC's main security function is to stimulate the economic development of Eastern Europe in such a manner that the governments elected in 1990 will not fail, and a nationalist backlash can be prevented. Function must take precedence over form — a rule that must be applied also to relations between the EC and the Soviet Union. Soviet economic development is also in Western Europe's security interests. Relations between the Soviet Union and the EC are also therefore extremely important, particularly facilitating the continued involvement of West European firms now that Gorbachev faces increasing domestic problems.

For the East, some patching will be necessary in order to preserve simultaneously some kind of leadership role for the Soviet Union and the full sovereignty of the liberated states. The Warsaw Pact and Comecon can only disintegrate further. There is little point in lamenting that development at this time on grounds of stability: one cannot have it both ways. Although they might have been a good thing — and, indeed, there may still be some point in making the attempt — institutional discussions between the two alliances on strategy, military postures and crisis management now seem to have little prospect of real impact for much longer. To institutionalize such discussions would give the Warsaw Pact legitimacy as a durable institution, which would be unacceptable for the East European states. Nevertheless, as noted above, provided that the Soviet Union itself does not collapse, considerations of balancing may again give the alliance opportunities to play an economic and political role.

The problem of how to include the Soviet Union in new security arrangements is thus a vexed one. The Soviet Union itself has indicated that it wants to speed up and use the CSCE process for this purpose. Would it be possible to discuss the preservation of common deterrence in such a forum? That is possible, but only in the form of a special committee comprising all involved parties. Could strategies and military postures be discussed? It discussions between the two alliances are excluded, a solution could be either to extend the CFE negotiations, which are formally conducted between individual states, to include other subjects, or to institute a European forum for discussing strategies and military postures on the basis of individual membership. Negotiations could then be conducted in *ad hoc* committees of that forum.

Could CSCE develop a crisis-prevention and crisis-management council, which could eventually become a form of collective security organization? The first phase of this suggestion seems possible, but the second runs up against the same reasons for the maintenance of common deterrence. Crisis prevention and crisis management are attractive concepts, but what can their content be? Crisis prevention is best served by common deterrence; and once the nuclear level has been reached, crisis management becomes a 'dangerous illusion'.[19] In the earlier phases in the development of a crisis, conflicts (in which crises originate) are prevented or mitigated in the first place through the appropriate management of interdependencies, both international and domestic (such as the position of national minorities within the nation). The EC, a European Environmental Agency, and East European economic cooperation have a more important role in this respect than a pan-European crisis council would have.

The containment of crises may be a different matter. If a local or civil conflict leads to a crisis, which means that it might develop into a military confrontation, European security demands that the parties should be lured or forced into negotiations, or that peace-keeping operations might become necessary. Could the CSCE fulfil such a role, without further institutionalization in the form of, say, a permanent European crisis council? In fact, an extension of CSCE might be useful, not so much for actual crisis management as for dealing with long-term security problems and threats.

But why should European security remain in the hands of Europeans alone? If in the coming years an armed conflict were to break out over, for example, the position of any or several national minorities in Eastern Europe, would anyone take the risk of intervening? The Soviet Union would certainly not, nor would NATO. Both would fear the that other side would find such intervention unacceptable — quite apart from the danger that such intervention would fail and thereby damage their prestige. Would joint intervention be feasible? Possibly: but in that case would the great powers not prefer the added legitimacy of operating through the Security Council of the United Nations? Europeans still tend to see Europe as a continent unlike any other; but after the burial of the bipolar structure, Europe may become — if satisfactory new security arrangements are not developed — as messy a continent as the others. There is in any case no reason not to consider the functions that a global peace-keeping regime might have for European security. Cyprus serves as a precedent for this. Such a peace-keeping regime must be based on generalized cooperation in the UN expressly for that purpose. A problem here, however, is the composition of the Security Council, which reflects the power distribution at the end of the Second World War. Nevertheless, cooperation between the great powers in a global peace-keeping regime might bolster their leadership role in global politics, which has been damaged by various unilateral interventions.

CONCLUSION

In the foreseeable future, neither economic nor security interdependencies can be regulated by one supreme European organization. The new general European security system such as is often proposed appears to be little more than a refuge from the complexity of present changes. Again, since function must come before form, what is required is a careful analysis of the interconnections between the functions that various institutions can fulfil. Europe remains best served by a complex network of institutions, overlapping one another in both membership and function.[20]

This listing of the various implications of the changing meaning of

security in Europe can only be provisional. Its aim has been to contribute to
the development of a framework for analysis that can withstand the rapid
course of events, even though time may prove the substance of specific parts
of the analysis and recommendations to be wrong or obsolete. It is unreal to
hope for an orientation as firm as what was possible during the bipolar
security order, but a new orientation based on a new perspective is surely
needed.

No matter how uncertain — and perhaps unstable — the future of Europe
will prove to be, it will no longer be based on the oppression of one part of
it. New security arrangements can now be built on democratic decisions and
voluntary participation. That may ultimately give them an even greater
stability.

NOTES

1. Although historically it would be more accurate to refer to Central Europe and
   the Balkans, considerations of the balance of power will continue to justify
   references to Poland, Czechoslovakia, Hungary, Romania and Bulgaria as
   Eastern Europe; for similar reasons, East Germany (the GDR) no longer
   belongs to that region.
2. For further analysis of the development and nature of common deterrence as a
   property of the nuclear age, see G. van Benthem van den Bergh, *The Taming
   of the Great Powers: Nuclear Weapons and Global Integration* (forthcoming).
3. Joseph Joffe, 'Europe's American Pacifier', *Foreign Policy*, No. 54 (Spring
   1984), pp. 64-82; Karen Dawisha, *Eastern Europe, Gorbachev and Reform*
   (Cambridge: Cambridge University Press, 1987).
4. On the development of Soviet military strategy, see David Holloway, *The
   Soviet Union and the Arms Race* (New Haven, CT, and London: Yale
   University Press, 1983), and Michael MccGwire, *Military Objectives in Soviet
   Foreign Policy* (Washington, DC: Brookings, 1987).
5. The term 'security community' was introduced by Karl W. Deutsch in his *Political
   Community at the International Level: Problems of Definition and Measure-
   ment* (Garden City, NY: Doubleday, 1954). It is used here somewhat differently.
6. The idea of a security dilemma goes back to Hobbes; it was more precisely
   formulated by John H. Herz, in his *International Politics and the Atomic Age*
   (New York: Columbia University Press, 1959).
7. The classic text on the difference between arms control and disarmament is
   Hedley Bull, *The Control of the Arms Race: Disarmament and Arms Control in
   the Missile Age* (London: Weidenfeld & Nicolson, 1961); see also Lawrence
   Freedman, *Arms Control: Management or Reform?* (London: Routledge, 1986).
8. See Richard K. Betts, *Surprise Attack: Lessons for Defense Planning*
   (Washington, DC: Brookings, 1982).
9. This is demonstrated clearly in Robert Jervis, *The Illogic of American Strategy*
   (Ithaca, NY, and London: Cornell University Press, 1984).

10. For a useful antidote to the popular 'doomsday' scenarios, see Alexander J. Motyl, 'Reassessing the Soviet Crisis: Big Problems, Muddling Through; Business as Usual', *Political Science Quarterly*, Vol. 104, No. 2 (1989), pp. 269-80.

11. For interesting speculation on the basis of the bipolar structure see Daniel Frei, *Risks of Unintentional Nuclear War* (London: Croom Helm, 1982), Ch. 5 ('International Crises as Catalytic Triggers'); for a historical and theoretical treatment, see Richard Ned Lebow, *Between Peace and War: The Nature of International Crisis* (Baltimore, MD, and London: Johns Hopkins University Press, 1981).

12. As the material on which my analysis is based had to be confined to newspaper reports and comments, there will be a paucity of footnotes.

13. The US government publication *Soviet Military Power*, which commenced publication in 1981 in order to document this assertion, stuck faithfully to this line up to 1987. That edition was critically annotated by Tom Gervasi in *Soviet Military Power: The Annotated and Corrected Version of the Pentagon's Guide* (London: Sidgwick & Jackson, 1988). Only in 1989 was this official assessment of Soviet military capabilities — that, after all, was its subject, rather than power as the capacity actually to deploy military prowess — given the subtitle 'Prospects for Change', and shorn of its gloomy rhetoric.

14. For an analysis of the gradual recognition by the Soviet Union of the meaning of nuclear war and deterrence — and the continuing pre-nuclear thinking of the Soviet military — see Stephen Shenfield, *The Nuclear Predicament: Explorations in Soviet Ideology* (London: Routledge & Kegan Paul, 1987).

15. Mikhail Gorbachev, *Perestroika: New Thinking for our Country and the World* (London: Collins, 1987), Ch. 7.

16. For a recent survey of the changes in Soviet strategy, see Terry McNeil, 'New Thinking in East-West Security' (paper presented to the annual conference of the British International Studies Association, December 1989); also Walter Clemens, *Can Russia Change? The USSR Confronts Global Interdependence* (Boston, MA: Unwin Hyman, 1990).

17. As long ago as 1946, Bernard Brodie wrote about that consequence of the atomic weapon: 'Thus far the chief purpose of our military establishment has been to win wars. From now on its chief purpose must be to avert them. It can have no other useful purpose': cited in Fred Kaplan, *The Wizards of Armageddon* (New York: Simon & Schuster, 1983), p. 21.

18. For a discussion of 'interdependency' as a bond between people as individuals, groups or states that can be both cooperative and hostile, see Norbert Elias, *What is Sociology?* (London: Hutchinson, 1978). The Soviet Union and the United States were so strongly interdependent as enemies that they were 'in continual jealousies, and in the state and posture of Gladiators, having their weapons pointed and their eyes fixed on each other', as Hobbes formulated it.

19. Richard Ned Lebow, *Nuclear Crisis Management: A Dangerous Illusion* (Ithaca, NY, and London: Cornell University Press, 1987).

20. For a fuller survey of institutional trends and problems of identity in Europe, see Egbert Jahn's contribution to the present volume.

11. Managing Economic Dependence
Alan H. Smith

At the end of the 1980s the East European economies were clearly experiencing a crisis in the sense that they were approaching a turning-point or a time for decision. The scale and symptoms of the crisis varied from country to country, but the basic problems were common to each East European economy and were systemic in origin. These problems included a major slowdown in the rate of economic growth in the early 1980s; reductions in the level of investment; poor agricultural performance; high energy and material intensity per unit of GNP; major environmental problems resulting from high energy use; cuts in hard-currency imports in the early 1980s resulting from the attempt to reduce hard-currency indebtedness, followed by increasing debt when import restrictions were eased; growing signs of consumer disequilibrium and shortages, resulting in queues and burgeoning legal and illegal secondary markets followed by escalating open inflation combined with continuing consumer shortages ('shortageflation') in the reform-oriented countries when domestic price controls were eased.

IMPORT-LED GROWTH AND THE GENERATION OF CRISIS

Although the East European economies have been suffering from a long-term secular decline in the rate of growth of industrial output since the Second World War, Western econometric studies attribute only a small part of this slowdown to a decline in the growth of inputs of capital and labour, and ascribe the majority to a loss of economic efficiency. More disturbingly, the poor growth performance of the early 1980s is more severe than would be expected by the secular decline in growth alone, with even official statistics indicating that several countries suffered from actual falls in output in one or more years.

The classic Stalinist growth model which was imposed on the East European economies in the early 1950s relied on a rapid rate of growth of inputs of labour and capital, energy and raw materials (especially to heavy engineering industries) to achieve a high rate of growth of output. This model differed from the West European pattern of post-war development in that it placed less emphasis on domestic innovation both in the development of new products and in cost-reducing processes. Limited economic reforms aimed at increasing the efficiency in the use of inputs were introduced in the 1960s but were abandoned in each East European country except Hungary, following the Warsaw Pact invasion of Czechoslovakia in 1968.

During the 1970s the East European countries pursued the strategy of import-led growth largely as a substitute for, rather than a complement to, domestic economic reform. The strategy had two basic components. First, it was an attempt to attract external financial capital to expand the rate of domestic investment without the need to cut domestic consumption by an equivalent amount. In the Polish case the policy was accompanied by a significant and unsustainable expansion of domestic consumption in the early 1970s which created major economic and social problems when the strategy collapsed at the end of the decade. Secondly, the strategy was an attempt to acquire the benefits of technology transfer from advanced capitalist corporations without relinquishing control over the detail of plant operation or over macroeconomic policies, including the size and structure of domestic investment, wage and employment policy, and so forth.

The strategy was a conscious attempt to imitate the investment activity of multinational corporations without permitting the latter full rights of ownership on East European territory. According to the 'product-cycle' model, investment by multinational corporations (initially those based in the USA) seeking lower-cost production bases and new markets was a major source of technology transfer to Western Europe in the 1960s and subsequently to newly industrializing countries in Southeast Asia and Latin America. By establishing wholly-owned subsidiaries in third countries, the multinational corporation provides an injection of financial capital into the host country and is responsible for any losses incurred if the investment fails. The products of the subsidiary are normally either used as components in the multinational's production process or are marketed under the multinational's trade name. Consequently, the multinational provides a market for the output of the plant and is required to maintain quality control and introduce subsequent technical innovations into the plant.

The import-led growth strategy involved a number of legal methods to acquire Western technology by purchases of licences, cooperation ventures including co-production agreements, and joint ventures involving minority Western equity participation. In general the restrictions imposed on Western corporations, particularly over quality control, manning and wage levels, meant that Eastern Europe provided Western corporations with a less easily controlled, higher cost and consequently less desirable production base than many newly industrializing economies. As a result, East European countries were less successful than those in attracting foreign investment, and they had to place greater reliance on hard-currency purchases of Western equipment embodying new technology, frequently in the form of complete installations. These 'turnkey projects' were supplied on credit, with the intention that credits would be repaid by exporting the output of the newly constructed plants back to hard currency markets.

East European imports from developed market economies grew from $4.1 billion ($4100 million) in 1970 to a peak of $22.3 billion in 1980. The major growth was concentrated on imports of machinery and equipment, which reached a peak of $6 billion a year during 1978-80. By that time, however, the East European economies were faced with the problem that straight purchases of machinery and equipment did not provide the economy with a once-off boost in technology but rather required continued supplies of components, spare parts and other imported inputs which were essential for the continued operation of the plant. At the same time the East European imports of foodstuffs from the West also grew from $1.5 billion in 1977 to a peak of $4.2 billion in 1981. Inadvertently, the East European economies had become increasingly dependent on imports from the West in order to maintain industrial production and to meet the demand for foodstuffs, while rising interest rates meant that an increasing proportion of hard currency earnings was required to service the debt.

THE COSTS OF DEBT REDUCTION IN THE 1980s

East European debt (net of assets at Western commercial banks) reached a peak of $62 billion in 1981.[1] Total East European imports from the developed market economies peaked at $22.3 billion in 1980, falling initially to $19 billion in 1981 as each East European country (except Bulgaria) reduced imports from the West in an attempt to reduce debt gradually. However, the loss of Western banking confidence in Eastern Europe in 1982 following the rescheduling of Polish and Romanian debt and the imposition of martial law in Poland resulted in a reluctance to provide new credits to Eastern Europe. The East European economies were forced to make further cuts in imports from the developed market economies: these fell to $14.3 billion by 1984. The burden of import cuts fell mainly on machinery and equipment, which declined from $6.2 billion in 1980 to $3.6 billion in 1984, and foodstuffs, which were cut from $4.2 billion in 1981 to $1.8 billion in 1984, as efforts were made to preserve imports of industrial components.

The most drastic import reductions were implemented by Poland and Romania, the countries which had embraced the strategy of import-led growth with the greatest enthusiasm, and which had become the two most severely indebted countries by 1981. Polish imports from the OECD were cut from $6.5 billion in 1980 to $2.9 billion in 1984. Imports of machinery and equipment fell from $1.8 billion to $0.7 billion. Imports of foodstuffs, amounting to $1.5 billion in 1980, grew to $1.7 billion in 1981 but were cut back after the imposition of martial law to $0.6 billion in 1983. Romanian imports from the industrialized West were cut from $3.9 billion in 1980 to $1.3 billion in 1983. Imports of machinery and equipment were reduced from $0.9 billion in 1980 to $0.2 billion in 1983, while imports of foodstuffs were cut from a peak of $0.9 billion ($50 per head of population) in 1981 to $0.3 billion in 1982 and only $27 million ($1 per head) in 1984.

These are the two most extreme examples, but they give an indication of the impact of import cuts on the domestic economies of Eastern Europe in the 1980s and demonstrate that these sharp reductions directly affected living standards as well as investment in new industrial capacity. Reduced imports of machinery and equipment have contributed to a failure to modernize industry and a consequent loss of competitiveness for East European industry in Western markets in the longer term.

THE RE-EMERGENCE OF INDEBTEDNESS PROBLEMS IN THE LATE 1980s

With the exception of Poland, where the size of interest payments exceeded the capacity for generating trade surpluses, the East European economies succeeded in reducing their net debt in each year from 1981 to 1984 by running surpluses in the balance of payments in convertible currencies. This strategy could no longer be sustained after 1985. As each country, except Romania, attempted to re-accelerate the growth of domestic output by boosting investment and relaxing constraints on consumption, imports from the industrial West, particularly of machinery and equipment, again grew faster than hard currency exports. As a result, each country except Romania was faced with a progressive deterioration in its hard currency trade balance over the years 1985-87, which became deficits in the hard currency balance of payments by 1987; the exception was the GDR, which benefited from direct access to West German markets. By the end of 1987, the level of net debt in each country, except Romania, exceeded the level at the end of 1985, even after allowing for currency fluctuations. The pattern of growth rates and trade deficits in 1988 varied from country to country, but there is at least some *prima facie* evidence to suggest that a deceleration of the growth rate was associated with an improvement in the convertible currency balance of trade and payments, and that continued acceleration of the growth rate was associated with increased imports and a deterioration in the balance of payments.

This analysis indicates that East European growth rates in the 1980s were constrained by the inability to generate a sufficient volume of hard currency earnings to service debt and to finance imports of machinery, equipment and industrial components. Kazimierz Poznanski has shown that the inability to export can be primarily attributed to a systematic inability to produce either the sophisticated manufactured goods demanded in Western markets (for example, synthetic drugs, computers or consumer electronics), or to produce and market less sophisticated manufactured goods (furniture, textiles, cars, iron and steel products and unsophisticated chemicals, and so forth) at prices, quality specifications and delivery terms that are competitive with newly industrializing economies in south-east Asia in particular.[2]

This systemic inability to export arises from three factors: first, problems created by the nature of the centrally planned economy itself; secondly, problems arising from the pursuit of Stalinist industrial priorities; and thirdly, problems created by the foreign trade system and the state monopoly of foreign trade in particular. It is now apparent that all three sets of problems must be overcome before any real progress can be made in improving economic contacts between Eastern and Western Europe.

Systemic problems created by the system of enterprise incentives involving the pursuit of bonuses linked to gross output, in particular, have been well documented.[3] They include poor quality of output, poor product ranges with insufficient attention to the specific demands of individual markets, insufficient attention to back-up services and the supply of spare parts, lack of attention to the delivery schedules, and so on. In addition, the prevalence of sellers' market conditions and the absence of competition have resulted in a disincentive both to bring out new product lines and to diffuse new technological innovation rapidly through the economy. Consequently, the majority of East European enterprises work with obsolete equipment producing obsolete commodities that are no longer in demand in West European markets.

The pursuit of Stalinist industrial priorities towards heavy industry also meant that planners attached a low priority to the production of consumer goods and were frequently unaware of the Western demand factors; they have therefore not branched out into the production of more sophisticated consumer goods. At the same time, excess domestic demand means that unsophisticated consumer goods can be absorbed in the domestic markets while the relatively soft Soviet market for consumer goods provides East European producers with little or no incentive to modernize their product range.

Finally, the Stalinist foreign trade system was essentially designed to inhibit trade flows that had not been sanctioned by the central planners. The state monopoly of foreign trade prevented enterprises and individuals from engaging in import and export operations, and meant that East European enterprises did not come into direct contact with foreign suppliers or markets. This isolation was reinforced by the separation of domestic wholesale and retail prices from world market prices, the inconvertibility of East European currencies, and the preservation of artificial exchange rates as *ex post* accountancy devices. The system remained essentially geared towards import-substitution rather than export generation and is ill-suited to generating exports of sophisticated manufactured goods.

WESTERN POLICIES TOWARDS EAST-WEST TRADE

Economic warfare and détente

Western policies towards trade with communist-ruled countries have been characterized by three basic attitudes. At one extreme is the view that could best be described as trade denial, or 'economic warfare' (see below); a central view is that trade with communist states should be largely unaffected by political considerations ('normalization', or passive détente); and a third view is that positive trade concessions should be offered in exchange for, or to promote, political concessions (active détente).

Attitudes in the US towards trade with the Soviet bloc following the Soviet invasion of Afghanistan in 1979 and the imposition of martial law in Poland in 1981 were largely determined by the principles of economic warfare. Hanson summarizes their rationale in the following terms: the USSR was seen as an inherently expansionist power whose objectives conflicted with those of the West. Proponents of economic warfare argued that it was prudent to weaken this adversary by limiting its productive capacity to the greatest possible extent relative to that of the West. This would also send a clear signal to the Soviet leadership that expansionary policies should be limited, and it might even stimulate popular dissatisfaction which could force a change in policies.[4]

Hanson contrasts this argument with the rationale of détente which prevailed in the 1970s. Supporters of détente argued that the USSR was not inherently expansionist but exhibited the opportunistic behaviour of a large power. As such, it appraised potential economic and political costs before embarking on policies that would invoke a Western reaction. Consequently, the Soviet leadership would be deterred from expansionist or aggressive behaviour if it feared that existing trade benefits would be withheld. The strategy of détente was the stimulation of economic interdependence. The more the Soviet Union was drawn into channels of trade and cooperation the greater would be the costs of political behaviour that threatened that cooperation. Furthermore, increased contacts increased the prospects for cooperation and lessened the possibility of misunderstanding by either party which could be damaging to mutual security.

The strategies of economic warfare and détente made little or no conscious attempt to alter the *status quo* of Soviet power in Eastern Europe in the pre-Gorbachev era. Proponents of economic warfare argued that the East European countries were, willingly or unwillingly, part of the Soviet bloc and full members of the Warsaw Treaty Organization. Although they did not discount the possibility that some East European countries (such as, in particular, Romania) might be dissuaded from wholehearted support for Soviet policies or even weaned away from the Soviet bloc by trade preferences, their basic attitude towards trade and cooperation with Eastern Europe was roughly the same as towards the USSR. Any trade that strengthened the Eastern European economies strengthened the Soviet bloc as a whole, while any weakening of those economies could require the Soviet

Union to divert resources away from military expenditure or expansionary policies. It was also argued that policies to limit the transfer of militarily useful technology to communist countries (administered by CoCom, the Paris-based 'Coordinating Committee') should be applied to Eastern European with the same vigour as to the Soviet Union. To the extent that CoCom increasingly became an instrument for the exercise of economic warfare for essentially political rather than purely security reasons in the early 1980s, limitations on the transfer of technology in such areas as telecommunications, digital con rol machinery and so forth have contributed to the lack of competitiveness of Eastern European industry. Ironically this has increased Eastern European dependence on Soviet markets for industrial products and on Soviet energy supplies paid for in soft currency.

The policy of détente involved greater economic cooperation between East and West without attempting to alter the existing political and economic system in Eastern Europe, and it *accepted de facto* the *status quo* of Soviet-East European relations. Limited détente involved passive tools to remove existing barriers to trade and 'normalizing' trade relations with Eastern Europe. This entailed granting official government credit support for exports to the countries of Eastern Europe, and easing import controls through tariff reductions, granting Most Favoured Nation (MFN) status, and allowing generalized preferences to less developed East European economies on largely commercial criteria, without differentiating among countries on political grounds and without explicit demands for political concessions. To the extent that energy and raw materials, which are subject to relatively smaller EC and US import restrictions, formed a significantly larger proportion of Soviet than of East European exports to the West, passive détente based on trade normalization rather than differentiation offered proportionally greater benefits to the USSR than to Eastern Europe and may have inadvertently increased the allies' dependence on the Soviet Union.

A policy of more active détente[5] involves positive measures to overcome the systemic obstacles to East-West trade and cooperation, including concrete trade promotion measures such as export subsidies to Western producers, favourable credit terms, allocation of central government resources to stimulating East-accepted West trade, the removal of tariff barriers and quotas, offering MFN status, the encouragement of scientific cooperation, and other similar measures.

Economic warfare and détente in the Gorbachev era

Since Mikhail Gorbachev came to power in 1985, the strategies of economic warfare and undifferentiated détente have had to be substantially revised, partly in response to a Soviet shift towards the use of diplomatic rather than military instruments to achieve foreign policy objectives. The virtual collapse of communist power in Eastern Europe in 1989 now necessitates a further reassessment of Western policy. It no longer appears tenable to regard as inherently expansionist a Soviet Union faced with a continued deterioration in domestic economic performance and growing ethnic and nationalist unrest that threatens the continued existence of its empire within its borders.

The Soviet leadership, too, has reassessed its trade and economic relations with both Western and Eastern Europe since the end of 1986, and this in part contributed to the events of 1989. The new Soviet leadership's initial trade policies were fashioned during the prevailing environment of 'economic warfare' in the early 1980s and emphasized increasing bloc 'invulnerability' to strategic or politically motivated embargoes. This policy placed greater faith in Soviet research and development and reduced emphasis on imports of Western technology. Soviet and East European investment was directed towards overcoming perceived long-term weaknesses in the bloc economies and the Soviet economy in particular, principally in the areas of R and D and technology, energy production and conservation, and the production of foodstuffs, in order to eliminate areas of vulnerability to Western action.[6] Simultaneously, Soviet officials made public noises about the need to improve the quality of East European manufactured goods exported to the USSR.

As the Soviet authorities became increasingly aware of the seriousness of the economic problems facing the CMEA (Comecon) economies, they also became less optimistic about the prospects of improving the quality of imports from Eastern Europe without radical reforms in the systems of planning and foreign trade in both the USSR and the Eastern European countries. The fall in world oil prices in 1986 (which resulted in a major deterioration in Soviet terms of trade with both the West and Eastern Europe) and the deterioration in Soviet domestic economic performance have greatly reduced the ability of the Soviet Union to bear even part of the cost of maintaining an inefficient economic system among its allies. The Soviet prime minister, Nikolai Ryzhkov, indicated at the CMEA session of July 1988 that the shift in Soviet attitudes towards more radical market-oriented reforms both at home and in the operation of the CMEA followed a reassessment of economic performance, which had revealed 'a far more serious economic neglect than had previously been supposed'.[7] Soviet policy towards economic reform in Eastern Europe under Gorbachev initially shifted from the imposition of a relatively uniform set of reform principles, which were to be implemented in each country, to a major relaxation of the political constraints to reform. Gorbachev's advisers also argued that political changes to break up the power of the economic bureaucracy and the *nomenklatura*, and social changes that would stimulate a more innovative and questioning society, were essential prerequisites to a successful economic reform. Even before the collapse or overthrow of communist power in East Germany, Czechoslovakia and Romania, and the Politburo coup in Bulgaria in the last weeks of 1989, the Soviet leadership had demonstrated that it would not intervene to prevent far more radical market-oriented reforms in Poland and Hungary, which included the transfer of large-scale industries into private hands, the development of capital markets, the possibility of enterprise bankruptcy and unemployment on a large scale, the introduction of currency convertibility and a reorientation of trade to the West.

Both EC and US trade policy towards Eastern Europe in 1989 evolved towards 'passive differentiation'. This involved active détente (offering trade concessions and limited economic assistance) towards countries that introduced major political and social reforms (Poland and Hungary), passive détente (trade normalization) to countries that introduced limited reforms (GDR, Czechoslovakia and Bulgaria), and trade denial to states that did not fulfil minimum requirements on human rights (Romania). This policy was explained by the EC in the following terms: 'by developing closer ties [with Eastern Europe] Western Europe can hope to stimulate this [reform] process which should lead to positive effects, not only on the living conditions of the East European peoples, but also on political evolution in those countries'. This would involve a 'pragmatic and flexible approach taking account of the special features of each individual case'.[8]

ACTIVE DÉTENTE AND WEST EUROPEAN ECONOMIC POLICY TOWARDS EASTERN EUROPE IN THE 1990s

It is to be hoped that the strategy of differentiating EC policy on trade and cooperation towards individual East European countries on political grounds will have become redundant following the political changes in Eastern Europe in November and December 1989, and that each East European country will become a potential candidate for the benefits of active détente if it maintains progress towards genuinely free elections and the introduction of market systems. Commitment to genuine political reform appears to differ substantially from country to country, and even after the event it is doubtful whether Romania, in particular, enacted genuinely free elections with full access of all participants to the communications media. Nor can the longer-term prospects be assessed with complete certainty. It was prudent, in the short term at least, to limit financial assistance until free elections had been held and their conduct approved, and the threat of withholding assistance should be maintained, to see how the new governments perform. However, the very speed of political change in Eastern Europe and the tendency of one or other country to leapfrog the others in introducing political changes suggest that short-term political criteria will no longer provide a satisfactory basis for the formulation of long-term economic policy towards Eastern Europe.

This suggests that the EC should formulate a general framework policy towards trade and cooperation with Eastern Europe, which would then be differentiated according to the specific economic conditions prevailing in each country.

What form should assistance take?

The most optimistic scenario is that the economies of Eastern Europe will be able to modernize their capital stock, retrieve their lost economic potential and achieve relatively high rates of growth in the second half of the 1990s. This scenario is based, first, on comparisons of income levels in Eastern Europe with those in comparable areas in Western Europe. Such comparisons suggest that the East European economies could virtually double their income levels by utilizing modern capital and equipment, raising industrial skills and adopting a more technically advanced structure of production. The experience of newly industrializing economies indicates that it is possible to achieve relatively high rates of growth by expanding production in areas of growing world market demand, rather than by concentrating on the domestic market. This was in part facilitated by attracting equity investment by multinationals, which provided short-term capital inputs and had a direct interest in improving product quality to world market standards, phasing out obsolete products, and training local work-forces and management.

In the medium to longer term, Eastern Europe offers Western investors the prospect of a relatively low-cost but well-educated labour force in close proximity to the EC market. A major part of EC policy should be geared towards measures to attract Western equity investment in the East European economies, combined with the initial reduction of trade barriers, such as tariffs and import quotas, on East European products in line with those offered to Third World countries. Ideally, this should lead to the eventual elimination of trade barriers with the intention of extending full membership to those East European states that apply for it.

This strategy carries two principal dangers. First, there is the risk that the East European economies will become excessively dependent on Western multinationals as sources of capital and markets, and will develop into 'screwdriver economies', consisting of assembly plants for foreign corporations and providing a low degree of added value. Secondly, improving East European access to EC markets will mean that the existing members of the EC will face growing competition in attracting inward investment and from new sources of low-cost production. The attendant problems of unemployment will the greatest in the geographically outlying areas of the EC, and in industries producing relatively unsophisticated manufactured goods. Both these dangers will be increased if industrial nations outside the EC establish assembly plants in Eastern Europe in order to bypass restrictions on the access of their products to EC markets.

The EC will need to protect the legitimate interests of its member states and will need to link more open East European access to EC markets to the fulfilment of conditions on fair competition. Protecting EC producers against unfair competition in the long run implies the development of genuine market prices, rational exchange rates, and the elimination of subsidies to industry and indirect subsidies which reduce wage rates in comparison with EC workers (for example, subsidies on foodstuffs, housing and public utilities). Similarly, East European producers will have to satisfy EC requirements that their legislation on such matters as work safety and environmental pollution meet EC standards, so as not to establish unfair advantages.

The strategy of marketization and industrial restructuring away from the traditional smokestack industries geared to the Soviet market and towards production for the EC market will require the East European economies to undergo an extremely painful period of adjustment. There is a very real danger that the short-term impact of the required adjustments will be so unpopular that social and political stability will be threatened before economic growth can be realized. The removal of price controls and subsidies on staple goods under the prevailing conditions of excess demand threatens to release hyperinflationary pressures if strict controls on the money supply are not introduced immediately. This will necessitate the removal of budget subsidies to loss-making industries, bringing the prospect of rapidly increasing unemployment as enterprises are closed or forced to make substantial reductions in their labour force to become genuinely competitive on Western markets. The social problems created by unemployment will be aggravated by the inadequate provision of unemployment benefits and facilities to ease the redeployment of redundant workers. These range from lack of information about new jobs, limited experience in 'job-searching', and the absence of facilities for industrial retraining to the limited development of the private housing market, which hampers labour mobility.

The most useful form of economic assistance will incorporate measures to ease the path of transition to a market economy in the short term, and to help the East European economies to develop flourishing domestic markets in capital and in wholesale and retail goods, and to improve their international competitiveness in the long term. Such assistance will involve the provision of immediate short-term assistance, in the form of grant aid and physical supplies, to overcome bottlenecks and consumption shortages (for example, food and equipment for its processing, storage and distribution, urgently needed medical supplies, and so forth). This would help to win popular support for reform while reducing excess money balances, thereby cutting demand-led inflationary pressures. The provision of this support, particularly food aid, should not conflict with the long-term objective of providing price incentives to boost domestic production, and it must be clearly demonstrated to be a short-term expedient. Ideally, food aid should be directly linked to policies to stabilize prices.

Longer-term measures should include grant aid to assist in the development of infrastructure whose export potential is limited but which is necessary to stimulate Western equity investment, for example, telecommunications, improved transportation, and pollution-control equipment; measures to stimulate foreign equity investment including the provision of information, and underwriting political risk; education and training in a range of industrial skills, from those required on the shop-floor to more sophisticated engineering and managerial skills including accountancy, marketing and personnel management, and training in the skills of central management of a market economy: economic administration, management of macroeconomic policy, monetary control, the formulation of accurate statistics, and so forth.

Financial assistance: throwing good money after bad?

The import-led growth strategy pursued by the East European economies in the 1970s failed because it paid insufficient attention to the convertible currency-generating capacity of investments, leaving the East European governments with insufficient export earnings to service debt and maintain imports of machinery, components and even food. The debt burden for which the East European governments had to take responsibility was increased by their reluctance to permit foreign risk-bearing capital in their economies. The debt burden is most severe in the case of Poland, where the convertible currency debt:export ratio approaches that of the most indebted countries of the world, and in Hungary, where per capita debt exceeds $2000. Bulgarian debt also has climbed alarmingly since the end of 1985. As for Romania, although it has become a net creditor nation, the human costs of Ceausescu's debt-reduction programme raise major questions about whether debt reduction on this scale can be achieved in democratic conditions.

A further round of government-to-government credits should be resisted in most cases, on the grounds that it will only add to the existing debt burden. Further credits to Eastern Europe should be linked directly to investments that will generate hard currency exports, or to the promotion of economic reforms that will stimulate international competitiveness, including measures to attract Western risk capital in existing enterprises and in newly constructed companies. One priority would be financial assistance to support the transition to a fully convertible currency. The introduction of full convertibility would provide East European governments with an internal discipline against monetary over-emission, and would act as a stimulus for Western investors to establish ventures producing for the East European as well as the West European market. This would be a major contribution to expanding Eastern demand for Western commodities, which would increase the size of the European market and create additional opportunities in both Eastern and Western Europe.

Why should the Western taxpayer pay?

The policy of active détente involves action by Western governments to encourage relations between Eastern and Western Europe that would not be

undertaken on strictly commercial criteria. This requires Western governments to provide guarantees and to underwrite extra-market risks for
profit-motivated Western institutions, and to meet the costs of training
programmes and providing other forms of financial assistance. These costs
will ultimately have to be borne by the Western taxpayer.

How can this expenditure be justified? The primary justification is
humanitarian and moral. The current economic and political circumstances
facing Eastern Europe are in no small part the result of negotiations between
democratically elected governments and financial institutions in Western
Europe and the imposed governments of Eastern Europe that were not
representative of their populations. Consequently, West European governments and financial institutions bear some moral responsibility for the current
economic situation in Eastern Europe.

Three specific cases can be cited in which the populations of Eastern
Europe were unwilling participants in processes that have damaged their
economies over the long term. First, the economic recovery of the West
European economies after the Second World War was facilitated by Marshall
aid which was denied to the populations of Eastern Europe through no choice
of their own. Secondly, the East European economies have been damaged by
the imposition of restrictions on the transfer of technology, albeit imposed in
the legitimate security interests of the West. Those countries that have
overthrown communist regimes at some personal cost are presumably entitled
to an easing of those restrictions and to assistance in overcoming their
historic effects on economic performance. Thirdly, a number of East
European economies, Poland and Hungary in particular, are saddled with a
high debt burden resulting from poor investment policies in the 1970s.
Western savers freely lent their money to financial institutions that freely lent
it to unrepresentative governments. Who should bear the cost of failed
investments: shareholders and lenders to willing participants, or the
descendants of unwilling populations?

In the more materialistic age that has emerged in the West in the 1980s,
the provision of financial and material assistance may have to be justified on
grounds of economic self-interest. It can first be argued that greater economic
cooperation *per se* between Eastern and Western Europe will contribute to
the removal of international tension and will result in a reduced need for
defence expenditure by Western governments. Secondly, there remains a real
threat that continued economic weakness in Eastern Europe will result in
political instability in the region, and inter-ethnic disagreements will act as a

source of wider political instability in Europe as a whole. Thirdly, the expansion of the European market to embrace the economies of Eastern Europe will bring gains from trade to both sets of participants, while economic failure in Eastern Europe will stimulate the exodus of skilled workers to Western Europe, with major political repercussions for government in both parts of the continent.

NOTES

1. All the figures in this paragraph are taken from various OECD sources.
2. K. Poznanski, *Competition between Eastern Europe and the Developing Countries in the Western Market for Manufactured Goods in Eastern Europe Economies: Slow Growth in the 1980s*, Vol. 2 (Washington, DC: Joint Economic Committee of the Congress of the United States, 1986), pp. 62-90.
3. See, for example, Philip Hanson, *Western Economic Statecraft in East-West Relations*, Chatham House Paper No. 40 (London: Routledge & Kegan Paul, 1986), p. 53.
4. Ibid.
5. This argument follows Hanson's distinction between weak and strong détente: see ibid., pp. 56-7.
6. See Nikolai Ryzhkov, in *Pravda*, 4 March 1986.
7. Nikolai Ryzhkov, in *Pravda*, 6 July 1988.
8. 'The European Community's Relations with Comecon and its East European Members', *Europe Information*, Brussels, January 1989.

12. Human Rights: A Change in Performance

Peter R. Baehr

For many years East and West used to differ strongly over the interpretation of international human rights norms. These differences have become smaller now that important changes are taking place in most of the countries of Eastern Europe. These changes refer to politics, economics, culture and communications, and include the field of human rights. Related to this is a change in attitude with regard to multilateral instruments protecting human rights. The issue has been raised as to how Western governments should respond to these changes.

Traditional differences in interpretation, especially between East and West, are by now well known. They refer broadly to a strong emphasis on the rights of individuals by the West versus more emphasis on community rights by the East, a related difference in emphasis on civil and political rights versus economic, social and cultural rights, and a somewhat stronger emphasis on international enforcement at least on the part of certain Western European governments, versus an emphasis on national sovereignty by the East. However, recent developments appear to indicate that Eastern European governments are now paying more attention to those very civil and political rights that used to be the *domaine exclusif* of the West. A major step forward was the adoption by the thirty-five European and North American participating states in the Conference on Security and Cooperation in Europe (CSCE) in Vienna in January 1989 of a concluding document which contained a new supervisory mechanism for what was called the 'human dimension' of CSCE (see below).

Three principal themes are dealt with in this chapter:

1. the extent to which there is indeed actual progress in the observance of human rights in most of the East European countries;

2. a change in attitude on the part of most East European countries with regard to multilateral instruments which protect human rights;

3. possibilities for Western countries to react to these developments.

DIFFERENCES OF VIEW BETWEEN EAST AND WEST

The reported changes must be seen against the background of traditional differences of view between East and West with regard to the formulation and interpretation of human rights standards. These differences have cropped up regularly since the Second World War. During the debates on the draft Universal Declaration of Human Rights in 1948 in the General Assembly of the United Nations, the Soviet delegate, Andrei Vyshinskii, made an explicit reservation with regard to the rights of individuals *vis-à-vis* their own states. Such notions were not of relevance to countries such as his own where there were no rival classes, he averred. In such a society, there could be no contradiction between the government and the individual since the government *was* in fact the collective individual. History had already solved that problem in his country. The state and the individual were in harmony with each other; their interests coincided. Later developments and publications gave evidence of continued differences of view between East and West with regard to the rights of individuals.

From the beginning, the Soviet Union also expressed views that differed from those held by Western governments with regard to the right of free expression. It felt that freedom of expression should not include the freedom to express, for example, fascist views. This was one of the reasons why the Soviet Union — together with Belorussia, Czechoslovakia, Poland, Ukraine, Yugoslavia and, *bien étonnés de se trouver ensemble*, Saudi Arabia and South Africa — abstained when the Universal Declaration came to a vote. In more recent Soviet sources this move is either called a 'mistake' or even entirely ignored: in a dispatch from Geneva a correspondent for *Moscow News* claimed that the Soviet Union was 'one of the drafters' of the Universal Declaration and that it had 'agreed to sign the Declaration'.[1]

Over the years, the Soviet Union and its allies used to state that they attached greater importance to economic, social and cultural rights, whereas the United States mainly stressed political and civil rights. Many West European states have also emphasized the importance of economic and social rights. This does not mean that the record of the socialist states in the field of economic and social rights has necessarily been better than that of Western countries. It should be noted that deficiencies in the field of economic and social rights have directly or indirectly led to the greater attention that is now being paid to civil and political rights, in the Soviet Union, for example. The Soviet Union's general view has always been that the principles of domestic jurisdiction and non-intervention should have preference, unless it is demonstrated that a violation of human rights contains a threat to international peace and security. *Apartheid,* fascism, national socialism, genocide, colonialism and racism are seen as such.

It should be noted that there exists a well-established view that the doctrines of East and West are so different that no common ground is possible with regard to human rights. On ideological grounds, neither side can accept the validity of a claim about human rights made by the other.[2] More recently, Howard and Donnelly have argued on theoretical grounds that communist society rests on a social utilitarianism that is fundamentally incompatible with human rights: 'Communism represents a thorough denial of human rights'.[3] They have been criticized for producing few empirical observations about the variation in human rights violations cross-nationally — a charge which they have strongly rejected.[4] Even granting their ideal-type characterization, it would still remain an open empirical question whether the states of Eastern Europe are moving substantially away from this 'communist' model towards practices more in line with human rights as understood in the West. Substantial recent evidence suggests that such an evolution is indeed under way.

RECENT CHANGES

In the age of *glasnost* and *perestroika* changes appear to have occurred — and are occurring at present — with regard to the practice of civil and political rights in the Soviet Union and in other Eastern European states. These changes are remarkable in view of the past record of these states in this area, and it is still too early to tell how fundamental and how permanent they will be. This issue is of course closely linked to the fate of the more general reforms, which are currently being introduced in the Soviet Union and its allies. The changes in the human rights field are the more noteworthy as they have been reported by some of the very non-governmental organizations and other foreign observers who used to criticize the Soviet Union and its allies on that score.

Free elections

The most spectacular recent phenomenon has been the holding of partially —
or wholly — free elections in the Soviet Union and elsewhere — 'free' at
least if compared to what used to obtain in those countries. In the USSR,
elections for the Congress of People's Deputies took place in March 1989. In
these elections, which for the first time offered Soviet voters a real choice
among different candidates, a great number of party regulars and even party
leaders were defeated. It can be seen as a major step away from the
traditional model. The elections in Poland in May and June 1989 concerned
35 per cent of the seats in the lower house of parliament — the Sejm — and
the entire Senate. Virtually all the contested seats were won by the
independent free trade union, Solidarity. Many communist candidates who
ran unopposed for the remaining 65 per cent of the seats failed to obtain
even the required 50 per cent of the vote in the first election round.

The Hungarian election law of 1983 decrees the need for at least two
candidates for each parliamentary seat; independent non-communist groups
have thus gained a real chance for political participation. New laws are in
preparation establishing the rights of parties, parliamentary elections and the
framing of a more democratic constitution.

Although shortcomings still remain if compared with democratic elections
of the Western type, the elections held in the Soviet Union, Poland and other
countries came remarkably close to the obligations as set out in article 25(b)
of the International Covenant on Civil and Political Rights ('Every citizen
shall have the right and the opportunity ... to vote and to be elected at
genuine periodic elections which shall be by universal and equal suffrage and
shall be held by secret ballot, guaranteeing the free expression of the will of
the electors'). An additional factor worth watching is, of course, the extent to
which these popularly elected bodies will be able to wield an adequate
measure of political control.

It remains to be seen what all of this will mean for the future of
communist party rule. In Poland a government mainly consisting of
non-communists took over in the autumn of 1989; the same happened in
Czechoslovakia in December 1989, and in the GDR and Hungary in the
spring of 1990. This means indeed a change of major proportions, the
consequences of which are not easy to predict. Moreover, the political
developments in Hungary and Poland had major repercussions in the GDR,
Czechoslovakia, Bulgaria, and dramatically in Romania. For the moment,

Albania remains the only country in the region which has remained apparently untouched by these developments, and even there signs of political relaxation began to appear in May 1990, particularly with regard to religious freedom.

Criminal law

In December 1988, *Izvestiya* published new principles of criminal law due to be adopted in 1989. However, from the point of view of international human rights norms these are not in all respects an improvement. The laws abolish internal exile but introduce new punishments. 'Arrest' means imprisonment of up to three months; 'restriction of freedom' is virtually identical with internal exile, but carries harsher penalties for prisoners who try to escape. A decree passed by the Supreme Soviet Presidium on 8 April 1989 amended the current laws against 'anti-Soviet agitation and propaganda', 'circulating anti-Soviet slander' and 'inciting national hatred' in a way that runs contrary to international standards on freedom of expression. The death penalty is retained as an 'exceptional measure of punishment' pending its total abolition, but its scope is restricted from eighteen offences in peacetime to six; it is also retained for legally specified crimes committed in a war or combat situation.[5] These laws are part of a major revision of criminal legislation which had been announced earlier, and they followed discussions in Soviet newspapers about the desirability of abolishing the death penalty, described as part of a steady international trend, particularly within Europe.

Reference was made in particular to the German Democratic Republic, which in July 1987 was the first socialist state to abolish the death penalty. Yet, in the GDR — at least during the early part of 1989 — discrimination and persecution on political grounds remained. Inhuman treatment, unhealthy labour conditions and strict disciplinary measures were often applied. Conditions in many East German prisons failed to meet minimum international standards. The rights of defence lawyers were restricted. A report published by Amnesty International in January 1989 said that secret trials, secret directives to lawyers and vaguely defined laws made it possible for the authorities to penalize almost any activity of which they disapproved. Laws which restrict freedom of expression, freedom of association, freedom of assembly and freedom of movement have been used to imprison hundreds of people, often after trials held *in camera*, which excluded even family members from the court.[6] In an update, published two months later, it was said that the human rights violations described in the report were continuing, and the GDR authorities also continued to deny that such violations were taking place.[7]

In Poland, instances of ill-treatment of detainees are not unknown. As of early 1990, the death penalty has not been abolished, but discussions have taken place on the possibility of establishing a five-year moratorium or outlawing the death penalty in peace-time. Since January 1988, an 'Ombudsman' has dealt with citizens' complaints and drawn the authorities' attention to abuses. This official cannot be deposed and has far-reaching authority to intervene and to bring matters before the administrative court.

In September 1988, the Hungarian Minister of Justice stated publicly that in his personal opinion the retention of capital punishment was unacceptable, even though more than 90 per cent of the Hungarian people allegedly favoured it. He announced that a general revision of the penal code would soon be embarked upon and that a decision would be taken on the death penalty.

Political prisoners

It has been reported that of nearly 600 political prisoners in the Soviet Union in 1985, more than half had been released in 1988. The number of prisoners sentenced for practising their religious beliefs had reportedly decreased considerably, though the exact number is not publicly known. The Burlatskii Commission (see below) recommended that the government pardon all prisoners serving sentences under laws limiting religious activities. Given that the Soviet authorities had always denied that *any* prisoners were detained for political reasons, Soviet sources have identified those released as persons 'who are referred to in the West as political prisoners'. Members of ethnic minorities are imprisoned in some countries in violation of the principle, agreed by the CSCE participating states, to 'protect and create conditions for the promotion of ethnic, cultural, linguistic and religious identity of national minorities on their territory' and 'respect the free exercise of rights belonging to such minorities'. Of particular concern are the situation of the Hungarian-speaking minority in Romania and of the ethnic Turks in Bulgaria who have been severely maltreated and even killed in the context of a forced assimilation campaign by the authorities.[8] Demonstrations in January 1990 against the restoration of full civil rights to Bulgarian Turks bode ill. Similarly, the newly-elected regime of President Ion Iliescu has made a poor start, in using miners to beat up peaceful demonstrators in June 1990.

The right to leave one's country

The Soviet government still does not recognize emigration as an inalienable right, but the number of Jewish emigrants is rising. In this connection it is interesting to note that the government has disbanded the 'Anti-Zionist Committee of the Soviet Public', formed in 1983; it was incorporated into a new committee that would focus on a wide range of human rights issues, the Burlatskii Commission.

In Hungary, since January 1988 citizens have had a fundamental right to leave the country — a right that is limited only by the need to obtain the necessary foreign currency. Polish citizens are reasonably free to leave their country for visits abroad, although, as in Hungary, there is a problem in obtaining foreign currency. In the German Democratic Republic the situation changed dramatically in the last months of 1989. Previously, the situation was rather curious: statistically, more East Germans travelled abroad than citizens of other communist countries; yet the penalties for unauthorized travel and the border controls were the harshest in all of Eastern Europe. Until November 1989, the Berlin Wall remained a strong physical as well as symbolic barrier to such travel. In Bulgaria, the right to leave and enter the country is still restricted: however, during 1988 reforms were introduced which may lead to the liberalization of procedures enabling individuals to leave. The position of Romania following the ousting of Ceausescu is still unclear, while Albania still maintains the strictest controls limiting the right to leave.

Freedom of expression

In the Soviet Union, more liberal rules are now in force with regard to the import of audio-visual material. Censorship has been diminished (but not ended), more critical pieces are allowed to appear in the Soviet press, and more formerly proscribed material is made available through the public libraries. The penal instruments for the suppression of anti-Soviet expressions of opinion are still in force, but are rarely applied nowadays; they are expected to be abolished under the planned reform of penal law.

In Hungary and Poland, also, there are more possibilities to express views in public than ever before. Jamming of foreign radio broadcasts has stopped. However, it is still virtually impossible — or at least very difficult — to obtain Western news media through news-vendors.

Imprisonment in psychiatric institutions

For many years, the Soviet Union confined political non-conformists in psychiatric institutions, although this was always officially denied. In 1983 the Soviet Association of Psychiatrists resigned from the World Psychiatric Association rather than face expulsion as a result of a report on the use of mental hospitals to imprison dissidents. More recently, reports in the Soviet press have accused individual psychiatrists of corruption and incompetence, and exposed cases of malpractice. In July 1987, for example, *Izvestiya* charged that Soviet citizens could be put into psychiatric hospitals arbitrarily and that the law offered them no redress. According to the lawyer V.M. Chkhikvadze, 'these violations of citizens' rights occurred, in some cases, owing to absence of clear-cut legislative rules regulating the conditions and procedure of psychiatric aid to patients'.[9] In January 1988, eighteen special psychiatric hospitals were transferred from police control to the Ministry of Health. Also, a statute was adopted giving people confined against their will in psychiatric hospitals and their relatives the right to contest their imprisonment with legal aid.[10] In the spring of 1989 a group of American psychiatrists visited Soviet mental hospitals to determine if dissidents were imprisoned there,[11] and the World Psychiatric Association decided in October 1989 to readmit the Soviet organization, along with those of Czechoslovakia and Bulgaria.

Contacts with human rights organizations

Changes are obviously occurring in the Soviet Union and its East European allies, although it is still too early to give a final judgement on whether the USSR has indeed made some good progress in the field of human rights. It is clear, however, that the government of the Soviet Union considers it important to improve its human rights record, or at least — as sceptics will argue — the *image* of its human rights record, in the eyes of the outside world.

This attempt to improve relations is shown, for instance, by the efforts made to improve contacts with international human rights organizations. In January 1988, a delegation of the International Helsinki Federation for Human Rights paid a much publicized visit to Moscow at the invitation of the Soviet Committee for European Security and Cooperation. During that visit, various aspects of human rights in the Soviet Union were discussed with public and semi-public authorities.[12] In April 1989, the International Helsinki Federation met in Warsaw — the first time it held a formal meeting in an East European country. The meeting included delegates from the United

States and Canada, a number of West European countries, and Hungary and Poland. However, the chairman of the Czech Helsinki Committee, former foreign minister and well-known dissident Jiri Hajek, was refused permission to leave his country to attend the Warsaw meeting. A month earlier, the Czechoslovak authorities had refused to receive a delegation of the International Helsinki Federation because of the inclusion of Hajek in that delegation.

Another important meeting was the one between representatives of Amnesty International and the Burlatskii Commission in Paris in May 1988. During this meeting, the human rights situation in the Soviet Union was discussed. In March 1989, an Amnesty delegation visited Moscow at the invitation of the Soviet Academy of Sciences. This was a far cry from August 1980, when the Soviet government newspaper *Izvestiya* carried an article in which it accused Amnesty of being maintained by imperialist secret services; it claimed that former Amnesty International staff and officials had links with British and United States intelligence agencies and that Amnesty was one-sided and over-critical of the Soviet Union in its reports. Since then, at least three books have been published in the Soviet Union about Amnesty International. The most recent one contains positive references to Amnesty staff people and to its 'solid reputation'.[13]

International supervisory mechanisms

Another important new phenomenon is the far more positive attitude of the Soviet Union and most of its allies towards supervisory mechanisms in the context of international conferences and organizations. Thus, the Soviet delegation greatly contributed to bringing the Vienna follow-up meeting to the Helsinki Conference on Security and Cooperation in Europe to a successful conclusion in January 1989. Also, the more positive attitude of the Soviet Union towards the United Nations has been widely noted.

The Soviet Union and some of its allies have become more positive towards requests for information on the part of international bodies. The familiar argument rejecting 'foreign interference' in supposedly 'domestic affairs' is heard less frequently nowadays.

CSCE

In January 1989, the Vienna follow-up meeting to the Helsinki Conference on Security and Cooperation in Europe adopted a concluding document which outlined a new supervisory mechanism with regard to the 'human dimension' of the CSCE. This mechanism contains the following four elements:

1. The CSCE states decided to exchange information and to respond to requests for information and to representations made to them by other participating states on questions relating to the human dimension of the CSCE. The states are obliged to supply this information.

2. If this exchange of information does not lead to satisfactory results, any CSCE state is entitled to convene a bilateral meeting with the other state in order to examine such questions.

3. If these measures do not lead to a solution, CSCE states are entitled to inform all other participating states about the questions concerned.

4. Finally, CSCE states are entitled to raise these problems at the annual conferences on the human dimension to be held in Paris (1989), Copenhagen (1990) and Moscow (1991) and the next follow-up meeting in Helsinki (1992).[14]

With one single exception so far — Romania — all participating states have accepted this new mechanism; moreover, Albania has indicated a desire to adhere to the Conference.

By 1 December 1989, this mechanism had already been used in 115 instances: for example, by the Netherlands and by Sweden and Austria against Czechoslovakia; by Spain (on behalf of the EC states) and Austria against Romania; by the United States against Bulgaria; by the United Kingdom against the Soviet Union; by the German Federal Republic against the GDR; and by Czechoslovakia against the Netherlands. It was used only once *within* a political bloc: by Hungary against Romania.

The Czech case referred to the arrest of the playwright Václav Havel and other members of the human rights organization Charter 77 for conducting a peaceful demonstration in the streets of Prague. The Czechoslovak authorities reacted positively to the request for information and subsequently bilateral talks were held between government representatives. For its part Czechoslovakia asked the Netherlands for information about alleged police brutality during a demonstration in Amsterdam against the operations in South Africa by the Anglo-Dutch oil company Shell. The matter of alleged Dutch police brutality was brought up during bilateral talks in Prague. It was furthermore mentioned by the Czech delegate in a working party at the Paris Conference. Thereafter, the Czechs have let it rest.

In April 1989, the twelve members of the European Community took the joint step, under the CSCE rules, of asking the Romanian government for information about the fate of twenty-four Romanians who had written to President Ceausescu an open letter of protest against the 'systematization project' of the destruction of villages: the Romanian government promptly reacted by calling this a matter of undue interference in its internal affairs. There thus exists a clear difference in the way the governments of Czechoslovakia and Romania reacted to allegations of human rights abuses in their countries. Both denied the substance of the allegations; but whereas Czechoslovakia showed itself willing to enter into a debate about them, Romania clearly rejected the right of other governments to discuss these matters as an interference in its domestic affairs.

The United Nations

Changes can also be observed in the attitude of the Soviet Union and its allies towards the implementation of UN Human Rights Conventions. The socialist states have *de facto* departed from the doctrine that a judicial or quasi-judicial communication procedure, initiated by a state or individual on the model of the European Convention on Human Rights, would violate national sovereignty.[15] Socialist experts, as members of international implementation organs, cooperate effectively in quasi-judicial procedures for the protection of human rights, although their governments still qualify them as an inadmissible interference with domestic affairs.

The Soviet Union has announced that it will ratify the optional protocol to the International Covenant on Civil and Political Rights. This will give individual Soviet citizens the possibility of lodging a complaint at the UN Commission for Human Rights against their own government. Deputy Minister Anatolii Adamishin announced to the UN Commission on Human Rights on 8 March 1989 that his government had recognized the compulsory jurisdiction of the International Court of Justice over the interpretation and application of a number of important international human rights agreements, notably those on genocide and torture.

The Hungarian government condemned fellow-socialist Romania for its human rights abuses. In March 1989, it co-sponsored a resolution in the UN Commission for Human Rights to appoint a special rapporteur to examine the human rights situation in Romania. The Soviet Union abstained, yet the resolution was adopted, in spite of strong opposition expressed by Romania, which considered this another illegal interference in its domestic affairs.

In another case relating to Romania, the Economic and Social Council of the United Nations took the unprecedented step of asking the International Court of Justice to give an advisory opinion on the application of Article VI, Section 22, of the UN Convention on Immunities and Privileges. It concerned the Romanian refusal to help to establish contact between UN Subcommission on the Prevention of Discrimination and the Protection of Minorities and its former rapporteur, Dumitru Mazilu, a Romanian citizen. Mazilu, who was charged with writing a report on human rights and youth, disappeared in Romania. The Romanian government rejected the notion that in his case the inviolability of experts who work for the United Nations should be applied. When ECOSOC voted on the resolution, its Eastern European members, among others, abstained.

THE WESTERN RESPONSE

The human rights record of many of the thirty-five CSCE states remains mixed. This is true of some Western states as well as of East European states. In their human rights record there is a distinct difference between Hungary, Poland and the Soviet Union on the one hand, (until recently) the German Democratic Republic, Czechoslovakia, and finally, Bulgaria and Romania on the other. In the first three countries more attention than in the past is being paid to their performance in the realm of civil and political rights.

The Eastern European countries, with the single exception of Romania, had by the end of 1989 accepted the newly established CSCE supervisory mechanism. This means that the notion that human rights is a matter solely within domestic jurisdiction would now seem to be a thing of the past. The Czechoslovak initiative to question the Netherlands about the way its police handled the Amsterdam demonstration should be welcomed. It indicates an acceptance by the Czechoslovak authorities of the notion that human rights performance on the national level is indeed a matter for monitoring by the international community.

Nothing, of course, is entirely certain in this field. Sceptics have warned against reaching over-optimistic conclusions. The American commentator I.F. Stone, shortly before his death, wrote that Soviet leader Gorbachev should not be trusted and that he was only trying to sell an old doctrine under a new name to the world community: 'He calls it "freedom of choice" or "freedom of socio-political choice". But it is really the old and anachronistic dogma of absolute national sovereignty and non-interference in so-called domestic rights'.[16] Nora Beloff argued in a letter to the editor that '... the publication of Solzhenitsyn's greatest novel, *The First Circle*, depicting *zec* life, should be the litmus test of Soviet literary freedom, just as the continued ban on *The Gulag Archipelago* testifies to the Politburo's continued dread of the truth about Party history'.[17] Her letter provides an excellent illustration of how quickly things may change: only a few months later it was officially announced that the Soviet Writers' Union had decided to lift the ban on the publication of Solzhenitsyn's works and the publication of *The Gulag Archipelago* began in the monthly *Novy mir* in August 1989. Nevertheless, she and other writers have been right in warning against too much and unfounded optimism.

Instead of giving way to either unfounded optimism or pessimism one should continue to monitor closely what is happening in the sphere of human rights in the Eastern European countries. The supervisory mechanism established at the CSCE meeting in Vienna, which includes three international meetings dealing exclusively with the 'human dimension', is a helpful tool. Of particular importance in this regard will be the meeting to be held in Moscow in 1991, the first such meeting to take place in the Soviet Union. A true 'litmus test' will be whether the Soviet Union will provide free access to that meeting for the Western press, and for political dissidents and representatives of non-governmental organizations. Many of the latter consider it inappropriate and in conflict with their independence and impartiality to attend international meetings of this kind only at the invitation of one of the participating states. In the spirit of openness and access to CSCE meetings non-governmental organizations should be granted independent access to the plenary debates of the Conference on the Human Dimension of the CSCE — in a manner similar to their position at the UN Commission for Human Rights. Regrettably, this was not possible at the Paris meeting in 1989. Western governments should insist that this independent access should be granted to non-governmental organizations in Copenhagen and Moscow. This will facilitate their independent monitoring role.

Western policy

The changes in the human rights record of the Eastern European states are mainly of a domestic nature rather than caused by Western policies. Moreover, when Western governments try to conduct an explicit human rights foreign policy, it is by no means certain — even after the event — to what extent such a policy has been successful. Thus, knowledgeable experts differ strongly over the extent to which President Carter's human rights policy was effective; the same is true of the efforts of the Reagan administration.

So far, there has been virtually no common West European policy relating to human rights in Eastern Europe. Yet, such a common policy — if agreed upon — would fit in well with the approach towards a common foreign policy envisaged in the Single European Act. Below, some suggestions are offered for ways in which Western governments — West European governments in particular — might help to encourage positive developments in Eastern Europe.

Overall, three lines of approach from the outside world, the West in particular, towards current developments in Eastern Europe would seem to be appropriate:

1. 'integration': human rights policy should be seen as part of an overall approach;

2. 'diversification': this would recognize the differences in development in the various Eastern European countries.

3. 'dialogue': to develop close — and when necessary critical — contacts at both governmental and non-governmental levels.

An 'integrated approach' takes into account the various policy fields in their mutual relationships. This is not only the case for human rights and security interests, which are closely interrelated, but for human rights and economic relations as well. The Dutch Helsinki Committee, in its comments to the Foreign Minister's 1988 policy paper on Eastern Europe, rightly criticized his failure to mention the use of economic instruments in support of human rights policy. Such economic instruments can be used by way of either positive or negative sanctions, depending on the country's dependence on foreign trade and its ability to find alternative trading partners.[18] It would be more effective if such policies were agreed upon as part of a common Western approach, rather than as the policy of single governments. The European Political Cooperation would seem to be a proper forum to start such a common approach. The initiative for this could very well be taken by small states such as the Netherlands or Belgium. If a common policy approach is agreed upon, the EC partners will then of course have to coordinate it with those of their non-European allies — the United States, Canada and possibly Japan.

Another aspect of such an integrated approach would be not necessarily to limit the expression of concerns over hum:.n rights to the East European region, but to extend it to parts of Western Europe and North America as well, if the need arose. Thus there would be ample reason to raise concern over the human rights situation in Turkey, where torture and ill-treatment of prisoners is still widely practised. It would contribute to the credibility of Western governments' concern over human rights situations if they were to use the CSCE mechanism in such cases as well — possibly in alliance with Eastern European governments.

Notions such as 'the communist bloc' or 'the world behind the Iron Curtain' have become increasingly out of date. In a recent EC survey of relations with countries of Eastern Europe the need for a diversified approach was clearly recognized. The European Community has indicated that it wants to stress the maintenance of bilateral relations with each of the separate East European states, taking into consideration their specific situation.

Such diversification must take into account current divisions of view among the East European states and try, where possible, to make use of such divisions. Already in 1989 Hungary clearly expressed its views with regard to human rights violations in Romania. Consultations with the Soviet Union might lead to a common approach to the Bulgarian government's treatment of its Turkish-speaking minority. Poland might be asked to discuss the human rights record of its East German and Czechoslovak neighbours.

A second aspect of diversification would be an increase in the assistance given to human rights movements and various forms of democratic opposition in the different countries, for both tactical and conceptual reasons. Again, the situation in the various East European countries clearly differs, so greater caution may be appropriate in some countries than in others. Next to moral assistance, the type of material assistance offered, for example in the form of literature, documentation and audio-visual apparatus, should respond to needs expressed by the groups concerned.

The attitude of the West towards nationalist movements in the region deserves very careful consideration. These movements offer an actual or potential grave threat to the very existence of such multi-national states as Yugoslavia and the Soviet Union. Clearly these groups should be allowed to express their demands in a peaceful and non-violent manner, in accordance with the provisions of major international human rights documents, such as the International Covenant on Civil and Political Rights. This is not, however, to say that the West should necessarily support the substantive demands of such ethnic and nationalist movements. Careful consideration should be given to the question of the conditions and circumstances in which such support should be offered, if at all. Here again, a diversified approach is strongly needed. In the field of human rights there is a great need for a continued and permanent dialogue between the countries of the East and the West. This should help to arrive at a common interpretation of the various international human rights norms, and to clarify these norms as a 'common standard of achievement'. Such dialogue should first take place at the governmental level. The meetings in the framework of CSCE offer a proper forum for such a continued dialogue. Relations between the Council of Europe and certain East European states are a promising new development. The Soviet Union, Poland and Hungary were the first to be granted (and to accept) the status of 'specially invited states'. The possibility of joining the European Convention on Human Rights has been mentioned several times. In a speech to the Council of Europe on 6 July 1989, Mikhail Gorbachev suggested that the Soviet Union might accede to some of the international conventions of the Council that are open to other states — on the environment, culture, education and television broadcasting. The Soviet Union was prepared to cooperate with the specialized agencies of the Council of Europe and was considering opening a Consulate General in Strasbourg.

The dialogue must, however, also be pursued at the non-governmental level. The scholarly community should be encouraged to study the state of human rights in East and West. This study need not to be limited to civil and political rights in the Eastern European countries which have been the main focus of this paper, but should include economic, social and cultural rights in East and West as well. Not only should attention be paid to the nature of the observed changes, but efforts should be made to arrive at valid explanations for such changes as well. Meetings of experts in various fields, exchanges of students, teachers and artists should be stimulated as part of a systematic and well thought-out cultural policy towards Eastern Europe. Mutual travel arrangements should be facilitated, in accordance with the agreements reached at CSCE. Such a dialogue in order to arrive at a 'meeting of minds' should, in other words, be pursued at all relevant levels of society.

CONCLUSION

In the pre-Gorbachev period the human rights policy of the Soviet Union and its allies was rather simple. As far as their foreign policy was concerned, it was mainly a matter of emphasis on non-intervention and national sovereignty, rejecting what was seen as international interference in internal matters and stressing the importance of economic and social rights. As far as domestic policy was concerned: rejection of the principle of the rights of the individual *vis-à-vis* his own state, suppression of dissident political views and rejection of freedom of expression except within the Marxist-Leninist framework. Things are not so easy any more. In the implementation of human rights, important changes are taking place which must be seen as part and parcel of developments in other fields. Thus, in the foreign policy of the Soviet Union a struggle is taking place between a traditionalist and a modernist point of view.[19] The traditionalist view is based on the idea of peaceful coexistence, emphasizing the continuation of ideological class struggle and isolation of Soviet citizens from the surrounding world. The modernist line dismisses the notion of class struggle as irrelevant in international relations, views foreign policy as a learning process, and favours increased Soviet contacts with the capitalist world. A similar struggle is taking place in the domestic policy area.

The result of this struggle will also determine the place of human rights in the policy process of the Soviet Union and the other East European states. If the traditionalist view wins, it can be expected that human rights will return to their previous oppressed position. Should the modernist view prevail, then it would mean a strengthening of the possibilities for a dialogue with the outside world in the field of human rights. The West, in particular, should try to encourage this type of dialogue.

NOTES

1. *Moscow News*, 1989, No. 9.
2. Mary Hawkesworth, 'Ideological Immunity: The Soviet Response to Human Rights Criticism', *Universal Human Rights*, Vol. 2, No. 1 (1980), pp. 67-87; Joshua Muravchik, *The Uncertain Crusade: Jimmy Carter and the Dilemmas of Human Rights Policy* (Lanham, MD: Hamilton Press, 1986), pp. 59-60.
3. Rhoda E. Howard and Jack Donnelly, 'Human Dignity, Human Rights and Political Regimes', *American Political Science Review (APSR)*, Vol. LXXX, No. 3 (1986), p. 811.
4. Neil Mitchell, 'Liberalism, Human rights and Human Dignity', *APSR*, Vol. LXXXI, No. 3 (1987), p. 923.
5. Amnesty International, external paper, January 1989.
6. Amnesty International, external paper, January 1989.
7. Amnesty International, external papers, March and May 1989.
8. Amnesty International, external paper, February 1989.

9. V. Chkhikvadze, 'A Socialist Conception of Human Rights and Human Dignity: *Perestroika* and the Rights of Man in the USSR', paper prepared for presentation at the Fourteenth World Congress of the International Political Science Association, Washington, DC, 1988, pp. 18-19.
10. *Amnesty International Newsletter*, March 1988, p. 7. For an early call by a Soviet lawyer for protection against forced psychiatric treatment, see N.S. Malein, 'O vrachebnoi taine', *Sovetskoe gosudarstvo i pravo*, 1981, No. 8, pp. 79-86, esp. p. 86 (reference supplied by Ron Hill).
11. *International Herald Tribune*, 23 May 1988, 7 November 1988, 28 February 1989.
12. See *On Speaking Terms: An Unprecedented Human Rights Mission to the Soviet Union* (Vienna: International Helsinki Federation of Human Rights, 1988); Max van der Stoel, 'Human Rights in the Soviet Union', *SIM Newsletter: Netherlands Quarterly of Human Rights*, Vol. 6, No. 1 (1988), pp. 74-9.
13. Oleg Vakulovsky, *'Amnesty' With and Without its Greasepaint* (unofficial translation prepared by Amnesty International), 1988.
14. Cf. A. Bloed, 'Successful Ending of the Vienna Meeting of the Conference on Security and Cooperation in Europe', *Netherlands Quarterly of Human Rights*, Vol. 7, No. 1 (1989), pp. 106-14.
15. Manfred Nowak, 'The Attitude of the Socialist States towards the Implementation of UN Human Rights Conventions', *Newsletter, Netherlands Quarterly of Human Rights*, Vol. 6, No. 1 (1988), p. 89.
16. I. F. Stone, 'The Rights of Gorbachev', *New York Review of Books*, 16 February 1989, p. 3.
17. *International Herald Tribune*, 9 February 1989.
18. Lynne A. Davidson, 'The Tools of Human Rights Diplomacy with Eastern Europe', in David D. Newsom (ed.), *The Diplomacy of Human Rights* (Lanham, MD: University Press of America, 1986), p. 28.
19. Kristian Gerner, 'Moscow and the Surrounding World: Perceptions of Gorbachev and his Entourage', unpublished paper (1988); Gerhard Wettig, '"New Thinking" on Security and International Relations', *Problems of Communism*, Vol. 37, No. 2 (1988), pp. 1-14.

13. The Future of Europe, Eastern Europe and Central Europe

Egbert Jahn

For forty years the East-West conflict had a decisive influence on political events in Europe and to a large extent in the entire world.[1] During this time the traditional national and regional identities and conflict configurations were overshadowed by the East-West conflict. The earth was, and still is, to an extent divided into two army camps, into two worlds or social systems and into two large socio-political factions in almost every country in the world. As a result of the conflict between these factions, Europe was separated into a Western Europe and an Eastern Europe, along a border stretching from Lapland to the Mediterranean. In a military, political, economic and cultural sense the border between systems was, and remains, a reality which has had a particularly far-reaching impact on people's lives, by no means merely superficial or ideological. However, since the mid-1980s, the older national and sub-national, continental and sub-continental identities and conflict structures have begun to emerge once again, in a modified form, from beneath the thick layer of Eastern and Western system identities and the East-West conflict. Not only do they modify the Eastern and Western loyalties, they even question in part their very existence. In this context, disintegrative tendencies in the Western and Eastern alliances go hand in hand with integrative efforts, whereby the system border is ignored. The integrative efforts are expressed bilaterally — for example, in the Austrian-Hungarian context, in the Italian-Yugoslavian context or the German-German context; regionally — for example, in the mid-European or the Balkan context; and also in terms of the continental-all-European context or even globally in the strengthening of global solidarity.

Since 1945 'Europe' has come to mean two things. Firstly, Europe is the place, the geographical continent from the Atlantic to the Urals, at whose centre the Western and the Eastern worlds divided. Secondly, Europe was and is simultaneously a political-cultural tradition and a political-cultural programme. In the latter sense, Europe and the West have been synonyms throughout long stretches of history: Europe ends at present on the Elbe, while Asia extends as far as Berlin, as the magazine *Der Spiegel* has remarked.

After 1945 many West European institutions appropriated the term 'Europe', but not because for the West Europeans Europe no longer existed beyond the Elbe. Western Europe would never be satisfied with being merely the 'European Community'. Beyond the system border lies for many West Europeans the *Europa irredenta*, the Europa *in spe*. This is the Europe which should liberate itself from Soviet communism and revert to its own tradition and fate along with Western Europe. Western Europe sees itself as the true Europe, which at the same time represents the core of a future united Europe.

'The East' has, since the early post-war period, stood for the communist state-managed economic and social system with a planned economy, and for the bureaucratic-socialist political order and the cultural and historical traditions and utopias connected to both systems. However, communist socialism is, neither in terms of origin nor in terms of its self-image, something Eastern, Asian or non-European.

Post-war definitions of both the West and the East contain considerable shifts of meaning as regards content and even geography, occasioned by the radical social and political changes of our century. The most important changes were the collapse of the European social and state system in 1914 and the proclamation and emergence of the new social and world-political concepts and powers of the Wilsonianism in the West and the Leninism in the East,[2] the temporary subjection of continental Europe under fascism, and the division and socio-political restructuring of Europe by the victorious powers following the conferences of Yalta and Potsdam. The post-war definitions of the West and the East have thrown the political topography into total confusion. Since 1945, or rather 1947, Athens and Ankara are deemed to lie in Western Europe, as do London, Paris or West Berlin. East Berlin, Prague, Warsaw and Budapest, on the other hand, evidently lie in Eastern Europe along with Lemberg (L'vov), Riga and Moscow.

The division of Europe into Eastern and Western Europe that knows no Central Europe, and which has reduced Northern and Southern Europe to peripheral provinces of Western Europe, is the result of the failed attempt in

1945 to unite Europe through force and give it a 'new order' under German national socialist domination and supremacy from the Atlantic to the Volga and beyond. The division did not begin with Yalta and Potsdam, a putative Anglo-American and Soviet plot to divide Europe into two by expanding 'from the edges', but with the two-front war waged by the national socialist German empire and the central powers allied to it — fascist Italy, Hungary, Bulgaria, Slovakia, Finland and so forth. From 1942 the only powers successfully to resist the use of military means by these central powers were the Soviet Union and Great Britain, with the USA in the background.

Europe's short period of unity from the centre — for many people 'Europe' remained for a long time after 1945 a fascist expression[3] — ended, along with the war, on 8 May 1945 with the unification of the Western and Eastern fronts in a military demarcation line between the troops of the Anglo-American Western powers and the Eastern power, the Soviet Union. The cold war between the Western powers and the Eastern power which began before the end of the war and reached its height in 1947, firmly established, after a few modifications, the demarcation line between the victorious powers as a line of division which would dominate for decades, in the form of the 'Iron Curtain' which separated a 'Western' from an 'Eastern' political system.

Today, however, the cold war is over, and the East–West conflict has changed its character fundamentally. The socialist system in Eastern Europe is undergoing significant political change. Relations within Western Europe and between Western Europe and the United States are also in a state of flux. The future of Europe, Eastern Europe and Central Europe seems extremely uncertain at the start of the 1990s.

MAJOR DIMENSIONS OF FUTURE EUROPEAN DEVELOPMENT

Not every spark becomes a flame and sets a whole area ablaze. Not every piece of politicized historical nostalgia results in a practicable programme for the future. And the dream of the old Holy Germano-Roman Empire or about a new United States of Europe will not inevitably lead to the emergence of a new super-state — be it a greater German one centred on Berlin, a Central European one focused on Prague, a Western European one centred on Brussels, or indeed a pan-European one centred on Moscow and stretching from the Atlantic to the Urals or Pacific. Nevertheless, the tendencies towards integration and unification will play an important role in the future history of Europe and of its constituent regions. In addition to the integrating trends, however, the trends towards national and sub-national fragmentation will be of major significance. Tendencies towards integration and those towards fragmentation are partly complementary, partly overlapping, and in part they contradict each other, provoking bitter disputes within and between states.

To predict how Europe will develop over the next, say, two decades is not possible. However, at least six major dimensions of European development can be indicated that will be crucial in shaping processes towards integration and fragmentation. These are: social systems, security, alliances, national policy, the formation of unions between states, and the communal aspects.

Three of these dimensions — namely, social systems, security and the communal aspects — have been examined elsewhere and will not be discussed here.[4] They will all, however, maintain a crucial impact on future developments in Europe. The system-related dimension of European development, that is the attempts to preserve, alter, combine, or eliminate the two economic and social orders in Europe, will probably remain the central issue of the development for decades to come. In fact, with the move towards parliamentary democracy and a market economy in several Eastern European states, the social dimension has drastically gained in importance within the past few years.

The security-related dimension will also continue to be crucial. The predominant security problem in Europe will continue to be that of the prevention of war between East and West. After all, war in Europe is merely unlikely, not impossible.

An important, if so far quite underdeveloped, contribution to the discussion about the future development is that concerning the communal dimension of the future of Europe.[5] Citizens' initiatives, associations, societies, parishes and districts constitute a multifariously diversified democratic infrastructure to modern society both in the West and, increasingly, in the East, and the further development of that infrastructure offers the best — and perhaps the only — safeguard against the despotic and tyrannical abuse of modern communications and of genetic, medical, transport, weapons and other technologies.

ALLIANCE POLICY IN THE PERSPECTIVE OF THE FUTURE

Since 1945 the alliance-related dimension of European development has been accompanied by a variety of ideas on the reorganization of the alliances. The *status quo* is undoubtedly favoured by a largely peaceful political context, since conflicting interests can seldom be coordinated in such a way as to bring about a change in the *status quo* that is capable of being carried through: that is to say capable, in a democratic or federal structure, of commanding majority support or indeed of eliciting consensus. As a rule, neither states nor alliances disintegrate peacefully.

As long as a major war in Europe remains unlikely, any extensive territorial reshaping of Europe will, despite all tensions at the national or East-West level, also be excluded. Without war, the national boundaries as essentially set out in the Paris Peace Conference treaties and modified in Yalta and Potsdam, will in all probability remain stable. And despite all the recurring crises within them, the alliances that grew up during the cold war are unlikely to be any less secure. In addition, expansions in alliances remain more likely than any shrinkages or re-formations.

Since 1945, however, the political significance of national and alliance boundaries has changed in three respects: first, as a result of the change in the security situation; secondly, as a result of the change in the societal structures within the states and alliances; and thirdly — a concomitant of the internal structural change — as a result of integrating and fragmenting processes in the system of states, some of which restore the institutions of the nation-state and nationalism, and some of which transcend them.

Given that for the foreseeable future the East-West conflict, in the form of a conflict of socio-political concepts and systems, will continue to be a crucial determining factor in development, it is clear that neither the military nor the economic alliances of East or West are suddenly going to break up or fuse. This also means that the two world powers will continue to be present politically, militarily, and economically in the west and centre of Europe. Conversely, the interests of the world powers — independent of their societal differences — and the interests of the alliance organizations help to perpetuate the conflict between the socio-political concepts and systems, without being, or becoming, its principal cause.

A constant, linear process of détente in the next, say, two decades remains unlikely: in other words temporary phases of East-West tension cannot be excluded, although these would not escalate into a new cold war. Nevertheless, there is a chance that the opposition between NATO and the Warsaw Treaty Organization (WTO) will continue to abate. Military confidence-building measures and arms control can reduce East-West confrontation, without completely eliminating the mutual threat. It may be assumed that the Western European process of integration within NATO and the Western European Union will continue. In Eastern Europe the WTO is likely to remain politically the chief integrating institution, at least for the time being. Simultaneous tendencies towards fragmentation are unlikely to lead to withdrawals from the military alliances but rather to pluralizing trends and to greater difficulty in political coordination, thus contributing to making the alliance unfit for aggressive purposesm (although Hungary has signalled its intention to leave the pact). From the point of view of peace it would make perfect sense to place an increasing number of troops — including non-German ones — under the jurisdiction of NATO and the WTO, so that they are no longer available for implementing national policies of aggression and intervention and are under international control. However, national reservations with regard to military sovereignty probably make such a policy for peace unfeasible for the foreseeable future.

A development that should be viewed in the same context is the intensification of economic, cultural, ecological and other communications across the East-West boundary. This is likely to modify, without entirely eliminating, the established economic division of Europe into two camps, the Western capitalist and the Eastern socialist. The EC and the CMEA will no doubt for a long time retain their characters as organizations specific to the relevant system and closely associated with NATO and the WTO. A break-up of CMEA and an eastward expansion of the EC or EFTA (the European Free Trade Association) as a move towards laying the foundation for a 'common European home' will continue to be unlikely in the coming years, although it can no longer be excluded. Even an integration of the neutral countries into the EC would not be without its complications. Success in the process of reform in Eastern Europe could bring with it a restructuring of CMEA to produce more efficient performance and integration. The pan-European trend, which will remain restricted, is more likely to give way to a more thorough-going globalization of a number of other institutions such as the World Bank, the International Monetary Fund, GATT, the OECD, and numerous special UN organizations; it may, however, also lead to the creation of new specific forms of organization for cooperation between the

EC, CMEA, and the neutral countries, or to a degree of revitalization of the UN's European regional organization, the Economic Commission for Europe (ECE), first established in 1947.

Major political and economic interests within and outside Europe militate against the notion that the partial overcoming of the boundaries between nations and systems in Europe will lead to a cutting-off of Western Europe and of Europe as a whole from the United States, Eastern Asia, and the African-Caribbean-Pacific (ACP) states; however, these interests will bring about a relative increase in the importance of Europe's borders with the outside world unless the internal European tendencies to integration are incorporated into the worldwide trend towards integration. The ideological overstatement of the issues, as expressed in catch-phrases such as 'common European home' or 'fortress (Western) Europe', should not mislead one into overlooking the fact that what we have here are not absolute alternatives — for example North Atlantic or all-Western integration (Western Europe, United States, Japan, and so on) versus all-European integration — but relative shifts in the world system.

The relationship between Western European and all-European integration[8] will be determined chiefly by the success — or failure — and the extent of the process of social reform in the Soviet Union and in the whole of Eastern Europe. The more intensive the reshaping towards a market economy and the development of foreign trade in Eastern Europe, the lesser the incentive for the formation of a close-knit political, military and, ultimately, also economic Western European unity. The process of reform in the eastern part of Europe favours all-European pluralization and the formation of both new all-European structures and national sub-continental identities. Such developments would also further temper the 'Western European versus North Atlantic integration' alternative and would mean that the American-Western European and also the Japanese-West European differences might be mitigated.

Western European identity will remain one among many other identities in Europe, partially modified by national and regional identities (for example, Benelux, Iberian Europe, the Nordic countries), and partially transcended by identities — such as the all-European, Northern Central European, Southern Central European, Austro-Hungarian, Baltic, and federal Balkan ones — that encompass both Eastern and Western states. These identities, which are founded on subcontinental proximity, overlap and partly conflict with sea-centred identities like the Mediterranean one — which has also managed to temper European-African distinctions — or the Baltic one, or again the upper North Atlantic one (Greenland, Iceland, the Faeroes, and so on).

Since states and peoples do not have to make an 'either-or' decision, provided successful prevention of war continues, the complexity of identities in Europe can continue to increase and the Eastern and Western identity as defined by their separate systems can continue to be modified. Denmark, for example, still does not have to opt either for Central Europe and the EC or for Nordic unity; Hungary does not have to choose between this or that Central Europe and CMEA; Austria does not have to opt for either Western or Central Europe; the Federal Republic of Germany does not have to choose between integration into the West and intense cooperation with the GDR (althoiugh certain choices have been made in 1990); Italy does not have to opt either for Western Europe or for closer relations with North Africa; Turkey does not have to choose between Europe and Asia; Britain does not have to choose between special relations either with the United States or with Commonwealth countries. European ambiguities are actually desirable from the point of view of world politics and peace. Only a war or a cold war necessitates clear-cut borders — to act as fronts.

NATIONAL POLICIES IN A STATE OF FLUX

The continuation of the East-West process of détente will also strengthen the national dimension of European development. In addition to the abatement of the East-West conflict and the differentiation in the positions with regard to security interests, the intensification of critical economic developments in West and East will give added impetus to nationalist and nation-state aspirations, which, it may be assumed, will not — are not intended to — cause the break-up of the existing alliances of states or indeed existing multi-nation states. In the United States and USSR too, the hopelessness of traditional imperial-missionary universalism will intensify American and Soviet or Russian nationalism and occasion repeated efforts at protectionism. Growing state and ethnic nationalism[9] will thus encourage above all the tendencies to the pluralization of societies and of alliances at the national level in both East and West.

The number of national variants of communist socialism and liberal-democratic capitalism will increase. In this connection, renewed attempts to develop national capitalist-socialist and democratic-socialist hybrid forms of the different societal systems, of which one example exists to date in

Yugoslavia, cannot be excluded. This applies particularly to the central part of Europe and to the countries with strong social-democratic or influential Eurocommunist parties. Furthermore, trends towards nationalist regression, as evidenced recently in Romania, Armenia and Azerbaijan, and as are also still present to a lesser degree in France, Italy, and numerous other Western European countries, cannot be discounted.

In the Soviet Union the social reform is inextricably bound up with a national reform that is bringing about a real international federalism in the country, instead of the Russo-centric pseudo-federalism that has existed up to now, and is at the same time pluralizing the Eastern alliance system, in order to give individual nations greater internal and external autonomy within the framework of the USSR, the WTO, and CMEA. The efforts at reorganization in the Soviet Union and in its alliance system are, at the same time, being met with very strong national, separatist and Russo-Soviet centralist resistance and may even be frustrated by this for a considerable period.

From the point of view of peace, the optimum solution would be if the non-Russians in the Soviet Union and Eastern Europe did not seek national emancipation via the circuitous route of national sovereignty but instead sought direct national autonomy within the framework of the existing Soviet, Eastern European, and all-European forms of association. This can work only if the Russians emancipate themselves from their despotic-imperial traditions and, at the same time, the non-Russians in the Soviet Union and Eastern Europe rid themselves of their uncompromising anti-Russian stance. Only in such a case could Western Europe also free itself of its super-militarized anti-communism and anti-Sovietism. Conversely, however, the mitigation by the West of the political and military threat, whether real or merely apparent, posed by the Soviet Union has been for the last twenty-five years, and continues to be, a constituent condition of the processes of emancipation in the Eastern part of Europe, and it will continue to be so in the future. On the other hand, lack of resolve by Western Europe in the defence of its freedoms, whether by military or non-military means — without wishing to export those freedoms by force to Eastern Europe — can only give succour to despotic imperial inclinations in the Soviet Union.

In principle it is easier for nationalism to develop in Western Europe, within the existing pluralist structures, and to counteract supranational tendencies. However, perhaps more salient is the absence of centralist, hegemonic structures that might stimulate and reinforce nationalism. This implies that a further reduction in nationalism in Western Europe, through the voluntary association of nations, is quite possible, so long as critical economic developments do not stimulate national antagonisms and calls for ethnic or nation-state protectionism. The real problem confronting Western Europe and NATO is the democratization of the supranational institutions, rather than the frequently evoked signs of dissolution.

Europe is not only confronted with the choice between either *status quo* or democratization, between either East or West. Social and nationalist regression, in which, in the name of 'national self-determination' and 'sovereignty', a policy of national economic, political, military and psychological segregation from the outside world is pursued, continues to be a dangerous potential development from the point of view of peace.

Another issue of great significance for the future of Europe continues to be the way in which the Germans and non-Germans tackle the German question. Radical attempts to change the configuration of states or the European security situation, such as is constituted by the efforts to bring about a peaceful unification of the two German states or — even more so — a restoration of the German Reich in its 1937 borders, bring with them the intolerable risk for Germans and non-Germans alike of tensions liable to lead to war. In the eyes of Germany's neighbours, the peaceful reunification of Germany means primarily the reunification of the Bundeswehr and the Nationale Volksarmee and the creation of a major economic and military power that no amount of neutralist or pacifist dressing-up can turn into another Switzerland or Finland. Germany cannot play the role of a disarmed Greater Liechtenstein. After the experiences with the 100,000-man army of the Weimar Republic, even pacifist trends in Germany are open to the suspicion of being merely transitional strategies, or unpremeditated transitional phenomena, leading to the political detachment of Germany from East and West and preparing the way for the country's ascent back to the rank of a militarily strong medium-sized power. German national pacifism could continue to be a historical vehicle firstly for reunification and later for rearmament to the rank of a great power.

Decades ago, for the Germans and Italians, and for those peoples who no longer had, or had never possessed, their own state, the desire for a nation-state in the centre of a Europe fragmented into tiny countries made sense for many reasons including that of security. Nowadays no German nation-state, whatever its boundaries and whichever Germans inhabit it, could afford the Germans greater security against war or aggression. Even the present peaceful attempt to create a German nation-state — merely by interpreting the right to self-determination as a right to reunify in the form of a nation-state — could considerably diminish the security of the Germans, if not threaten their very existence.

The fear non-Germans have of a German nation-state is a hard political reality, even though the development of the German political consciousness since 1945 does not in fact indicate any risk of German imperial leanings towards the revision of ethnic structures in erstwhile Eastern Germany and Sudetenland, or towards the domination over non-German peoples. Even the prospect of a non-imperial, petty German, capitalist-democratic economic power in the centre of Europe could be pushed through only in the face of considerable opposition from Germany's neighbours.

Détente has reopened the German question. The more the military antagonism between East and West dwindles and the greater the tendencies towards convergence and tolerance become, the more virulent hopes and fears once again become about the emergence of a German nation-state as a major power. Since neither Germans nor non-Germans have any interest in prolonging major tensions in order the better to be able to justify the division of Germany, the prospect of further East-West rapprochement and closer East-West cooperation calls for new German and non-German answers to the newly opened German question, since this is an issue that is crucial for the future of Central Europe and of Europe as a whole.[11]

Until 1990, there was no likelihood of a Federal Republic of Germany beimg taken over by communists and joining up with the GDR, or even of a GDR fully restored to capitalism being joined to the FRG, since such a move would cause a significant shift in the international correlation of forces. Any signs of a dual-system policy on Germany — a confederal or indeed federal unification of two German states with differing societal systems analogous to the Chinese strategy of reunification — were not apparent until recently. Renewed endeavours to bring about a pan-German state through a policy of pacifist or sparsely armed democratic-capitalist neutrality were perceived, as in the 1940s and 1950s, as a threatening shift in the security balance, demanding therefore the most delicate handling.

If, contrary to such expectations, the complete national *and hence also military* unification of Germany should nevertheless be pushed through, this would result either in the dissolution of the residual NATO or in the latter's increased integration and armament. The confrontation between East and West, in a new configuration, would be renewed at a considerably intensified level. A heavily armed pan-German state can only be realized by force in the face of the mistrust of Germany's neighbours, a mistrust that is deeply rooted in German imperial history; and such a move would inevitably evoke associations with the historical events leading up to March 1939, which took place under the ideological pretext of the exercise of Germany's right to national self-determination.

The border between West Germany and the Netherlands, and even that between West Germany and Austria, has already attained — or will attain in 1992 — about the same significance, or insignificance, as the border between Hesse and Bavaria. In a civilized Europe, détente will, through peaceful, persistent, painstaking work, also bring the boundary between the two hitherto existing systems in Germany and Europe down to the level of that between West Germany and the Netherlands. The postulate of the West German Constitutional Court that the border between Thuringia and Hesse should be qualitatively no different in law from that between Bavaria and Hesse can only be translated into reality by social and political means, by decades of steadfast policy of peace and détente, following formal relations between the two separate German states. In the meantime, as the Berlin Wall and the barbed wire along the frontier between the two systems are broken up and sold off to tourists or converted into museums, the Germans have to learn to tackle the societal conflict in Germany itself through policies aimed at peace, in addition to resolving the colossal economic, ecological, political and psychological consequences of half a century of separation.

IS UNIFICATION OF EUROPEAN STATES VISIBLE?

Closely bound up with development not only in alliance and national policy but also in policy on security and societal systems is that dimension of the future of Europe that relates to the formation of unions between states. The détente in East-West relations, the differentiation of security interests, and the increasing economic and political strength of the allies of both world powers have prompted fantasies about programmes for the long-term formation of new alliances between states and the conversion of existing alliances into federations.

Hopes of a quite radical restructuring of the European system of states seem especially widespread in the centre of Europe. Yet there is little indication that any new federal-type combinations of states will actually materialize during the next two or three decades.

Cooperation between smaller states in Western Europe will probably intensify but, for national and alliance reasons, will not — either in the case of the Benelux states or in the case of the Scandinavian countries — attain federal proportions. In Eastern Europe national interests vary so widely that there will probably not be any closer amalgamation of the Soviet Union's smaller alliance partners in the future either. The latter prefer to seek special relations with their Western European neighbours or with the EC. In this connection, there could also be closer state relations between the Balkan countries, or between the south-central European countries of Hungary, Austria, and Yugoslavia — and perhaps also Italy, transcending the division between the former systems. However, central and south-eastern European plans for union can at best provide only an ideology and cannot serve as a feasible political programme for inter-state cooperation.

The original plans for a closer linkage of the 'socialist community of states' within the framework of the WTO, or indeed of CMEA, must now be regarded as a thing of the past. For the foreseeable future the tendencies to fragmentation will surely predominate here.

Following the frequent predictions, over the last few decades, of the break-up of the EC, this now seems overcome by an unexpected thrust towards integration. EFTA as an alternative and extended medium for cooperation has, historically, dwindled to the point where it now has only residual functions. The extent and objects of integration continue to be politically disputed.[12] Should more neutral states be accepted — for example, should Ireland be followed by Austria, Switzerland, and Sweden? Is the EC prepared to take on board the economic, social, religious and ethnic problems that come with acceptance of Turkey into its ranks, or is it able to accommodate the political consequences for NATO of a long-term exclusion of Turkey from the EC? Should socialist states — and perhaps one day even a radically reformed Soviet Union — also be accepted into the EC in the longer term? Or should the EC become the second pillar within the North Atlantic community — not only economically but also in respect of foreign and security policy? Should the United States of America (with the increasingly close association of Canada and Mexico) be presented with a partner and competitor of equal weight with NATO, possibly even rendering NATO superfluous?

Politicians of the EC often extend their claims with regard to integration to cover the whole of Europe, and this strikes quite a chord in central and south-eastern Europe. Shall we end up seeing a race to integration between the Soviet Union and a European Union, with these two vying to recruit the states that lie between the EC and the USSR, thus turning central and south-eastern Europe once again into an endangered 'intermediate Europe'?

A successful renaissance of German plans for central Europe is probably unlikely. The Federal Republic has, in the course of forty years, become so integrated both economically and socially into the West that, despite all internal Western differences, there cannot again be any illusion about the Germans occupying an independent economic and military position of power in central Europe. The bases of Friedrich Naumann's deliberations in regard to a central European world power have in many respects been overtaken by history or else were destroyed by national socialism.[13] In Germany, political musings on central Europe will probably remain confined to peripheral groups of the right or left, or if not will at best give those elements of German politics that cherish German national or pan-European aspirations something to toy with. A delimitation from Western Europe and the United States and a limited rapprochement towards the Soviet Union could bring the Federal republic nothing but disadvantages in almost every respect, and particularly with regard to economics and security. The first Rapallo — in conjunction with Locarno — may not have been a tragedy[14] but a chance to establish a European peace order; but a second Rapallo would without any doubt be a farce, with German power fantasies as the main theme.

For the relevant political forces in the Federal Republic, the cultivation of nostalgia for central Europe is at best a means to an all-European end, namely the extension of the economic and social influence of Western Europe — in practice, primarily of the Federal Republic — to the Eastern part of Europe, across the divide between the systems. In this connection, traditional conservative thinking, geared towards the future build-up of macro-state power, will be envisaging a primarily Catholic-Protestant, Western style, capitalist-democratic Europe from Poland to Portugal, destined one day, in the form of a European Union, to stretch all the way from the Soviet to the American Union. Such a Europe implies a shift of the boundary between the systems from the Elbe to the Bug.

Social democratic and democratic socialist (including Eurocommunist) thinking will, from the point of view of security policy, also tend towards this kind of Europe, extending between the two superpowers from Poland to Portugal; however, in the event of more radical democratic reforms in the Soviet Union, it will also be receptive to the idea of bringing the Soviet Union into the process of European unification. The notion of the 'reunification of the European labour movement' could, in the extreme case, develop within the European left into a sharper distancing from the capitalist United States and to closer cooperation between an economically and militarily strong social-capitalist western and central Europe and a democratic-socialist Soviet Union, on the basis of equal rights.

Possibly the most favourable — and, if détente continues, the most likely — development from the point of view of peace is if there is no establishment of a European federation during the next few decades — neither a Western European one from the Atlantic to the Elbe, nor a Western European or pan-German one extending to the Oder, nor a petty-European one from the Atlantic to the Bug, nor a great-European one from Gibraltar to Vladivostok.

Of all the European projects for union, the much-vaunted idea of a united Europe from the Atlantic to the Urals is the most senseless and the most obviously unrealistic amongst all the utopian fantasies. Such a unification of Europe would presuppose a split not only of the Soviet Union but also of the present Russian and East Slavic area of settlement. This could not be achieved without a disastrous war — and probably not even through war at all.

NOTES

1. See Werner Link, *Der Ost-West-Konflikt: Die Organisation der internationalen Beziehungen im 20. Jahrhundert* (Stuttgart: Kohlhammer, 1980); Manfred Görtemaker, *Die unheilige Allianz: Die Geschichte der Entspannungspolitik, 1943-1979* (Munich: Beck, 1979); Richard W. Stevensen, *The Rise and Fall of Détente: Relaxations of Tension in US–Soviet Relations, 1953-84* (Urbana and Chicago, IL: Macmillan, 1985).
2. Arno J. Mayer, *Wilson versus Lenin: Political Origins of the New Diplomacy 1917-1918*, 2nd ed. (New Haven, CT: Yale University Press, 1963).
3. Max Beloff, *Europe und die Europäer: Eine internationale Diskussion* (Cologne: Verlag für Wirtschaft und Politik, 1959), p. 37; Alain Finkielkraut, 'What is Europe?', *The New York Review of Books*, 32 (19/1985), p. 10.
4. For an extensive analysis of the security dimension, social systems and the communal aspects of the future developments in Europe, see Egbert Jahn, *Europe, Eastern Europe, and Central Europe* (PRIF Report 1/1989), pp. 45-56 and 70-3.
5. Chadwick F. Alger and Saul H. Mendlovitz, 'Grass-roots Initiatives: The Challenges of Linkages', in Saul H. Mendlovitz and R.B.J. Walker (eds), *Towards a Just World Peace: Perspectives from Social Movements* (London: Butterworths, 1987), pp. 333, 347; Richard A. Falk, 'The Global Promise of Social Movements: Explorations at the Edge of Time', in ibid., pp. 363ff.
6. For a different opinion, see Stevenson, *The Rise and Fall of Détente*, p. 188;

Fred Halliday, *The Making of the Second Cold War* (London: Verso, 1983), p. 19.

7. Christoph Royen, *Osteuropa: Reformen und Wandel. Erfahrungen und Aussichten vor dem Hintergrund der sowjetischen Perestrojka* (Baden-Baden: Nomos, 1988).

8. Peter Bender, 'Westeuropa oder Gesamteuropa?', in Werner Weidenfeld (ed.), *Die Identität Europas* (Munich: Hanser, 1985), pp. 235-54.

9. 'Neuer Nationalismus und nationale Minderheiten', *Osteuropa-Info*, No. 61 (2/1985).

10. Social nationalist systems are all those regimes that are not either liberal-democratic, communist, or aristocratic/monarchist, including *inter alia* fascist and populist regimes, which all cultivate an integral nationalism founded on a broad social basis.

11. For a particularly well argued case for this, see, for example, François Fejtö, *Die Geschichte der Volksdemokratien*, Vol. 1 (Graz, Vienna, Cologne: Styria, 1972), pp. 463f.

12. Daniel Frei, 'Integrationsprozesse: Theoretische Erkenntnisse und praktische Folgerungen', in Weidenfeld (ed.), *Die Indentität Europas*, pp. 113-31.

13. Friedrich Naumann, *Mitteleuropa* (Berlin: Reimer, 1915), pp. 263ff.

14. Renata Bournazel, *Rapallo — ein französisches Trauma* (Cologne: Markus, 1976).

Index